PIMLICO

158

THE CASE OF MARY BELL

Gitta Sereny is of Hungarian-Austrian extrac-
tion and is trilingual in English, French and
German. During the Second World War she
became a social worker, caring for war
damaged children in France. She gave
hundreds of lectures in schools and colleges in
America and, when the war ended, she worked
as a Child Welfare Officer in UNRRA
displaced persons' camps in Germany. In
1949 she married the American *Vogue*
photographer Don Honeyman and settled in
London, where they brought up a son and a
daughter and where she began her career as a
journalist.

Her journalistic work is of great variety but
has focused particularly on the Third Reich
and troubled children. She has written mainly
for the *Daily Telegraph Magazine*, the
Sunday Times, *The Times*, the *Independent*
and the *Independent on Sunday Review*. She
has also contributed to numerous newspapers
and magazines throughout the world.

Her other books are *The Medallion*, a novel;
The Invisible Children, on child prostitution;
Into that Darkness, on Franz Stangl, com-
mandant of the Treblinka extermination
camp; and, forthcoming, a biographical re-
evaluation of Albert Speer.

THE CASE OF MARY BELL

A Portrait of a Child who Murdered

GITTA SERENY

With a new preface and appendix by the author

PIMLICO

". . . As more exposed to suffering and distress;
Thence also, more alive to tenderness."

To Don

PIMLICO
An imprint of Random House
20 Vauxhall Bridge Road, London SW1V 2SA

Random House Australia (Pty) Ltd
20 Alfred Street, Milsons Point, Sydney
New South Wales 2061, Australia

Random House New Zealand Ltd
18 Poland Road, Glenfield
Auckland 10, New Zealand

Random House South Africa (Pty) Ltd
PO Box 337, Bergvlei, South Africa

Random House UK Ltd Reg. No. 954009

First published by Eyre Methuen 1972
Pimlico edition, with a new preface and appendix,
1995

7 9 10 8

Papers used by Random House UK Limited are
natural, recyclable products made from wood grown in
sustainable forests. The manufacturing processes
conform to the environmental regulations of the
country of origin

Printed and bound in Great Britain by
Mackays of Chatham plc, Chatham, Kent

ISBN 0–7126–6297–9

CONTENTS

PREFACE TO THE PIMLICO EDITION

When I first saw Mary Bell, on 5 December 1968, the opening day of her trial at the Newcastle upon Tyne Assizes, I was there to report for the *Daily Telegraph Magazine*. I had recently undertaken to write a book on cruelty to children, and this strange case of the alleged murder by two girls, one thirteen, the other eleven, of two small boys, one four and one three, seemed a possible extreme example of cruelty by child to child.

But as I sat through the nine days of the trial, my purpose changed. In Court and in the press, Mary Bell was called a "fiend" and a "Svengali". The Court would decide that she—and basically she alone—had committed the murders, and when the other child was acquitted, the whole country seemed to breathe a sigh of relief. The older girl being found innocent created an equation acceptable and even welcome to society: fate, or some terrible wrath of God, had produced a freak: one monstrous child, a "bad seed", the uniqueness of whose evil could be seen as confirming the probity and virtue of society at large.

My difficulty, almost from the first day, was that I could not believe it. I had, very quickly, met the families of the little boys who had been killed and their pain was atrocious to see. And, of course, I knew that one or both of the girls had killed four-year-old Martin and three-year-old Brian. But somehow I could not associate the concept of evil with Mary Bell. In the context of the events, the suffering of the small boys' parents, and the anger, not to say panic, in the media, there was one, to me overriding, impression I knew I would not be able to express in the articles I was commissioned to write. But it was precisely this impression that would change my original plan and would bring me to write this book. This feeling, much easier to describe today when, twenty-six years later, we have lived through the violent Jamie Bulger murder, was that the murder of the two little boys in Newcastle was not at all an illustration of cruelty by child to child.

There was a strange absence of violence in those murders which—and this is what one could not say at the time—were carried out, it seemed to me, almost with tenderness. This inversion, even perversion of emotion, I know, is as frightening as anger, and in these circumstances perhaps even more puzzling. But somehow I could not reconcile it with evil: to me, this strange, intelligent and isolated child just seemed horribly hurt.

Twenty-six years later, in Preston, at the "Bulger trial", as it became known all over the world, we would find striking parallels but equally significant disparities.

Here too, two ten-year-old boys had accused each other of kidnapping and torture, but both denied having initiated the killing. The vast difference, however, was that in this case the victim was a child only just out of babyhood, entirely unknown to either of the boys, and was killed, not as a dreadful "game", not out of some aberrant sense of curiosity, but with a ferocity really beyond human understanding. Not surprisingly, perhaps, in the absence of any explanation whatsoever, the *vox populi*, yet again, decried the two child perpetrators as "evil".

There were further parallels between these two cases, almost three decades apart. The most important one (because of which my publishers and I have decided to add my report on the Bulger case—written in February 1994 for the *Independent on Sunday Review*—as an annexe to this book) is the total bewilderment which the court and jury in both these significant cases manifested when they were confronted with the children's testimonies.

This "bewilderment" was and is symptomatic of the unfitness of that formal venue for the trial of children, even for murder. And the identical reactions of the court and public opinion in 1968 and 1993 also demonstrated how terribly little we have learned in a quarter of a century, how little progress we have made.

In 1968, I had become increasingly concerned each day of Mary Bell's trial about the incomprehension and the partisanship of the Judge. In 1993, even though the Judge in the "Bulger case" was infinitely more knowledgeable and professional, and clearly aware of the deficiencies in the proceedings, his actions and decisions were inevitably determined by the system he served. For me, sitting through an almost exact replica of the 1968 trial, much of it had a distressing quality of *déjà vu*. And during the breaks and the sixteen evenings of the trial days, I found, yet again, that every lawyer, every court official, virtually every police officer and every member of the media I spoke with, had grave misgivings about the case and, yes, the venue of the trial.

In Newcastle, Brian Roycroft, one of the finest social workers in the country, took over as Children's Officer in the summer of 1968. Not long afterwards he became Director of Social Services and, thanks to him, I received enormous help from all who worked there.

In Liverpool, where the police and voluntary organizations readily responded to me, the local authority social workers and the teachers were, not surprisingly perhaps, officially gagged.

But even where officials consented to speak—in 1968 *and* in 1993—what they voiced were private opinions: officially, unlike capital cases involving children in other Western countries (or proceedings in the far more knowledgeable and enlightened Juvenile or Family Courts in Britain), no-one was allowed to seek the *reasons* for these tragedies.

"Due process" in British High Courts allows only the facts of the case to be presented: and according to these facts—which certainly established that eleven-year-old Mary Bell in 1968, and Robert Thompson and Jonathan Venables in 1993, had killed— there *was* no reason, and so these children, who had most certainly committed evil deeds, were stamped "evil" and tried, convicted and sentenced as adults.

So first in 1968 in this book about Mary Bell, and then again in 1994 in the articles about the boys who killed Jamie Bulger (which are reprinted at the end of this book), I decided to ask the questions a British Court is not in a position to ask, and to protest against a judicial system which is totally outdated.

How, first of all, can it be right to subject young children to the awesome formality of a jury trial? How can a jury be expected to understand the thought processes, the emotions or language of children? How can it be justifiable in the last half—now the last decade—of the twentieth century, to deny children, who have committed the ultimate crime and therefore presumably gone through an ultimate trauma, immediate access to some kind of therapy—this on the pretext that if they were allowed contact with psychiatrists for any other reason than to establish their capacity to distinguish between right and wrong, it could "contaminate the evidence"?

Indeed, unless we continue to subscribe to the antediluvian concept of evil birth, do we *need* psychiatrists to inform us that a child who kills does so because it has suffered profoundly disturbing experiences and is in fact a sick child?

Let me state swiftly here that I do not subscribe to the thesis that all criminals are sick and in need of hospitalization rather than imprisonment. I think there are greedy, dishonest and brutal people about, and when they commit crimes they must be punished. There are also mad people around—the Yorkshire Ripper and Ian Brady, to name only two—and even though it is only too possible that childhood experiences have caused or at least contributed to their abnormalities of mind, I have no hesitation in saying that they should be permanently restrained from contact with society.

It is possible that this could apply to a child; it is possible for children to be sufficiently hurt to be damaged for life. But an enlightened society cannot presuppose this. An enlightened society, it seems to me, has to believe in the essential guiltlessness of children. And if a child's intrinsic goodness fails, then this enlightened society must surely ask the question why.

Why should a child want to kill another child it has no obvious grudge against, or does not even know? Where does the fantasy, which no doubt underlies this act, begin, and why? And what causes, forces or enables a child to take that fatal step from fantasy to enactment?

In the case of the two boys who killed James Bulger—and we will not know for a long time which of the two was the moving force in this awful act—we now know, which the Court did not, that both of them had for years gone through profoundly upsetting childhood experiences. Unhappily, they found each other at a dangerous critical time in both their lives and, supporting each other, together breached that fatal line which neither would probably ever have crossed on his own.

The parallel with the case of Mary Bell is evident, though there it was clear that her co-defendant, two years older and much loved by her family, was mentally fragile, and that clever little Mary, emotionally abused for years by a seriously disturbed mother, was the leader.

The mystery in both these cases is, how was it possible that relatives and neighbours, teachers and social workers had not recognized the danger, had not understood that these were children approaching a crisis point?

I found in many people I met in Newcastle, and then in Liverpool, an extraordinary collective sense of guilt and unease. In 1968–69, there was little compassion for Mary Bell, and in 1993–94 virtually none for Robert Thompson and Jon Venables.

Nonetheless, in retrospect, there was in both these pivotal cases a public awareness that an undefined failure of—or deficiency in—society had contributed to these dreadful events.

All of Mary Bell's family (as well as, later, the immediate families of the two Liverpool boys) were fully aware of what I was doing. All the information I have about Mary's family life (and, later, that of Robert Thompson and Jon Venables) was given to me by relatives motivated only by a desire to help, and who showed great courage and honesty in doing so. Mary's mother, who was the principal source of all her troubles, not unexpectedly rejected every opportunity to tell me her own story. And Mary's maternal grandmother, in an impossible conflict of loyalties, understandably added only marginally to this account. (It is, I think, of considerable significance in a comparison of the two cases, in terms of their nature and the place and time in which they occurred, that while Mary Bell's extended family stood firm in mutual support throughout and after these events, Jon Venables's parents and Robert Thompson's mother were deserted by practically all their relatives and most of their friends.)

In these pages I criticize the provisions which were eventually made for Mary Bell. The authorities involved have always known of my misgivings and it was therefore all the more to their credit that they co-operated with me on a number of occasions, including inviting me to conferences at the Home Office and enabling me repeatedly to visit the unit where Mary was held. It would be very wrong if my remarks here led to the impression, even at this late date, that there was ever even the slightest element of indifference in the official attitude toward Mary Bell. On the contrary, considering the number of children whose needs were just as pressing as hers, her case received throughout an extraordinary amount of attention and consideration.

Twenty-six years on, things have regressed rather than progressed. We live in an age where neither parents, schools, churches, nor for that matter police are willing or able to exercise authority. Parents are too busy or too depressed; teachers are over-extended and unsupported by parents; churches have become largely irrelevant to the young; and the British police— once upon a time a model for the whole world—are seen as a penalizing rather than as a supportive body. The life of human beings in this last decade of the century is not ruled by thought, or morality, but almost entirely by economics; by money despairingly earned and, ever more of it, desperately needed; by money controlled—given or refused—by what has become a much too powerful and entirely materialistic state, and by values which, largely dictated by money, are reflected in much we read, and see on the ever-present screen.

Within this atmosphere of having and needing, our children exist in a moral void. Shoplifting and car-thieving are considered a sport by children as young as seven; burglary is becoming a profession for young teenagers; violent child criminality, much of it drug-related, is ever increasing, and the only solution the government of the day has presently found is the creation of five secure training units which, staffed by private security firms appointed after competitive tendering, will attempt to re-educate, or "train" as they are calling it, about 200 "persistent young offenders" between 12 and 14 years old.

While I am not as horrified as some experts in penal reform at the idea of possibly quite tough educational and work-training centres for kids who have come to reject all structure, the very idea of allowing semi- or non-experienced personnel anywhere near either the re-education or supervision of child offenders is highly questionable. Furthermore, changing the Criminal Justice Bill in order to allow the government to create punitive provisions for two hundred youngsters seems yet again a purely political gesture when what is needed are enlightened re-education facilities probably for several thousand rather than a few hundred.

In the final analysis, however, it is society itself, through the family framework on which its stability rests, that needs strengthening and safeguarding, in each instance from the moment a child is born. The offending child is a symbol of family—and more than that, of societal—breakdown.

Cases such as Mary Bell's, and now the one of the boys who killed James Bulger, are the extreme; they are, one might say, the expression of ultimate anger, the final cry for help.

But, in the wake of the huge outcry following the murder of James Bulger, it is important to point out, once again, that these cases are so far very rare. Over the past two and a half centuries, there have been 27 recorded cases in Britain of children under fourteen killing other children, and four more who killed adults. This is no more than one such case per decade and the incidence in other Western European countries is about the same. But it is true that as family pressures continue to intensify and other cases of child violence proliferate, these extreme cases are likely to increase too. And it is shameful that Britain, which led the world in radical social reforms following World War II, today limps behind most Western nations in resources for children's psychiatric and social services, and that the British judicial system, with regard to capital crime committed by children, has remained unchanged for centuries, almost as if we still lived in the age when children were whipped and hanged.

Twenty-five years ago, when I decided to undertake this book, I did so with considerable reluctance. I was profoundly conscious of the moral problems involved, not only in writing about someone who was still a child, but even more, in setting up a permanently available record of the unhappy circumstances of Mary Bell's child-life which she herself—and, I already thought then, any children she might eventually have—would one day have to confront. But, the persistent incomprehension of Mary's situation, demonstrated by the circumstances of her detention, persuaded me that nothing would help Mary then, and other children after her, except a public exposition of her case.

Some changes were eventually made, partly, I was told, as a result of public pressure after the publication of this story. Above all, the authorities determined never again to be found lacking in the provisions available for seriously disturbed children, and further secure units were set up, theoretically including psychiatric care.

But, as we saw again in Liverpool in 1993–94, it was all still too little and too late. The reason such tragedies happen is that there is still too much ignorance within families about how to live and how to love. And a state which is ruled by a dogma of non-interference in private lives—which, admittedly, of course, can save enormous sums of money—is showing ever less compassion for troubled adults, far too little care for troubled children, and entirely lacks the courage to separate children from parents when the relationship is manifestly destructive.

The fact is that, in a modern state at the end of the twentieth century, it should be impossible for social services to remain unaware of crises in crisis families; it should be impossible for children who behave conspicuously in school not to be noticed and attended to; it should be considered outrageous that either men or women caring for children on their own are not provided unstintingly with human and financial assistance.

Prevention of cases such as those described in this book is entirely dependent on knowledge: knowledge about relationships, between men and women, husbands and wives, parents and children, brothers and sisters, extended families and friends.

In both of the extreme cases I examine here, all these relationships, which normally nourish children's lives, were limited, faulty, damaged or had broken down. All these children needed to leave home in order to be safe, and all of the immediate families needed intensive social-service—and psychiatric—help if they were to be equipped to care for their children.

In this book, both I hope a guideline and a warning, I describe as much of the relationships as possible, though necessarily seen through the eyes of involved adults.

Ultimately, however, the only people who can one day help us towards complete understanding and thereby allow us to come much closer to achieving means of prevention, are the "children" themselves. So far, this has never been tried.

In the case of Mary Bell, she was released from prison in 1980 when she was 23 and has since, though living "under licence" (supervision by the authorities), achieved, I think, a kind of triumph, by creating a normal life for herself. It is my hope that one day, soon, she and I will talk again. This time I will hope to learn from her directly rather than through others, what happened to and in her during the first ten years of her life, and during her twelve years of detention—the last two of which, it is worth noting, under the stewardship of a wise prison governor, were evidently of benefit to her. Then perhaps, with the help of this intelligent young woman who has managed to emerge comparatively safely on the other side of a kind of hell, only some of which was of her own making, we can achieve a further step along the rocky path to understanding.

And, although the acts committed by the two boys who murdered Jamie Bulger were somehow infinitely worse, perhaps ten or more years from now Robert Thompson and Jon Venables—if they are lucky enough to receive sensitive help in prison—will also have changed and grown sufficiently to understand themselves and to communicate this understanding to others.

It is only if we learn to understand the impulses which preceded the acts described in this book that we may, at some point in a more enlightened future, manage to eliminate the circumstances which in Britain alone, twenty-seven times during more than two centuries, have driven children to murder children.

ACKNOWLEDGMENTS

This book could not have been written without the help of a great many people. I owe thanks above all to my family and close friends who have lived it with me for so long; to John Anstey, Editor of the *Daily Telegraph Magazine*, for the original concept; Miriam Rosenthal Hodgson, my editor at Eyre Methuen, for her unflagging support in face of many problems; my old Newcastle friends Olive and Hans S. for the solace of their home on so many occasions; Helene Thimig Reinhardt for her help at a crucial moment; and Dr. Christopher Ounsted for his valued advice.

The enlightened support of the Newcastle civic authorities, many of whom, at their request, I did not name, made it possible for me to document this account. The Chief Constable of Northumberland, Mr. C. H. Cooksley, Q.P.M.; and, above all, Superintendent James Dobson, B.E.M., made it possible for me to document the account of the police investigation. Mr. Brian Roycroft, appointed as Newcastle's Children's Officer shortly before the trial took place, was one of the people I was not allowed to name at the time. Today, however, when he has just retired after twenty-one years as one of the most enlightened Social Service Directors Britain has ever had, I can say that without his passion for social justice and, I think because of it, his help to me over the years, there are many things I would have found difficult to do.

This now applies, too, to all those, in Liverpool and Preston, none of whom I can name at this point, who supported my efforts to find out the truth about the two boys who killed Jamie Bulger. A very special thanks here to Liz Jobey, Editor of the *Independent on Sunday Review*, whose involvement with this story went way beyond the bounds of "duty"; I'm thankful I can write for her.

All those whose honesty, compassion, and concern have

prompted them to stand by me during my work on both these harrowing tales: the families concerned, their neighbours and friends, doctors and lawyers, police officers, social workers and teachers—all of them should know that I admire their courage and that I am grateful to them for their trust and—many of them—for becoming my friends.

Gitta Sereny
London, August 1994

AUTHOR'S NOTE

Except for the principals, names of all children who were more than marginally affected by the events described in this book have been deleted, equally those of Mary Bell's family except for her parents.

By agreement with the Chief Constable of Northumberland the surnames of all policewomen who were concerned with Mary Bell have been deleted.

The account of the trial is taken verbatim from the transcript, with dots indicating deletions.

PROLOGUE

The eighth day of the trial at Newcastle Assizes was a cold, bleak day in December. It rained outside, the interminable mid-winter drizzle of the English north. The paneled courtroom—the central heating turned on to capacity "because of the children"—smelled of wet hair and wet winter coats. The room was packed but quiet. The lights were on, the faces of the onlookers as well as participants strained and pallid. The atmosphere was one of unease; the audience in the public gallery looked as if—no less than the jury— they were there out of necessity, not by choice.

"Members of the Jury," Mr. Justice Cusack began his summing up. He sat on his throne-seat on the raised and blocked-off dais, in his white wig, red robe, and ermine; the High Sheriff in full regalia sat on his left, his Clerk in morning dress on his right. But he spoke quietly and slowly, in brief sentences, using familiar words and phrases. In a deliberate attempt to humanize and simplify the proceedings, he tried to bridge the gulf between himself and the Jury by speaking to them as man to man, as mind to mind.

> It is an unpleasant thing for any Court to have to try a case in which it is alleged that two little boys, one aged three, the other aged four, lost their lives by murder. It is even more unpleasant and distasteful when it is alleged that the persons responsible are two girls respectively aged eleven and thirteen. . . .

The two girls, Mary, eleven, and Norma, thirteen, separated by two policewomen in plain clothes, sat not as is customary in the dock, but in the center of the Court, in the second row, behind their counsel, near their solicitors, in front of and within reach of their families. Their hair brushed shiny, their gaily colored cotton dresses always freshly washed and ironed, their cardigans spotless, they sat there, five and a half hours each day, throughout the trial. This was their duty, and their privilege; the law prescribes that the Accused hear all that is said for and against them; only this way can they protect themselves and be protected. Only this way can justice be preserved.

> I have no doubt [continued Mr. Justice Cusack] that some people may feel that it is out of place to try girls of that age by Judge and Jury with all the formality of an Assize Court. But, leaving aside altogether for the moment the details of this case, it is an unfortunate fact of human experience, isn't it, that quite young children can be wicked and sometimes even vicious.... Who, Members of the Jury, could hope to understand and assess the intricacies of this case and reach a fair judgement upon it, if they had not heard the evidence which you and I have listened to for so many days, and heard it probed and examined by advocates whose duty it is to place the facts fairly and squarely before the Court? I say these things to you so that you may understand why this trial takes place at all and in case you should be puzzled by it. It has had many painful aspects. It has had its distressing moments. But, distressing moments sometimes arise too in the trial of adults, because it is an unhappy thing that the Criminal Courts, for the most part, are not concerned with the successful things of life, but are concerned with life's shadows.
>
> Members of the Jury, the truth of the matter is this: that Parliament in making the Law has said that any child over ten years of age may be tried on a criminal charge. You and I are bound by the Law and we must administer that Law as it is and not as it might be if it were re-written, perhaps nearer to the heart's desire. And you above all, in reaching your decisions, must be governed, not by hearts but by your heads, and that is an important thing to have in mind. There has been, of course, every kind of emotion in this case, and everybody who has listened to it, must have been subject to ... astonishment, dismay, horror, pity. Put all that aside. Judge the case only on the facts as you find them to be, having listened to the evidence. Don't be swayed either by sympathy for the two girls who are so young and find themselves

on so serious a charge, or by sympathy for the parents and relations of those two little boys who lost their lives tragically, whoever or whatever may have been the cause of their deaths. . . .

PART ONE

SUMMER 1968

In the early afternoon of Saturday, 11 May 1968, the police and an ambulance were called to the Delaval Arms, a pub in the Scotswood district of Newcastle upon Tyne: a small boy, John G., aged three, had been found injured in the vicinity of the pub. The next morning the police took statements from two girls who had found him: Norma Joyce Bell, thirteen, and Mary Flora Bell, ten, who were neighbors but not related.

Norma Bell's statement read:

> I am 13 years of age and live with my mother and father at 68 Whitehouse Road, Newcastle-upon-Tyne. I attend Whickham View Benwell Lower School.
>
> About 1.30 p.m. on Saturday, 11 May 1968, I was playing in the street with my friend Mary Bell and we met John G. We took him to the shop at the bottom of Delaval Road for some sweets. We then took him back to the top of the steps at Delaval Road/Whitehouse Road and told him to go home.
>
> Mary and I then went and got some wood from the old houses in Coanwood Road and brought that home to our mothers.
>
> We then went to play on the car park beside the Delaval Arms.
>
> While we were playing there Mary told me that she could hear some shouts from the direction of the old sheds beside the Delaval Arms.
>
> We went over the grass and through the wire fence and found John G. behind the sheds. He was bleeding from the head.
>
> We jumped down and picked him up but could not lift him up onto the grass. We climbed back onto the grass and pulled him up by his hands.
>
> We shouted to a man who was passing on Scotswood Road

but he would not help. Then we saw another man on Scotswood Road and shouted for him and he carried John to the Delaval Arms where an ambulance and the Police were sent for.

I have never seen John playing down there before and I have never taken him down there.

signed: N. Bell

Taken at 68 Whitehouse Road between 11.30 a.m. and 11.55 a.m., 12 May 1968 by Sgt. 462 Thompson.

Mary Flora Bell's statement read:

I am 10 years of age and attend Delaval Road Junior School. I live at 70 Whitehouse Road with my mother.

At 1.15 p.m. on Saturday, 11 May 1968, I left the house to play with my friend Norma Joyce Bell, 68 Whitehouse Road. We were playing in the street when we met John G., 60 Whitehouse Road. He started to cry so Norma and I took him to the shop at the corner of Delaval Road and St Margaret's Road to get some sweets.

Norma got him some sweets and we took him to the steps at Whitehouse Road and told him to go home.

We then left him and went to the empty houses in Coanwood Road to collect sticks. We got some sticks and took them home to our mothers.

We then went to Vickers Armstrong Car Park beside the Delaval Arms and started to play. While we were playing I heard John shouting 'May' and 'Norma'. This seemed to be coming from the empty sheds next to the Delaval Arms.

We went through the grass and through the fence and found John staggering around behind the sheds. He had bleeding from his head and had been sick all over his coat.

We jumped down and tried to get him up onto the grass but could not, so climbed back up and took hold of his hands and lifted him up onto the grass.

We shouted to a man who was passing along Scotswood Road but he would not help. Then another man was walking along Scotswood Road and we shouted to him. This man took John to the Delaval Arms where an ambulance and the Police were sent for.

I don't know how John got down behind the sheds, I have never taken him there to play before.

signed: Mary Bell

Taken at 70 Whitehouse Road between 10.40 and 11 a.m., 12 May 1968 by Sgt. 462 Thompson.

That same evening, 12 May 1968 at 9:30 P.M., Mrs. Watson of 48 Woodlands Crescent, Newcastle upon Tyne 5, made a complaint to the police alleging that her daughter Pauline, aged seven, and two friends, Cindy Hepple, six, and Susan Cornish, six, that afternoon between 4:30 and five P.M., in the sandpit of the Woodlands Crescent Nursery, had been assaulted by one of two older girls: Norma Joyce Bell, aged thirteen, or Mary Flora Bell, aged ten. The blotches on both sides of Pauline's neck—she said later—remained visible for three days.

In a statement taken the next day by Police Sergeant A. Lindgren and Woman Police Constable I. Charlton at the Watsons' home, Pauline Watson said that at about 4:30 P.M., Sunday 12 May 1968, she had gone to the Nursery at the end of Woodlands Crescent with Cindy Hepple, Wendy Hepple, and Susan Cornish, and that two big girls had come in.

> The smallest one of the two girls told me to get out of the sandpit [she said]. I said no. She put her hands around my neck and squeezed hard. The bigger girl was behind the hut, playing. The girl took her hands off my neck and she did the same to Susan. Me, Cindy and Susan all ran home. The girl who squeezed my neck had short dark hair. I don't know this girl and had not seen her before.

At 4:30 P.M. on 13 May, Woman Police Constable Jean Birkett took a statement from Norma Joyce Bell:

> I am 13 years of age and I live at 68 Whitehouse Road, Newcastle-upon-Tyne, with mam, dad, five sisters and five brothers. I go to Whickham View (Lower) School and I am in Class 5.
>
> After tea (about 4.40 p.m.) yesterday, Sunday 12 May

1968, I went with Mary Bell who lives next door, up to Woodstock Road to see some hens that were up there. We stayed up there for a while and then we came back down home. Then we went along to the Nursery to play. We were playing inside the fence that was around the Nursery. There were two other girls there. One was called Pauline Watson but I don't know what the other one was called. We were talking to these two girls. Mary was talking to Pauline saying, 'Do you know Mary Bell?' The girl said, 'Yes, you are Mary Bell.' Mary said, 'No, I'm not.' Mary then said to Pauline, 'Can you fight Mary Bell?' Pauline said, 'Yes, I can fight you.' Then Mary went to the other girl and said, 'What happens if you choke someone, do they die?' Then Mary put both hands round the girl's throat and squeezed. The girl started to go purple. I told Mary to stop but she wouldn't. She did this for a while and then she put her hands round Pauline's throat and she started going purple as well. Both Pauline and the other girl were crying. Another girl, Susan Cornish, came up and Mary did the same to her. Susan had some rock (sweets) and Mary took this off her. I said to Mary, 'There'll be trouble,' and then Mary asked me if I wanted some rock. I said, 'Yes', and had a little piece from her. I then ran off and left Mary. I'm not friends with her now.

Signed: N. Bell
Witness: C. Bell (mother)

Between 6:55 and 7:10 P.M. Monday, 13 May 1968, Woman Police Constable I. Charlton took a statement from Mary Flora Bell at Tower View Section Police Station.

I am 10 years of age and I live with my mammy, two sisters and one brother at 70 Whitehouse Road, Newcastle-upon-Tyne. I go to Delaval Road Junior School.

After tea (about 4.45 p.m.) yesterday, Sunday 12 May 1968, I went out with my friend Norma Bell who lives at 68 Whitehouse Road. We went to the Nursery next to Woodlands Crescent. We got in through a hole in the fence. There were two other girls there. One is called Pauline Watson and the other is Cindy Hepple. Norma and I were talking to these two girls. Norma said to Pauline, 'Do you know Mary Bell?' Pauline said, 'Yes'. Norma then said to Pauline, 'Can you fight Mary Bell?' Pauline said, 'No.' Norma said, 'Do you wish that Mary Bell was dead?' Pauline said, 'No'. I told Norma to shut up and I went behind a shed to play. When I was behind the shed I heard Pauline scream. I came from behind the shed and I saw Pauline running away towards the fence. She was holding her throat and screaming. I asked Norma what had happened and she said that Pauline had fallen and hurt her throat on the edge of the sand pit. I didn't see Cindy then. I then walked down home with Norma and went in the house.

> Signed: M. Bell
> Witness: E. Bell (mother)

Mary's headmistress at the Delaval Road Junior School told me that Mrs. Bell (Mary's mother) came to see her on Monday, 13 May 1968, told her about the alleged sandpit incident, and asked her to "get to the bottom of this accusation against her daughter." "She seemed honestly concerned that I should find out the truth," said the headmistress, "so I called Pauline in and asked her to tell *me* honestly who had squeezed her neck. She said, 'Please Miss, I don't know the girl,' and she wouldn't say anything else. Of course, by this time everybody was talking about it. When I took her to the door I saw Mary Bell waiting just a little way down the corridor. I didn't know what to believe."

On 15 May 1968, Police Sergeant Lindgren enclosed the statements in his report to his superintendent, and said that in view of the home circumstances of the two older girls the Childrens Department had been notified. His report continued, "When the three children were seen by me about 9.30 p.m., Sunday 12 May 1968, they bore no marks or injuries to substantiate the complaints. The parents have been advised to take out a private summons for common assault if they so wish. They are satisfied with the action taken by the police and do not intend to take action themselves.

"The girls BELL have been warned as to their future conduct."

CHAPTER ONE
SCOTSWOOD

Newcastle upon Tyne shares the·curious characteristic of many of Britain's industrial cities of looking empty even when the streets are full, poor even in relatively affluent times, gray even in brightest sunshine. But, lying 275 miles north of London, with a population of about 250,000, it has a large number of good schools and hospitals, a university of repute, a famous medical school, a progressive Council with one of the best social service departments in the country, and all the trappings of a lively metropolis: a large shopping district with branches of several London stores; two daily and one Sunday paper; two theaters, cinemas, restaurants, three large hotels, two of them hypermodern, a new airport open to intercontinental jets, and a maze of one-way streets creating insuperable traffic problems. Newcastle also has some of the most beautiful surrounding country in Britain, and its own dialect, "Geordie": "Gizabroonjack," for example, means "Give me a pint of brown ale," "hyem" stands for "home," "wor lass" is "my wife" or "the little woman." "Thordeeincanny" means "They are doing very well." "Canny" can also be translated as "pretty," or again as "many" (in which case the phrase might be "aycannyfew.") When a child thinks that it is going to be punished it speaks of being "wronged," and in a phrase like "She asked me something," the word "us" replaces "me," all somewhat bewildering to the outsider.

Newcastle is the urban center for many nearby mining villages and shipyards. Coal mining has for some time been a dying industry in Britain, and the shipyards throughout the economically depressed 1960s suffered from labor troubles and increasing competition from abroad. Throughout that decade, Newcastle had the dubious distinction of having the highest crime record (35,882 indictable crimes in 1970), the highest rate of alcoholism (six to eight pints of brown ale per night the accepted norm), and one of the consistently highest unemployment figures of any city in Britain (4.2 percent against the national average of 3.5 percent).

Despite these disadvantages the people of Newcastle are warm and friendly and nowhere more so than in the partly very poor working-class districts such as Scotswood where half the men are frequently out of work.

Scotswood, an area covering half a square mile inhabited by around 17,000 people, lies on a hill three miles from the city center. In the late 1960s, large tracts of Scotswood land were cleared for re-building. Already in the streets nearest to the city several ten- to twelve-story monsters had been built to take the overflow from streets like Woodland Crescent, Whitehouse Road, and St Margaret's Road, which were still lined with condemned houses. If the streets of Scotswood could be described as being in layers, then St Margaret's Road would be the first layer at the foot of the hill and Whitehouse Road, running above and parallel, the second. Both these streets look out over railway tracks, a large tract of waste land—the "Tin Lizzie"—Scotswood Road, the huge Vickers plant, the River Tyne, and the city.

Whitehouse Road, wide and windswept on top of the hill, is a clean and elegantly curving street, with generous pavements, ample space for bicycling and parking, and a spectacular view of the city. The red-brick, terraced, semidetached houses, here as well as in St Margaret's Road and all the nearby streets, date from between the two world wars and are Council property. Many of the gardens are well cared for with shrubs, flowers, or, if nothing else, a little grass. Someday, this street, because of its position, could become "fashionable" and the houses "converted" into valuable "period" properties.

But, for the present, most of the tenants pay the Council £2.20 rent a week (about $5.50) with rebates available in hard times. They huddle around the coal-fed fireplace in the front room—the only heating; watch slot-television; fight to keep up payments to the "tallyman" or "clubs"; live with the constant threat of unemployment, and try to cope with anger, lethargy, despair, and their destructive effects: petty crime, gambling, and drink for the men, nervous breakdowns for the women, and fights and demoralization for the children. Despite these hardships many of the houses in

Scotswood are neat and clean, many of the parents kind and honorable, many of the children intelligent and bright-eyed.

In May 1968, June and George Brown and their children, Martin and Linda, were such a family.

CHAPTER TWO
MARTIN BROWN

25 May 1968: Four Years and Two Months Old

The Browns' house at 140 St Margaret's Road is the same as most of the others: downstairs the kitchen and sitting room, upstairs two bedrooms and a bath. But the front room is warm and tidy—with a settee and comfortable armchair, a pleasant rug on the floor. The fire is almost always kept burning; somehow these houses always retain the damp of the long days of rain.

On Saturday, 25 May 1968, Martin got up around 6:30 A.M. as he always did. He was four years and two months old and had a sturdy body and a ravenous appetite, wavy, light blond hair, a round mischievous face, a fair complexion, and blue eyes—"shiny blue," as his mother said later. He loved his one-year-old sister Linda, and his "Mam" June, and "Dad" Georgie, whom he more often than not called by his first name.

He also loved the Bennetts, the next-door neighbors. "They loved him like: he was that kind of lad—grown people could talk to him," his mother told me later. Rita Finlay, June's older sister, lived two blocks down the street with her four children, and he loved her too.

Martin and Linda's bedroom was the smaller of the two. There were Martin's bed and Linda's cot, no sheets but plenty of blankets and pillows, a teddy, a doll, and a few plastic cars. On Saturdays and Sundays, the Browns had a lie-in, so Martin was careful not to make a sound when he went down to the scullery to get himself a piece of bread and a glass of milk. When he'd finished his downstairs, he brought some up for Linda. He stood on tiptoe and, leaning over the side of the cot, carefully held the cup for the baby, waiting patiently while she ponderously chewed and rechewed her piece of bread. "He always did that," said June. "I'd hear him coax her, 'Come on, Linda, drink yer milk.'" Later he got her up and dressed her, and just before nine they went in to wake up their mother. "He had his breakfast around nine," June said. She is blonde with long hair and a fringe (bangs), and a slightly tremulous, warm smile. "Sugarpops," she said, "them were his favorites. He got his anorak—I was in the scullery—I heard him call, 'I'm away, mam, tara Georgie'; that was the last I saw or heard of him."

Later that Saturday morning—though they didn't remember exact times—John Hall and Gordon Collinson, two workmen from the Newcastle Electricity Board, noticed a small boy in a blue anorak watching them disconnect power cables from derelict houses in St Margaret's Road. They had put up a railing around the hole in the ground where they worked and a canvas tent against the ever-threatening rain.

Martin probably came and went all morning, because at eleven he dropped in on his Aunt Rita at 112 St Margaret's Road. Rita Finlay, a little blowzy, with shoulder-length black hair and a quick temper, is a mother-earth figure. She yells easily and laughs easily, spends easily and, no doubt, gives easily too. "I love kids," she says, and one believes her. "I had an arrangement with June—she worked, you see, so our mam had Linda, and I had Martin every day while she was out at work; except Saturday and Sunday. Saturday I'd have a late lie-in and then I'd clean my house from top to bottom. And I'd do my hair like, to step out you know, at night. Well, that Saturday morning I woke up with Martin's face looming over me. 'Fita,' that was what he called me, 'are you going to get up?' he says, and I don't mind telling you, I was mad, I really was. 'Will you get out of here?' I screamed at him—I hate to say it now, but I did, I really did, I let him have it and I pushed him out, 'you get out of here. . . .' My mam had come by too. Martin, he was crying, and she said, 'Now, there's no need to shout at him,' and she gave him an egg on toast. He was standing munching it on the stairs and still crying; so I went to him, you know, and I says, 'Now you stop crying. It's all right. Is it all right now, Martin?' and he nodded like. No, I don't remember seeing him go then—we didn't think to watch when they came and went, you know—all the kids are all over the place—Martin—everybody was his friend. . . .

"Norma Bell and Mary Bell came in later," Rita went on. "Norma was a nice girl—I loved that girl, I really did. I felt that close to her. She was always here—she loved my John, who was three then. She loved baby-sitting and she was that good with him. I didn't like that other one, that Mary Bell, but they were always together, so they came here together too. It was a lovely day, that Saturday. I'd said I'd give the kids their dinner in the garden. But I was first going to see my mam, and I had enough common sense not to leave the bairns alone ever. So, when I came back from seeing my mam—it must have been about a quarter to three—because I knew I'd have to buy some things for dinner, and Dixon's shop across the road opened at three (after lunch)—those two girls must still have been here, waiting for me to come back."

It was just about then that Martin was noticed again. "He came in just before Dixon's shop opened," said June Brown, "to get some money off Georgie for his lollipop—I didn't see him."

Dixon's shop is a small, wooden shack, ten feet back from the street. The window is full of sweets, pencils, blocks of paper, cigarette advertisements, cheap lighters, red-ribboned boxes of chocolates, ice-creams and darning wool. There are thousands of such shops all over the country, still the principal source of casual shopping for many families and the main suppliers of sweets and ice-cream for their children.

At five minutes past three, Martin Brown stood in a queue of children, waiting to buy his lollipop.

Mr. Dixon's son, Wilson, an organist by profession, had known Martin since he was born. He had come over from Winlanton, six miles away, as he frequently did on busy days to help his father. "I went down to the shop about five past three," he said. "There were many young children outside. Martin was among the crowd when I opened the shop and served one or two other children. By that time it was ten past three. When Martin wanted to be served he was standing with his fingers in his mouth. I scolded him because his hands were filthy. I served him and several other children. He went out. By that time it would be about a quarter past three. I think he bought a lollipop."

"I was in Dixon's shop," Rita Finlay says. "Wilson Dixon says now I wasn't, but I was: because I remember him smacking Martin's hands because he'd had his fingers in his mouth and he was all black from playing. 'Can I come up and have my dinner?' Martin said, and I told him, 'go back home and wash your hands.' 'I can wash them at your house,' he said, so I let him. And I gave him bread and he took a knife to put on butter. 'Don't use the butter,' I said, 'use margarine—the best butter is for tea.' He was angry. 'I'm not coming to your house bloody no more,' he said. 'I won't come again. . . .' But he couldn't stay mad for long. 'Oh, don't be like that, Fita,' he said and then he went and that was the last I saw of him."

The old condemned houses in front of which the men from the Electricity Board were working were only a few yards up and on the other side of the street from Rita Finlay's house. At 3:30 P.M., just fifteen minutes after Martin Brown had been seen by Wilson Dixon, three boys, John Henry Southern, sixteen; Walter Long, thirteen; and Fred Myhill, eight, entered No. 85 to look for scrapwood which they needed to build a pigeon dovecote. The house was boarded up in front, so the boys got in through the back yard. Going up to the first floor, Walter Long went to look in the front and the two other boys into what had been the back bedroom. When Walter heard one of them shout, he ran to see what was going on.

A small boy was lying in front of the window, on his back on the rubble-covered floor, with his arms outstretched and with blood and saliva coming from his mouth.

Fred Myhill, the youngest of the three, fled at once, and Walter and John ran out to get the electricians, who were having a cup of tea in their shelter outside No. 85.

"We knew the little boy right away," said John Hall. "I'd given him some biscuits earlier on," said Gordon Collinson. "We hadn't seen him again after lunch," John Hall continued.

"I ran to call an ambulance," said Gordon Collinson. The call, officially recorded by the ambulancemen, was received at 3:35 P.M.

"I gave him the kiss of life," said John. "I just held him in my arms all the time. He looked dead to me like. His body was cold."

Walter Long felt sick after he and John Southern had brought the workmen up, and went to another room to get some air. While he stood with his head out of a window overlooking St Margaret's Road, he saw two dark-haired girls walking toward the house. The road was otherwise empty at the time. They stopped directly underneath his window and the smaller one, whom he knew—Mary Flora Bell—said to the other, "Shall we go up?" "Howay then, let's go up," Walter says he heard the taller one reply.

The girls then climbed through a partly boarded-up window on the ground floor of the house next door, No. 83, went through into the back yard and through a partly demolished outhouse into No. 85. Walter Long stopped them as they came up the stairs, he told the court later.

"Get away down," he shouted.

"That's all right—the police know I'm here," he says Mary Bell replied. "They weren't allowed up though—they were told to go away," he said.

"It seemed like just minutes after I'd last seen Martin," says Rita Finlay, "there was a knock on the door and when I went, it was them two: Norma and Mary; and I said, 'What do yous want?'

" 'One of your bairns has had an accident,' the other one said first—you know, that Mary. 'No,' she said, then, 'I think it's your June's. But there's blood all over . . .' But I thought it couldn't be Martin—I'd just put him out. It had to be John. I hadn't seen him in some time . . . I'd put on some sausages to cook and put half my hair in curlers after I'd put Martin out—that's how little time it was since. But them two girls had come two times before to say that a bairn had had an accident; both those times I said, 'Did you tell his mother?' Both times they said, 'No, we came to tell you.' So I says, 'Why tell us, go tell his mam.' So when they came this time I thought they were having us on. But then I seen this woman wave to us from the street and I dropped everything, sausages and all, and I didn't even think of the bairns—I just left them and ran. Even when I got there, I didn't really believe it. I tripped over a brick in the back yard and pulled myself up on somebody and when I looked, it was Mary. There she was next to me again. She said, 'I'll show you where it is.' I was going hysterical, I told her to get out of my way and followed a man up some stairs into a small bedroom where I saw Martin in the arms of another man. He looked asleep like. I kept saying, 'He'll wake up in a minute. He's asleep—that's all.' "

"It was about 3:35 or a bit later," June Brown recalls, "when

Georgie talked to somebody at the door. He turned round—when I saw his face I knew. I knew something had happened. Georgie stayed with Linda—I just ran. I didn't know where it was, but I turned into the old houses, I just knew it was there. When I got there, Rita was there and she kept saying, 'He's just asleep,' but I knew—I knew he was dead. When they brought him down I saw him—his face was—you know, graylike, mouselike—I knew. . . . They tried to revive him in the ambulance. I watched them, but I knew."

The police, informed by the hospital just after 3:40 P.M. that Martin was dead, sent a sergeant and constables from the uniformed division (who are in charge of accidents) straight to the scene. They arrived after Martin's body had been removed. As far as they could see there was no sign of a struggle or fall. There was a hole in the ceiling, but it was diagonally opposite where Martin had been found. He couldn't possibly have fallen across the room.

There was a thick layer of dust everywhere, and none of it had been disturbed except where, of course, all the people who had handled Martin had stood, or squatted with him in their arms. That evening, the pathologist, Dr. Bernard Knight, carried out a *post mortem* and found it impossible to determine the cause of the boy's death. Martin had been fit, well nourished, and healthy. There were no external injuries except a trivial knee bruise. His clothing was not torn nor damaged, nor were there any broken bones. The only abnormality the internal examination revealed was a small hemorrhage in the brain which was slightly swollen.

"I thought at first that the most likely possibility was poisoning," Dr. Knight said, "because of the circumstances and because there were empty bottles found in the house. But this was later ruled out when the analysis revealed no drugs or chemicals."

"They asked us hundreds of questions," June Brown said, "whether anybody in the family had had fits and all that—it went on for days. They took me to see Martin. I don't know what I thought he'd look like. They warned me, about the autopsy like, but I didn't think. How can we know what it's like? But when I saw him, you know, with brown sawdust in his nose and everywhere, I . . . I said nobody else was to see him."

Dr. Knight said later that another possible explanation—asphyxia—had occurred to him, but strangulation which left no pressure marks whatever seemed quite impossible; Martin's neck had been unblemished. So he had discarded it.

The Uniformed Division, for some reason without further inquiry, accepted that Martin's death had been an accident, and the C.I.D. (Criminal Investigation Department) was never brought into the case.

"The day after Martin died," Rita Finlay said, "it was a Sunday—those two girls, Norma and Mary, came and asked to take John out. I thought it was very good of them. With having four children I was a bit upset and I said, 'If you dress him you can take him, but you will have to make sure he is tidy.' They washed his face and combed his hair and they took him away. They came every day after that to play with him, or to take him to the shops. They kept asking me, 'Do you miss Martin?' and 'Do you cry for him?' and 'Does June miss him?' and they were always grinning. In the end I could stand it no more and I told them to get out and not to come back. I couldn't think, you know, why they were doing it, but then I was upset like so maybe I just didn't think."

That Sunday, 26 May, was Mary Bell's eleventh birthday, and Mary and Susan—Norma Bell's eleven-year-old sister who also occasionally played with Mary—took Mary's Alsatian for a walk in Hodkin Park. "Mary asked us whether I'd sent her a birthday card," Susan said, "and I said I had. But Mary said I hadn't and chased me all the way back to our house with her dog and then she tried to strangle me."

When Susan's parents heard her scream they dashed out, they say, and saw Mary and Susan standing near the front door of the house, Mary with both hands around Susan's neck.

"I chopped Mary's hands away," says Mr. Bell, "and gave her a clip on the shoulder. She said, 'I'm going to tell my dad,' and I said, 'You do that.' But I heard no more about it. After that I didn't let Susan play with her no more."

Woodlands Crescent is a small curved street at the end of Whitehouse Road. The Day Nursery, well staffed and equipped to take care of the children in a community where a large number of mothers go out to work, is in an old two-story house, with a gabled roof. The window frames and door are painted white, there are flowering hedges and small lawns in the front and a playground and sandpit in the back.

On the morning of Monday, 27 May, the teachers arriving at the Nursery found that it had been broken into over the weekend. Slates had been removed, it had been entered through the loft, and large amounts of school and cleaning materials were scattered and smeared round the room. Among the wreckage the police found four pieces of paper, with words scribbled on them in childish writing.

> "I murder
> so that
> I may come
> back,"

said Note one. Note two had the letters "BAS. . . ." at the top, and underneath,

> "fuch of
> we murder
> watch out
>   Fanny
> and Faggot"

Note three said:

> "WE did
> murder
>   Martain
> brown
>   Fuckof
>   you Bastard"

Note four read:

> "You are micey
> y becuase
>   we murderd
> Martain Go
>   Brown you better

> Look out THErE
>   are Murders about
> By FANNYAND
> and auld Faggot
>   you srcews"

The young policeman who had come in answer to the Nursery teachers' telephone call decided that the notes were a nasty prank. He took them back to the station, gave them to the Station-Sergeant, and they were filed away in a drawer. But the Nursery was a valuable property and had been broken into before, so it was decided to install a beeper alarm system in the loft.

That same morning, 27 May, Mr. F.'s class at the Delaval Road Junior School worked on their school "Newsbook" in which, every week, they were encouraged to record current events and interesting things they'd noticed.

Mary Bell drew a picture which showed the outstretched body of a child lying on the floor of a room under a window. Next to the body is a bottle and above it, written partly in capital letters, the word TABLEt. To the left, a man, a cap on his head and a tool over his right shoulder, walks toward the body. Above the drawing, on the left, the date: 27568. Underneath it says:

> On saturday I was in the house. and my mam sent Me to ask Norma if she Would come up the top with me? we went up and we came down at Magrets Road and there were crowds of people beside an old house. I asked what was the matter. there has been a boy who Just lay down and Died.

When the teacher glanced through the forty books at the end of that day, Mary's entry did not strike him. It was only when, many weeks later, he found her newsbook behind a radiator, that he realized that she was the only child who had written about Martin Brown's death.

Four days after Martin had been found, Mary Bell knocked on the door of the Browns' house. "There was another girl or maybe girls down the garden path," June Brown says. "Mary smiled and asked to see Martin. I said, 'No, pet, Martin is dead.' She turned round and said, 'Oh, I know he's dead. I wanted to see him in his coffin,' and she was still grinning. I was just speechless that such a young child should want to see a dead baby and I just slammed the door on her."

On Friday, 31 May, the automatic alarm that had been installed at the Woodlands Crescent Nursery went off in the West End Police Station. The two policemen, who got there within minutes, found two girls in the Nursery Yard. They had broken in by removing slates and climbing through the roof. They were Mary Bell and Norma Bell.

The girls were questioned but positively denied ever having done it before. They were charged with "Breaking and Entering" but were released into their parents' custody until the case could be heard in Juvenile Court, which, as the court calendar was very full, would be months later.

About a week after this, a twelve-year-old boy, who lived near the Nursery and knew both girls, joined them when they were playing near the Nursery sandpit, and saw Mary "tripping Norma up." Norma fell, and Mary jumped on top of her and scratched her face and arm. "I am a murderer," Mary screamed, which made him laugh. But he says he stopped laughing when Mary pulled Norma's hair and kicked her in the eye. He says she then pointed in the direction of the house where little Martin had been found and said, ". . . that house over there, that's where I killed . . . Brown," and that made him laugh again, because Mary Bell was such a show-off and everybody knew it.

On 7 June, the Coroner's inquest on Martin Brown left the cause of death open and Martin's body was released for burial.

"There were so many flowers," Rita Finlay said.

A few days later a crowd of Scotswood residents marched on the Civic Centre to protest against the deplorable housing conditions which allowed such accidents to happen.

Five or six weeks later, toward the later part of July, Mary Bell was visiting the Howes, neighbors at 64 Whitehouse Road. The family consisted of the father and five children from two marriages: four boys and a girl, fourteen-year-old Pat. The mother of the two youngest boys had left them eighteen months before, and Mr. Howe, who had suffered from ill health for many years, was in hospital at the time. Pat, slim, blond, and childlike, but responsible beyond her years, had left school and was keeping house and looking after her two small brothers, Norman, seven, and Brian, three. The oldest boy Albert, twenty-three, was at that time courting a pretty twenty-year-old, Irene, who was also there that day when Mary Bell came by. "Mary was showing us some pictures she had drawn," Irene said, "and she said, 'I know something about Norma that will get her put away straight away.' We asked her what it was and she said we'd tell the police if she told."

When they assured her that they would not, Mary said, "Norma put her hands on a boy's throat. It was Martin Brown; she pressed and he just dropped."

"When we asked her what she meant," Irene said, "she showed us by putting her hands on her own throat. Then she left."

No time was lost in letting Norma's family know about the rumors Mary was spreading. "You'll get wronged," people told Mary. "You wait till Norma's dad tells yours. Will you get it!" Later that day, Mary went and apologized to Norma Bell's mother for what she had said.

CHAPTER THREE
BRIAN HOWE

31 July 1968: Three Years and Four Months Old

Brian Howe had fine, curly, very light blond hair, a strong, small body, a pink-and-white complexion, and a face that, still with the contours of babyhood had a tentative and vulnerable quality. On Wednesday, 31 July 1968, he was three years and four months old. He hardly knew his mother because she had left them when he was only a year and a half, but he loved his father, his step-sister Pat, his brother Norman, and his black-and-white dog, Lassie. Rita Finlay's three-year-old son John was his best friend, and he loved Rita too.

"Pat was always over here," Rita Finlay said. "I used to go and wake her up on my way to taking John to the Nursery and then I'd take Brian too: I'd take them one day and she the next—then she'd wake *me* up. I loved little Brian," said Rita, "different like from the way I loved Martin—but I loved him. That day I was taking my kids to the Nursery and I went to wake up Pat on my way and pick up Brian. I knocked at the Howes' door but they didn't answer. I said to myself, she must be having a lie-in. The woman at the Nursery asked where Brian was."

At lunch time, though, Brian and John met up and they went out to play. Rita went looking for them about 1:30 P.M., she says. "I found them sitting on the ground watching the men pull down one of the old houses. I went mad. I screamed at the men and said didn't they know better—a brick could fall down and kill them—how could they let them sit there? And then I hit the lads so hard, one after the other, my hands were stinging. I put John to bed and I gave Brian some biscuits and sent him home, and told him to tell Pat he'd been to the old buildings but she was not to hit him, because I'd already hit them. That's the last I saw him."

Between two and three that afternoon—it turned out later—

Brian was noticed by a number of children, all of whom saw him playing in the street, with his brother—and two girls on bikes. Lassie was with him, they all said.

"Sometime that afternoon those two lasses—Norma and Mary—came," said Rita, "and Norma asked, 'Where's my boyfriend?' She meant our John. Yes, I am sure she really loved him: she was on about him more than about her own brothers and sisters—she had ten of them you know. I told them the lads had been to the old buildings and that I'd put John to bed. Norma said, 'Put Jacqueline to bed,' as if that had anything to do with it. And then they left. It was such a beautiful day out that day. I nearly got John up and let him go with them. If I had, maybe it would have been him they'd got rather than Brian. . . ."

It was very likely after leaving Rita Finlay's that Mary and Norma came upon Brian playing with the two little girls on the corner of Whitehouse Road and Crosshill Road. And it was him they took for a walk.

At about 3:20 P.M. Pat Howe came back home after spending several hours with friends in another part of the city. She asked Irene, who was still staying with them, where Brian was and was told that he was out playing. About four o'clock, Albert told Pat to go and look for him in the streets.

One of the first people she asked was Maxine Savage, who lived at 66 Whitehouse Road, next to Norma Bell's house. She talked to her on her backsteps—where Maxine was sitting with Mary Bell —but Maxine hadn't seen Brian.

"Are you going to look for your Brian?" Mary asked. "Yes," Pat answered, "Are you coming to help?" Mary Bell was always ready to do anything at a moment's notice. "Yes," she said. Just a few seconds later Norma Bell came up. She said she'd come too, of course. Pat also asked several boys who were about on their bikes to look for Brian and they all went off in different directions. "Howay," Mary said, "let's go down Davy's way first. . . ."

Davy's was a shop at the far end of St Margaret's Road, one of the places where the children congregated quite often. But he wasn't anywhere on the way there, or near the shop, and they started down the hill, across the railway toward the Vickers Armstrong car park—another major attraction for the children of

Scotswood, who had no playgrounds. But he wasn't at the car park either, and they went back up on the railway bridge from where they could see all over the "Tin Lizzie"—the 400 or 500 yards of waste ground full of old building materials, oil drums, and "tanks" just on the other side of the tracks, which the children used as an adventure playground. "He might be playing behind the blocks [they were huge concrete boulders]," Mary Bell said, "or between them." But Norma said firmly, "Oh no, he never goes there."

Pat didn't think so either—not alone he wouldn't anyway, and from where they were standing there wasn't anybody to be seen. "We'll have another look around for him up top," Pat said, "and if we don't find him by seven o'clock, we'll go to the police." Norma ran off saying she was going to play with Linda Routledge. Pat and Mary went the other way to Hodkin Park. There they met Pat's boyfriend and they all came back together. Later Pat came past Linda's house at 59 Whitehouse Road, saying she was going to phone the police. "You coming with us?" she asked Norma, who was still there playing with Linda. But Norma said, "No."

From up the road came the sound of Mary's dad, Billy Bell, calling her in for supper—it was 7:30 P.M.

They found Brian at 11:10 that night. He was lying on the ground, between two concrete blocks on the "Tin Lizzie." His left arm was stretched out from his body, and his hand was black with dirt. Lying on the grass nearby was a pair of scissors with one blade broken and the other bent back. His body was covered with a carpet of long grass and purple weeds—which grew all over the "Tin Lizzie." There were scratch marks on his nose, traces of bloodstained froth at his mouth, his lips were blue, and there were pressure marks and scratches on both sides of his neck. He was dead.

"We'd all been out looking for him for hours," said Rita Finlay, "June and me and—oh, hundreds of people it seemed like. We'd look one way and then another and then come back and have a cup of tea and a sandwich—spam or cornbeef or whatever—and then go out again. By the time they found him we were back home though—it was dark. We could hear the sirens going with all the police cars rushing down there. People called to each other out of their doors, asking what was happening. I don't know who knew first—it went from street to street and house to house."

Mary Bell—a light sleeper at the best of times—came downstairs at 11:30 and joined her dad, who was standing outside the front door watching the commotion in the street. "What's going on then?" she asked.

"They've found Brian Howe," he said, "over on the 'Tin Lizzie.' "

"Oh," said Mary.

Detective Chief-Inspector* James Dobson of the C.I.D. was asleep when his telephone rang at one A.M. (Some time had been lost trying to reach his chief, who was not at home but expected any minute.) "They said the boy Howe had been found under suspicious circumstances, believed stabbed." James Dobson is tall, short-haired, wide-shouldered, with sharp blue eyes, a ready sense of humor, and a sympathetic mind carefully masked by his northern, trenchant manner. Like many others he was to become deeply involved and very troubled by the consequences of this case.

"I pulled on some trousers and a sweater over my pajamas," he recalled, "and I rushed out. I remember it was a clear night. I got over to Scotswood at 1:10 A.M. I could see it from a long way off—they had arclights up by that time. I parked up on the road and as I walked down to the 'Tin Lizzie'—the strange thing, looking back—I suddenly thought of Martin Brown. There wasn't any reason: I'd had nothing to do with that case. But where I stopped was just across from where he'd been found. And it ran through my mind that there must be some connection." The immediate area had been surrounded by uniformed policemen. "There were a lot of people around, but somehow it was very quiet. What I heard most was the clanking of the railway—it's very loud at night."

The bulk of the night was taken up with details. The pathologist's examination established that Brian had been dead for several

* Now Superintendent.

hours. "After that," Mr. Dobson explained, "we took him to Newcastle General for further tests, and we sent for his step-brother, Albert Howe, to identify him formally. Albert had been crying before he came in," Mr. Dobson said, "and he burst into tears again when he saw the body. It was all very sad. We then took him across to West End Police—he made a statement and then we sent him home in a police car."

The *post mortem* revealed three scratch marks on the right side of Brian's neck and two on the left. There were also a series of compression marks on his nose, suggesting that someone had pinched his nose on both sides. In the midline of the scrotum there was a small area of superficial skin loss and a similar one on the tip of the boy's right ring finger. There were six puncture wounds on his thighs and legs: two on the outside of his left thigh, three on the back, and one on the right calf. All these and the mark on his scrotum were superficial wounds which had only punctured the skin.

The pathologist, Dr. Bernard Tomlinson, concluded that the child had been strangled and that little force would have been required to kill a boy of three in this manner. He thought it was unlikely that the attacker was an adult because an adult usually used very much more pressure than was necessary. Equally, the curious playfulness (rather than brutality or viciousness) of the disfigurements pointed to a child or children. The scratch marks on Brian's neck, he thought, were probably caused by his struggling against the person who was attacking him, and he put the time of death between 1:30 and 5:30 P.M., but most likely more exactly between 3:30 and 4:30 the previous afternoon. (Strangely, no such suspicious marks appeared on Martin Brown's neck, considering, in view of his mother's remarks to me later, that he, too, must have struggled. In view of the absence of such marks, Detective Chief-Inspector Dobson's suddenly thinking of Martin Brown on his way to investigating the Brian Howe case is an all the more remarkable instance of the importance of police intuition.)

"There was no doubt, no doubt whatever that it had to be a child who'd killed him," Chief-Inspector Dobson said. "But who? And why?"

The "Murder Room" at Newcastle's West End Police, the headquarters for the investigation, was a hive of activity all night. "Murder cases are always special, whoever the victim, and wherever it is," Mr. Dobson said. "But there was something different about this, from the start. All of us felt a great sense of urgency, of anxiety, and of concern."

Preliminary statements were taken, questionnaires carefully composed which would be used to collect statements from all neighborhood children of certain ages, and thousands of these forms were mimeographed. "We called in a hundred C.I.D. officers. The acting Chief Constable, Mr. Gale, said I could have anyone I needed. Those who had telephones were phoned—we sent cars for the others. When they were all assembled, I organized them into teams and told them we'd be working around the clock until we solved it. They started at eight in the morning and except for snatches of sleep now and then we didn't stop for eight days."

During the first twenty-four hours a thousand homes in Scotswood were visited, and 1,200 children between the ages of three and fifteen, and their parents, were given the mimeographed questionnaires to fill out.

"The place was swarming with police," June Brown remembers. "But people were worried—really worried, especially everybody who had small children. We kept looking out for them, calling after them."

"We were real nervous," Rita Finlay added, "but the kids themselves felt it too. They were 'bunching'—know what I mean?"

"There were, of course, a lot of inconsistencies in many of the answers in the questionnaires," Mr. Dobson said. "You know what kids are. We saw several of them several times. I looked more thoroughly at the forms of about a dozen children." Among those who were visited repeatedly by the police because of unclear replies were Norma Bell and Mary Bell.

Detective-Constable Kerr visited Norma Bell at 4 P.M. on 1 August to ask her to clarify her answer to question 8 ("Do you know anyone who played with Brian? If so:—Name and address ...").

"Of course, they were overcrowded," Detective-Constable Kerr says of the family. "But they gave me the impression of a close and happy family." He talked to Norma, her mother, and several of the other children. "I thought Norma was peculiar," he said. "She was continually smiling as if it was a huge joke. Her mother kept saying, 'Didn't you hear what he asked? Answer the question.' "

Norma finally gave Detective-Constable Kerr a supplementary statement:

> The HOWE family moved in to our street about one year ago and little Brian HOWE started to play with my brothers John Henry and Hugh Bell.
>
> Brian also used to play with John and Jacqueline Blackett, 111 St Margaret's Road, Newcastle-upon-Tyne. They all used to play round about our street, St Margaret's Road, and in different back gardens. I have never seen any of them playing near the railway lines, behind the Delaval Arms public house. I have only been down there about 2 or 3 times, and the last time was months ago.
>
> The last time I saw Brian HOWE was about 12.45 p.m., Wednesday, 31 July 1968, when he was playing with his brother and two little girls on the corner of Whitehouse Road and Crosshill Road. I cannot say who the little girls were.
>
> Between 1 p.m. and 5 p.m. that day, I played in my street with Gillian and Linda Routledge, 59 Whitehouse Road. We were making pom-poms. [Next to this sentence, on the statement, appears the police remark "verified."]

After leaving Norma Bell's house, Detective-Constable Kerr went next door to No. 70, to see Mary. In her case he was checking her replies to questions 6 ("... When did you last see Brian?") and 9 ("Were you playing behind the Delaval Arms Public House near to the railway lines between 1 P.M. and 5 P.M., Wednesday, 31 July 1968?").

"It was a very different atmosphere in there," he said. "No feeling of a home, just a shell. Very peculiar ... the only life one felt was that big dog barking. Mary was the most evasive child I'd ever come across. And her father was very odd. I asked him, 'You be her father?' and he said, 'No, I am her uncle.' 'Where are her parents?' I asked and he answered, 'She's only got a mother and she's away on business.' All the questions I asked *her,* she was continually looking at him for guidance."

Detective-Constable Kerr wrote to Mary's dictation:

> I last saw Brian Howe in Whitehouse Road about 12.30 p.m. Wednesday, 31 July 1968, when he was playing with his brother. I did not go near the Railway Lines or the waste ground near there at all on Wednesday, 31 July 1968. I have been down there before, but it was at least two months ago.

Later that evening, Detective-Constable Kerr saw Norma once more—by this time it was 7:05 P.M. This time she added a little more information:

> Further to my first statement, I would like to say that on Wednesday, 31 July 1968, I met Mary Flora BELL . . . in the pathway of my home. This was about 11.30 a.m. in the morning. We went out to play in our back garden and for a few minutes in her back garden. We stayed there until I went in for my dinner at 1.30 p.m.
>
> At 2.30 p.m. I went and called on Mary Flora BELL and we went to Davy's shop which is at the end of St Margaret's Road. We stayed at the shop about half an hour, and played with Elaine the daughter of the owner of Davy's shop.
>
> We walked back along home, then Mary Flora BELL went into the house for about 10 minutes. I went into my own house.
>
> About 3.15 p.m. that day I went out the back way and met Mary Flora BELL. We crossed our back garden, went up the garden path, and into Whitehouse Road, and we just played in the street until about 5 p.m.
>
> I then went over to Gillian and Linda ROUTLEDGE's house and we sat on their front step making pom-poms. As far as I know Mary Flora BELL just went into her house.
>
> I didn't see her again until 7 p.m. in the back lane behind our house, when she was on her own. I don't know where she had been.

On the next day, 2 August, Detective-Sergeant Docherty went to see Mary about some further inconsistencies in *her* answers. It turned out she, too, had remembered something else. She said that on the Wednesday afternoon Brian Howe was killed, she saw a little boy, A., standing by himself in Delaval Road, and he was covered with grass and little purply flowers. She said she had seen A. play with Brian Howe a lot and that she had seen him hit Brian for no reason at all. And that he had hit Brian around the face and neck. She further said that she had seen A. play with a pair of scissors "like silver-colored and something wrong with the scissors, like one leg was either broken or bent." "And I saw him trying to cut a cat's tail off with those scissors," she remembered.

"A.," said Chief-Inspector Dobson, "was eight. When we read Mary Bell's statement mentioning those scissors we had found lying in the grass near Brian Howe's body, they had not been photographed or described by any of the newspapers. We spent two days on A. He was the first child I saw myself. He was a kid who was not very quick for his age—but he stuck to his story and it was confirmed by others. Of course, in cases where children are involved, one is prepared for parents to cover up for them. But in those two days we didn't only see his parents—we saw everybody who had, even remotely, anything to do with his story. But everything the boy—and his father—said was borne out by the statements of all the other people: A. had played with Brian Howe until Brian went away. In the afternoon he went with his mother, grandmother, and stepfather to the airport. They came back at 7:45 and had tea at their house in another part of Newcastle. After that he played there in the street till he went back to Scotswood with his grandmother, at ten P.M. This was confirmed by a man the stepfather knew who had seen them at the airport that afternoon. Everything A. had said had proved true. But Mary Bell had said that she saw A. with those scissors: how did Mary Bell know about those scissors which could have been used to make those puncture marks on Brian's body? How could she know enough to describe exactly what they were like?

"Those two girls, Mary Bell and Norma Bell, had already changed their statements twice," Chief-Inspector Dobson said. "By that time we had pretty well eliminated everybody else. I had not seen them yet, but they had remained in a pocket of my mind: it had to be them, or one of them."

On 4 August at 7:45 P.M., Detective-Constable Thompson

went back to talk to Norma once more about her whereabouts on 31 July. He pointed out to her that she had said she had been playing with her brothers and sisters during those hours, but several other people had said that they had seen her in the streets with Mary Bell and Mary Bell's dog, who was known all over Scotswood for his ferocity.

She insisted for quite a while that what she had said in her two statements was true, but then suddenly began to cry and said, "Can I talk to you without my dad being here?" Her father left the room, and Norma said, "I was down Delaval Road with Mary and the dog. Mary took me to see Brian." Detective-Constable Thompson then stopped her, called her father in, and said he was taking Norma to the police station. She said, "I don't want my father there." Mr. Bell agreed that she should go alone.

Meanwhile Detective-Constable Kerr had once again called at No. 70. Mary came to the door. "I said, 'Can I come in?' She said, 'No.' I asked her why not. 'My uncle's not in,' she said. I asked here where he was and she said at the pub and I told her to go get him. Billy Bell was very hostile when they got back and Mary was again continually looking at him. Of course, I believed he was her uncle—I had no reason not to. And I had the feeling that this uncle was only passing through—you know, not living there. I got no further information from them that evening."

Chief-Inspector Dobson saw Norma Bell for the first time at 8:10 P.M. that night, in her father's presence. "She was pale and nervous," he said, "her eyes darted from one of us to the other and there was this nervous smile that turned to tears at the drop of a hat."

"Norma," he told her, "I am Chief-Inspector Dobson, this is Detective-Inspector Laggan, and you already know Detective-Constable Thompson. I am obliged by law to tell you that you are not obliged to say anything unless you wish to do so, but that anything you say may be taken down in writing, and may be given in evidence. . . ."

"Now," Mr. Dobson continued, "I understand that you have something you want to tell me about the death of Brian Howe."

"I went with Mary Bell down to the blocks the day that Brian was lost and I tripped over his head," she said.

"What do you mean, you tripped over his head?"

"When I went into the blocks I tripped over something. I looked down and saw it was Brian's head. He was covered with grass but I could see all his face. He was dead."

"What happened then?"

"Mary said, 'I squeezed his neck and pushed up his lungs. That's how you kill them. Keep your nose dry and don't tell anybody.'"

"How do you know he was dead?" Chief-Inspector Dobson asked.

"His lips were purple. Mary ran her fingers along his lips. She said she had enjoyed it."

"Did you see anything else on his face?"

"What do you mean?" Norma asked.

"Was there any blood on his face?"

"No, there was no blood, but he had a funny mark on his nose."

"Were his eyes open or shut?"

"They were open."

"Did you see any other part of his body?"

"Just his arm, which was out at his side, his hand was black. I could only see his red jersey."

"Which arm could you see?"

"It was his left arm."

"Did you see anything near Brian?"

"No, but Mary showed me a razor and said she had cut his belly. She pulled his jersey up and showed me the tiny cut on his belly. She hid the razor under a block and told me not to tell my dad or she would get into trouble."

"Could you show me where the razor is hidden?" Mr. Dobson asked, and Norma replied, "*Yes.*"

At 8:30 P.M. Norma was taken to the spot where Brian had been found dead. "It's under there," she said and pointed to the corner of a concrete block. Mr. Dobson pulled the grass away from the bottom of the block and under the edge of the block was a silver-colored razor blade. He went back to Norma who was standing some yards away. "What sort of razor was it that you told me about? Was it one that opens like a knife?"

"No," she said, "it was a razor blade." He showed it to her. "Is that it?"

"That's it," she said.

"Show me where you saw Brian lying, and where his head was."

She pointed to the space where the body had been found. "It was there," she said, "but that hole wasn't there—it was all grass."

Chief-Inspector Dobson told her to lie down next to the hole and show him the position the body had been in. Norma lay down, on her back, with her left arm bent out at a level with her shoulder, palm uppermost, and her head on one side, in exactly the position Brian's body had been found.

Less than half an hour later, at 9:10 P.M., Mr. Dobson saw Norma again at the police station, in her father's presence. He asked her whether she wanted to make a written statement about what she had told him earlier and she said, "Yes." The following appears in the records:

> I, Norma Joyce Bell, wish to make a statement. I want some-
> one to write down what I say. I have been told that I need
> not say anything unless I wish to do so and that whatever
> I say may be given in evidence.
>
> Signed: Norma Bell
>
> On Wednesday, when Brian Howe got lost I was in St Mar-
> garet's Road back lane. May Bell, that's what I call her, but
> her proper name is Mary, come up to me and said she was
> taking the dog out. She went in and got the leader and we
> went away with the dog on the leader. We went down to the
> car park near Scotswood Road . . .

At this stage Norma stopped and looked anxiously at her father. Chief-Inspector Dobson asked her whether she wanted her father to go out and she said, "Yes." He said that a policewoman could come and sit with her.

> We went through the wire netting, then a few yards to the
> blocks [Norma continued after her father had left]. We
> walked in among the blocks and I tripped over something. I
> looked down and saw it was Brian Howe's head. He was
> lying on his back and his left arm was out by his side with
> the palm up, it was covered with black dirt. May said, 'Keep
> your nose dry, he's dead.' I could see his head and nearly
> all his jersey. It was a red pattern. His legs were covered
> with grass. Round his lips were purple. May touched his
> lips and his nose, there was a funny mark on his nose. His

eyes were open. I knew he was dead by his face. She got hold of my neck under the chin and said that was how she had done it, by squeezing his lungs up and she enjoyed doing it. She said she took him there to harm him. She said, 'Don't tell your Dad or I'll get wrong.' May got a razor blade from under the corner of a block and showed me it. She said, 'Don't tell anybody' and put it back under the block. That was where I showed you tonight. She said she had cut his belly and she pulled his jumper up and I saw a tiny red mark somewhere on his belly. There was a man on the top of the railings at the other side of the railway line, he was shouting to some kids who were playing further along and I heard one shout 'I'm coming, dad'. We thought the man was coming over to the blocks so we went across the waste ground and jumped down into Scotswood Road. Howe's dog came with us. We went up the steps onto Delaval Road and May let her dog off the leader. We went up past Davy's shop onto Whitehouse Road. It was about 4 o'clock then and we had been at the blocks about ten minutes. When I got to our gate I went across to Yvonne Coleman's opposite and played with her and Linda Routledge, Gillian her sister and David Jones. Jacqueline Coleman was there and we made pom-poms. May took the dog in and I didn't see her for a long time. About quarter to seven I went over to Savage's back door and Pat Howe and May was there. May said to Pat, 'Are you looking for your Brian?' Pat said, 'I haven't seen him for a long time, are you coming to help look for him?' May said, 'Yes' and I said 'Yes'. May said, 'Howay lets go down Davy's way first?' We all went down to the car park and May said to Pat, 'He might be playing behind the blocks and he might be in between the blocks.' Pat said, 'We'll just look around for him and if we don't find him by seven o'clock, we'll go to the police station at the top.' I went back to Linda's and they went up to the top of Whitehouse Road. Pat came back and asked me if I would go to the phone with her cause Brian was lost, but I said 'No' and I just played with Linda till half past eight. I went home and stayed in. Yesterday or the day before, May said that it was in the paper that an 11 year-old or a 14 year-old girl had killed Brian and would be caught by that night. She was happy when she said that.*
When we were looking at Brian on Wednesday, May said

* No paper carried such a report.

she was not frightened of dead bodies cause she had seen a few. I didn't tell anybody about it cause I was frightened and if I had snitched May could have taken anyone else's bairn. The last time I saw Brian was about dinner time when he was playing with Norman. I forgot to say when we left Brian, May put some purple flowers on top of the grass that was over Brian.

Cert: I have read the above statement and I have been told that I can correct, alter or add anything I wish. This statement is true. I have made it of my own free will.

It took Norma an hour to give this statement. At 10:30 P.M., with her father's agreement, she was taken to stay at Fernwood Remand Home, a County Council Children's Home for girls in Newcastle.

Chief-Inspector Dobson and two police constables went to Mary Bell's home two hours later—at 12:15 A.M. on Monday, 5 August. The house was in darkness except for a blazing fire and the television which was going full blast. The children, Mary, B., C., and D., were asleep upstairs.

"In a murder inquiry," Mr. Dobson said, "you have to forge ahead. You ignore the time of day or night; when you have to see somebody you see them, never mind who they are or what time of day it is."

Billy Bell was watching television. "He said his wife was away. I said I wanted to question Mary at the police station and he refused to wake her up. I said it would be easier for her if he woke her up and got her dressed, but if he wouldn't, we were prepared to go in and do it."

Billy Bell then asked them to wait outside. After a moment he came out, closed the door behind him, and said he was just going across the road to get his sister, Mrs. S.

"I thought he'd gone to get her to sit with the other kids while he came with Mary," said Mr. Dobson, "but actually it was Mrs. S. who came in the car. She was very good too. She sat in the back with Mary, she had her arm around her, held her, and all the way to the police station she kept talking to her, very sensibly you know, very nice, telling her to tell the truth."

Billy Bell's sister Audrey is small, slim, and attractive, with a careworn face which lights up when she smiles.

"I took them straight up to my room," Mr. Dobson said. "We didn't have to go through the main office, but anyway it was a quiet night. I got some tea brought up right away and biscuits. We all had some. But Mary didn't seem very bothered—she was fresh-faced, chirpy, and confident. She was completely alert in spite of being woken up like that." The Chief-Inspector cautioned her and told her he was making inquiries into the death of Brian Howe on Wednesday, 31 July 1968. "I have reason to believe that you can help me with these inquiries," he finally said.

"I know about him dying," Mary answered, "because I helped to look for him when he was missing. I was with Pat Howe and Norma."

"Where were you in the afternoon?" Mr. Dobson asked.

"Playing. I played with Norma."

"Did you go down to the railway near the concrete blocks that day?"

"No, I never went there. I never go there. I have only been there once a long time ago. I went down to the car park with Pat and Norma when we were looking for Brian."

"Did you see Brian that day?"

"Yes, about half-past twelve. He was playing with his brother in Whitehouse Road."

"I have reason to believe that about 3:45 P.M. that day you went to the concrete blocks with Norma and you saw Brian Howe between the blocks."

"I never," she said.

"Where did you go with your dog?" Detective-Inspector Laggan asked.

"I went to the park."

"Who were you with?"

"I was by myself."

"Are you sure you were by yourself?"

"No, I remember, I was with Norma."

"Did you see anyone you know in the park?"

"No, there was just a man and a woman with a pram."

"When did you come back?"

"About half-past four. I sat on Maxine's step."

"What were you wearing that day?"

"This black dress [she indicated the one she had on] and my white blouse."

"I have reason to believe you were wearing your gray dress that day," said Detective-Inspector Laggan.

"No, I wasn't," Mary answered. "I haven't worn it for weeks."

"Did you play with Brian very much?"

"I never played with him. He's only little. I sometimes brought him from the Nursery. That was before the school holidays."

"I have reason to believe that when you were near the blocks with Norma a man shouted at some children who were nearby and you both ran away from where Brian was lying in the grass. This man will probably know you."

"He would have to have good eyesight," she replied.

"Why would he need good eyesight?" Chief-Inspector Dobson asked quickly.

"Because he was . . ."—she paused for a few seconds—"clever to see me," she continued, "when I wasn't there. I am going home," she said then and got up.

"You can't go home yet," Chief-Inspector Dobson said.

"I'll phone for some solicitors," she said, "they'll get me out. This is being brainwashed."

"I have reason to believe that, when you were in the blocks with Norma, you showed her something which you said you had done something to Brian with," Chief-Inspector Dobson continued. "Then you hid it."

"I never," she said.

"Norma showed me where this thing was. I now have it," the Chief-Inspector told her.

"What was it?" Mary said. "I'll kill her."

"Do you wish to make a written statement saying where you were that day?" Mr. Dobson asked.

"I am making no statements," Mary answered. "I have made lots of statements. It's always me you come for. Norma's a liar, she always tries to get me into trouble."

"The whole interview," Mr. Dobson recalled later, "had gone very slowly. My first impression of her was that she was a 'kook'

—she was very defensive, fidgeting, she kept jumping up saying she was going, she wasn't staying there. She sat silent for intervals and questions had to be repeated to her. At one stage I received a telephone call and she said, 'Is this place bugged?' And in the end she had admitted nothing. I had her there half the night—three hours—and she just stuck to her story; she didn't know a thing. Of course, it could have been true. It could have been Norma doing it all. At that time we had not yet made the connection with the sandpit incident, nor with Martin Brown. At 3:30 A.M. we sent Mary back home."

That morning, 5 August, at eleven A.M., Mr. Dobson took Norma Bell once more to the place where Brian had been found and asked her again to lie down in the position in which she had seen Brian. "We had to make sure—it's always a matter of asking the same things over and over. But she lay down in exactly the same position—no change."

Norma had lunch in the policewoman's office, and at 1:45 P.M. Mr. Dobson saw her again at the West End police station. "Before we could ask her anything, she said, 'I want to tell you what I missed out of my statement last night. What I told you is true, every bit, but I was there three times.'" Mr. Dobson cautioned her again and asked her whether she wanted to make a written statement about this.

"Yes," she said, "but I don't want anybody here, not my dad, just you."

"Detective-Constable Thompson will have to be here."

"All right," she answered, "he's one of your men."

"She was very excited," Mr. Dobson said. "Falling over herself wanting to be helpful. Her face looked drawn now, she was twitchy, wriggling in her seat, again looking from one side of the room to the other even though there was no one there and nothing to look at."

Norma gave Mr. Dobson what was to be her fourth statement:

> I want you to write my statement down, I don't want my dad here, but your men can come in. The statement I made yesterday was all true but I missed the first bit out. I want to tell you all the truth now. Last Wednesday about 1 o'clock I was playing with May and about 3 o'clock we saw Brian

Howe playing with his brother. They were playing with two little lassies on bikes. They live on the corner of Crosshill Road and Whitehouse Road. They were beside the garden gate and his brother gave Brian a pair of scissors. We both went with Brian. May said we would take him. We went down Crosshill Road, and through the hole in the fence near Dixon's shop. We went over the railway lines. I had taken the scissors off Brian in the street and I carried them. We climbed over the fence at the bottom of the bank, then over the fence at the other side. I climbed over first and May bunked the bairn over. May said, 'Look at that big tank, we'll all get in.' The tank was further along from the blocks. There was a hole in the side of the tank. May got in first, I bunked Brian up to May, then I got in. It had a stinky smell so we all got out again. May then said, 'The blocks Norma howay,' and we went along to the blocks. Then May said to Brian, 'Lift up your neck'. Just when she said that there were some boys playing around and Lassie, Brian Howe's dog was barking. She had followed us down. May said to them, 'Get away or I will set the dog on you'. The boys went away. May said to Brian again, 'Lift up your neck'. She put her two hands on his neck, she said there was two lumps you had to squeeze right up. She said she meant to harm him. She got him down on the grass and she seemed to go all funny, you could tell there was something the matter with her. She kept on struggling with him and he was struggling and trying to get her hands away. She left go of him and I could hear him gasping. She squeezed his neck again and I said, 'May, leave the baby alone,' but she wouldn't. She said to me, 'My hands are getting thick, take over.' Then I ran away. I went back the way we had come.

I went into Whitehouse Road where I played with Linda Routledge and the other kids I told you about. About twenty minutes after, May come up and asked me to go back down. I forgot to tell you that when I ran away and left Brian and May, I left the scissors on the grass. We went round by the car park. We didn't take the dog that time. That was when I tripped over Brian's head like I told you in the other statement. On the way down May found a razor blade on the path. I didn't tell you before that when I lifted Brian's head and shoulders up a bit and patted his back but his hand fell on one side and I layed him down again. I felt his pulse but it wasn't going up and down. May pressed the razor blade down on Brian's belly a few times in the same place. She lifted his jersey and that's when she did it. I didn't see any blood. That was when she hid the razor blade and said, 'Don't tell your dad or I'll get wrong'. The scissors were in the corner near the blocks beside Brian's feet where I left them. We went back to Whitehouse Road, May went away and I went into the house. About 5 o'clock I saw May outside. She had just had her tea. We took her dog down to the car park again and then went to see the bairn again. May said she would make him baldy and she cut a lump of hair off his head near the front, she put it on the grass above his head. She pressed the scissors onto his belly a few times but not hard. That was when the man shouted at them kids and she hadn't time to cut any more hair off before we ran away. The hair she put on the grass was separated a bit. She put the scissors on the grass somewhere beside him on the side where his dirty hand was. We went onto Scotswood Road and back up to Whitehouse Road. I saw May again about a quarter to seven when we looked for Brian with Pat.

"Could you draw Brian and put in the place where Mary pressed the razor blade?" asked Chief-Inspector Dobson.

She drew a little body lying with legs spread, and arms outstretched. There is a line drawn across just above where the bellybutton would be and there are some marks (some bigger, some smaller) above it and several more below.

"The top marks are where she pressed the scissors and the bottom ones where she pressed the razor blade."

Norma finished at 3:30 P.M. "We left her with the policewomen in their office. Dr. Tomlinson and I re-examined Brian's body," Mr. Dobson says. "We now saw five faint but clearly outlined marks, slightly brown at the edges [on Brian's belly] which had not been visible at the *post mortem* examination on 1 August. We discussed this at great length. It was the first time in either the pathologist's or my own experience that we had found incisions which were made so freshly after death that they were invisible until decomposition set in. I don't know whether this was the first time anywhere—probably not. But it must be very rare indeed."

The marks—obviously razor cuts—were later to be described as appearing to form a letter, or letters: three of them looked like the letter "N," but in conjunction with the fourth one there also seemed to be an attempt to transform it into the letter "M." (An interesting possible parallel to this emerged later when a handwriting analysis of the "We Murder" notes concluded that the girls had each written consecutive letters of some words or had alternately written the words of the notes. See page 113.)

At 4:30 P.M. that afternoon, Norma was again taken to the "Tin Lizzie" and asked to point out the tanks and the two points where she claimed to have crossed the railway with Mary and Brian. At 4:45, at West End police station (only minutes away by car) Mr. Dobson confronted Norma with eight pairs of scissors. "Can you tell me if any of these are the ones Brian had last Wednesday when you took him to the blocks?" he asked.

Norma immediately picked up the scissors which had been found. "She threw them on the desk and said, 'That's them.' "

"I saw her again several times on 6 August," said Mr. Dobson, "both at the Children's Remand Home and at West End police station. I asked the same questions over and over. She never backtracked an inch. Either she was a masterful liar or she was speaking the truth."

Brian Howe was buried on 7 August, a brilliant, hot summer day.

"There were at least two hundred people," Mr. Dobson says. "Masses of flowers. A lot of people cried who had nothing to do with Brian's immediate family. It was very sad.

"Mary Bell was standing in front of the Howes' house when the coffin was brought out. I was, of course, watching her. And it was when I saw her there that I knew I did not dare risk another day. She stood there, laughing. Laughing and rubbing her hands. I thought, My God, I've got to bring her in, she'll do another one."

Mary's mother Elizabeth Bell, called Betty, was still away on one of her regular trips—people said—to Glasgow. Billy Bell had been summoned that afternoon by the Durham police to answer some questions on a minor charge that was pending against him. It turned out that his sister Audrey, loyal as ever, had gone with him.

"I sent a woman police sergeant at 4:30 P.M. to get Mary," Mr. Dobson says. "We had expected that Billy Bell's sister would be there to look after the other children. When the policewoman realized that she had gone along to Durham, she brought all the children in. We settled the other three in another office with some toys and tea and a policewoman to look after them until their aunt came to get them later that night."

Chief-Inspector Dobson saw Mary in his office as before. "She was very apprehensive," he said. "She was pale and tense. She gave me the impression that she knew the time of reckoning had come." He cautioned her again and asked her first to tell him which dress she had worn on Wednesday, 31 July.

"I had my gray one on part of the day, but I changed into my black one sometime in the afternoon," she said. "I want to tell you the truth but I'll get wrong," she added a moment later.

"Do you mean that it is not true that you changed your dress?"

"No," she said, "I mean about when I was there when Brian died."

Mr. Dobson stopped her at this point and telephoned the New-castle General Hospital—just a few blocks away—to ask that a Nursing Sister be sent over to sit with Mary while she would make what Mr. Dobson was certain would turn out to be the decisive statement. As a rule (in Britain) minors under sixteen years are not questioned about a crime unless a parent or an independent person of the same sex is present.

Sister H. said she was "a bit shaken when they said what it was for, but you know, I didn't have to do anything: I just sat there."

Chief-Inspector Dobson asked Mary whether she wanted to make a written statement, and she said, "Yes."

> I, Mary Flora Bell wish to make a statement. I want someone to write down what I have to say. I have been told that I need not say anything unless I wish to do so, but that what-ever I say may be given in evidence.
>
> Signed: Mary F. Bell
>
> Brian was in his front street and me and Norma were walking along towards him. We walked past him and Norma says, 'are you coming to the shop Brian' and I says, 'Norma, you've got no money, how can you go to the shop. Where

are you getting it from?' She says, 'nebby' (Keep your nose clean). Little Brian followed and Norma says, 'walk up in front'. I wanted Brian to go home, but Norma kept coughing so Brian wouldn't hear us. We went down Crosshill Road with Brian still in front of us. There was this coloured boy and Norma tried to start a fight with him. She said, 'Darkie, whitewash, it's time you got washed.' The big brother came out and hit her. She shouted, 'Howay, put your dukes up.' The lad walked away and looked at her as though she was daft. We went beside Dixon's shop and climbed over the railings, I mean through a hole and over the railway. Then I said, 'Norma, where are you going?' and Norma said, 'Do you know that little pool where the tadpoles are?' When we got there, there was a big, long tank with a big, round hole with little holes round it. Norma says to Brian, 'Are you coming in here because there's a lady coming on the Number 82 and she's got boxes of sweets and that.' We all got inside, then Brian started to cry and Norma asked him if he had a sore throat. She started to squeeze his throat and he started to cry. She said, 'This isn't where the lady comes, it's over there, by them big blocks.' We went over to the blocks and she says, 'Ar—you'll have to lie down' and he lay down beside the blocks where he was found. Norma says, 'Put your neck up' and he did. Then she got hold of his neck and said 'Put it down'. She started to feel up and down his neck. She squeezed it hard, you could tell it was hard because her finger tips were going white. Brian was struggling, and I was pulling her shoulders but she went mad. I was pulling her chin up but she screamed at me. By this time she had banged Brian's head on some wood or corner of wood and Brian was lying senseless. His face was all white and bluey and his eyes were open. His lips were purplish and had all like slaver on, it turned into something like fluff. Norma covered him up and I said, 'Norma, I've got nothing to do with this, I should tell on you, but I'll not.' Little Lassie was there and it was crying and she said, 'Don't you start or I'll do the same to you.' It still cried and she went to get hold of its throat but it growled at her. She said, 'now, now, don't be hasty.' We went home and I took little Lassie home an all. Norma was acting kind of funny and making twitchy faces and spreading her fingers out. She said, 'This is the first but it'll not be the last.' I was frightened then. I carried Lassie and put her down

over the railway and we went up Crosswood Road way.
Norma went into the house and she got a pair of scissors and
she put them down her pants. She says, 'go and get a pen'.
I said 'No, what for.' She says, 'To write a note on his
stomach', and I wouldn't get the pen. She had a Gillette
razor blade. It had Gillette on. We went back to the blocks
and Norma cut his hair. She tried to cut his leg and his ear
with the blade. She tried to show me it was sharp, she took
the top of her dress where it was raggie and cut it, it made
a slit. A man come down the railway bank with a little girl
with long, blonde hair, he had a red checked shirt on and
blue denim jeans. I walked away. She hid the razor blade
under a big, square concrete block. She left the scissors beside him. She got out before me over the grass on to Scotswood Road. I couldn't run on the grass cos I just had my
black slippers on. When we got along a bit she says, 'May,
you shouldn't have done it cos you'll get into trouble', and
I hadn't done nothing I haven't got the guts. I couldn't kill
a bird by the neck or throat or anything, it's horrible that.
We went up the steps and went home, I was nearly crying.
I said, if Pat finds out she'll kill you, never mind killing
Brian cos Pat's more like a tomboy. She's always climbing in
the old buildings and that. Later on I was helping to look for
Brian and I was trying to let on to Pat that I knew where he
was on the blocks, but Norma said, 'he'll not be over there,
he never goes there,' and she convinced Pat he wasn't there.
I got shouted in about half past seven and I stayed in. I got
woke up about half past eleven and we stood at the door as
Brian had been found. The other day Norma wanted to get
put in a home. She says will you run away with us and I said
no. She said if you get put in a home and you feed the little
ones and murder them then run away again.

She signed the statement at 6:55 P.M.

I have read the above statement and I have been told that
I can correct, alter or add anything I wish. This statement is
true, I have made it of my own free will.

Mary Flora Bell

"Do you know it's wrong to squeeze a little boy's throat?" Chief-
Inspector Dobson asked.

"Yes," she replied, "it's worse than Harry Roberts; he only did train jobs."*

"She felt nothing," said Sister H. "I've never seen anything like it. She said all those awful things they had done but she didn't *feel* a thing. I felt she was a very intelligent child. But she didn't seem like a child at all. Her vocabulary—I have a boy of eleven— he couldn't use the kind of words she used. All that evening I repeated to myself what I'd heard. And even so, I couldn't believe it. . . ."

Sometime during those two hours Chief-Inspector Dobson had brought up Martin Brown. "It was in my mind from the beginning that there was some connection between Martin's and Brian's deaths," he said. "That afternoon I just told her that I believed she and Norma had broken in the Nursery School and written the notes and she admitted it at once. But that was all I said about it that day: I was having my team re-interview all the people concerned: it was necessary to get far more details than were available so far if we were going to look at it as a possible murder; we had to start all over again and get the facts."

At eight P.M. that night he charged Mary. "I am arresting you on a charge of murdering Brian Edward Howe on 31 July 1968," he said, and she answered, "That's all right with me."

At 8:30 P.M. Norma was brought in. "Do you know it's wrong to squeeze a little boy's throat?" he asked and she said, "Yes." When he told her he was arresting her on the charge of murdering Brian she replied angrily, "I never. I'll pay you back for this."

Ten minutes later he saw the two girls together. "Do you wish to say anything in answer to the charge? You are not obliged to say anything unless you wish to do so. But whatever you say will be taken down in writing and may be given in evidence. You are charged as follows: In the city and county of Newcastle upon Tyne on Wednesday, 31 July 1968, you did murder Brian Edward Howe contrary to common law."

This time Mary said nothing but Norma said again, "I never, you know," and cried.

---

* Harry Roberts was actually found guilty, on 12 December 1966, of murdering three policemen in Shepherds Bush, London.

CHAPTER FOUR
REMAND

"I Hope Me Mum Won't Have to Pay a Fine"

The cells at the Newcastle West End police station, used only for overnight detentions, are along a narrow corridor on the ground floor at the very back of the building. There are six of them, about eight-foot square, each with a cot and small ceiling light. A door from the cells leads to the "washroom"—which has a sink and a gas ring for making hot drinks.

The two girls spent the first night after their arrest in two small rooms at the end of another little passageway that leads from this washroom to the main office. These rooms, specifically intended for juveniles who require care and observation, are considerably less isolated and lighter than the "cells," because, if youngsters for any reason have to be kept there overnight, the doors to the brightly lit corridor are usually kept open, with a woman police officer sitting just outside.

Two policewomen, Pauline Z. and Lilian Y., were assigned to guard Mary and Norma that night. "We came on at ten," Pauline recalls. "When we arrived they were chatting away—I think they were both lying on a cot in one of the rooms. They told us right away that they'd had fish and chips for supper. 'Mr. Dobson bought them for us,' Mary said—sort of proudly, you know. We took them along to wash their faces and hands—there wasn't anything for them to change into for the night but we tried to settle them down as comfortably as possible. It wasn't bad," Pauline said. She is a humorous young woman with a direct and warm personality. " 'Course, it was a hot night, and they were that wrought up—they couldn't sleep. I sat with Mary, and Lil sat with Norma." She shook her head. "But oh, it was a night. They kept shouting to each other through the doors. . . ."

"They made such a racket," Policewoman Y. said. "We finally

told them to shut up. At one moment I heard Mary shout, 'I'll kill my mother.' "

"I am not sure she said that," said Pauline. "It may have been 'I'll *kick* my mother.' "

"They were going to be charged in Court the next morning. They were charged twice, you see—first in the ordinary Magistrates' Court that next morning, Thursday, and then the Wednesday afterwards in Juvenile Court because Juvenile Court only sits once a week. Mary didn't talk much to me about the case that night. She wore broken shoes, and she was more concerned about that than anything else. 'I told Mum I needed new shoes,' she said. 'I sent her a message. I just hope she'll get new ones to me. What will people think if they see me like this?' I kept on hoping she'd go to sleep. At one moment I said, 'Why don't you go to sleep?' and I sort of chatted to her quietly for a bit and after a while she said that she was frightened she'd wet her bed. 'I usually do,' she said. I told her not to worry about it but she did—she kept going to the bathroom. She didn't wet her bed. But she didn't really sleep either.

"Later on that night," Pauline went on, "I was sitting in the chair at the foot of her bunk and she was lying on it—she suddenly started singing. Do you know *The Northumberland Mining Song?** Cilla Black sings it. She knew every word of it, she had it absolutely right. She has a very good voice." Again Pauline shook her head. "I can't explain, but to hear that kid sing like that in those cells, that night . . ."

> Oh, you are a mucky kid
> dirty as a dustbin lid
> when he hears the things you did
> you'll get a belt from your Da
>
> You look so scruffy lying there
> strawberry jam tats in your hair
> 'tho in the world you haven't a care
> and I have got so many

* Words & New Music Adaptation by Stan Kelly. © Copyright 1964 Heathside Music Ltd., London, England. TRO-MELODY TRAILS, INC., New York, controls all publiaction rights for the U.S.A. and Canada. Used by permission.

Oh you have your father's face
you're growing up a real hard case
but there's not a one can take your place
so go to sleep, for mammy.

"That's what she sang and she hardly slept at all."

Mary's mother was not in Court for her appearance the next morning but the children were not unsupported: Billy Bell, his sister, and Mary's grandmother from Glasgow came. And so did Norma's parents. The children were seen about ten minutes before the normal Court convened, and, as the magistrates sat as a Juvenile Court, the papers would report only that two juveniles had been remanded in custody for the murder of Brian Howe and the room was empty except for those directly involved.

"It took about three minutes," Mr. Dobson said. "The magistrates granted the application for legal aid and then both girls were taken to Remand Homes: Mary to Seaham and Norma to Carlisle. The decision where to send them was mainly based on where there was space, and, of course, where there were adequate security provisions."

The police as well as the Children's authorities were stunned. "I'd give my eyeteeth if it hadn't been children murdered and children concerned in it," Mr. Dobson was to say shortly afterwards.

"One could hardly take it in, and it became more unreal, more unbelievable every day," said Brian Roycroft, Children's Officer* for Newcastle. A young man of exceptional ability and initiative, he had only taken over his job in June and had hardly had the time to get the reins into his hands or familiarize himself with individual family situations.

Newcastle Welfare authorities were familiar with the circumstances of Norma Bell's family. Not because any of them had ever been in trouble with the law—they hadn't. But because they were a family of eleven children who, with several serious illnesses and accidents in rapid succession, had had more than their share of troubles and were receiving help from various departments.

Brian Roycroft was to discover however that there was very

---

* Now Director of Social Services.

little in the files about Mary Bell's family. This absence of information and Mary's parents' distrust and resentment of "Authority," their reluctance to cooperate in the subsequent inquiries into her background by police, social workers, and psychiatrists, were to be one of the main stumbling blocks in the efforts to find explanations for Mary's actions and, later, ways to help her.

On 14 August the girls appeared in Juvenile Court and were remanded again. Again Norma's parents and Mary's relatives were in Court: Mary's mother, too, had been found in Glasgow and was persuaded to attend.

When it was over, Norma was taken back to Carlisle and Mary went to Milton House, Croydon, near London.

"It was a ridiculous performance: I took her to Croydon; me and Cathy V.," said Policewoman Lynn W., a comfortable and cheerful-looking girl. "Here we were, at the railway station with this kid everybody was on about, how dangerous she was and how the whole country would be up in arms if she got away and all that, and then there was all this hargie-bargie about getting a private compartment on the train: there wasn't the money for it—£25. You wouldn't believe it, would you? If it hadn't been that we knew the stationmaster, who got us one anyway, I don't really know what we would have done. We got settled, you know, pulled down the curtains and all that so nobody could see in. Mary—she'd been zooming to and fro between the window and her seat and suddenly she said, 'I hope me mum won't have to pay a fine.' I thought that was a funny thing to say for a kid who was supposed to have killed two little boys. But she meant it, you know, that's what she was worrying about.

"Cathy went to get some eats, you know, orange drinks and sandwiches and all. (Cathy didn't like May—I think May knew.) She was cheeky you know—at first I didn't like her either. Anyway, after Cathy went, she suddenly sat still in her seat. I looked at her and I suddenly thought, why, she's nothing but a little kid, and she suddenly looked all pale and tired and I put my arm around her. You know, she'd been all excited, and nobody would have thought she had a thing on her mind, but then she leaned against me, you know, she went all limp, soft you know, and I . . . well, as I said, I hadn't liked her at first but, I don't know how to explain it, I forgot all that, and she had lice crawling all over her head and down her collar and shoulders, and I knew they'd get on me. . . ." She laughed. "I did catch one, too . . . and I just held her and she started to talk about having to go back into Court the next week. You know, they have to go on remand every week until the trial. 'Me mum will be there,' she said. 'I hope me mum won't be too upset.' 'She was upset this morning,' I said, 'she was crying.' 'I know she was, but she didn't mean it. I think she doesn't like me. I'm sure she doesn't. She hates me.' 'She's your own mum,' I said, 'she must love you.' 'If she loves me, why did she leave?' she said then.

"I didn't know what she meant, so I didn't say anything. She asked me what I did before becoming a policewoman, and I said I was a nurse. She asked me where I worked and I said in the children's ward at Newcastle General Hospital. 'You did?' she said. 'I've been in the hospital a couple of times, but it was long ago.' I asked her what she'd been in for, but she wouldn't say. She clammed up then. I never knew why. I've thought about her a lot," Lynn added. "She was a canny kid. I didn't like her at first," again she sounded puzzled about her own reaction, "but later . . . I think I could have become very fond of her. She did that to one: one thought about her. But," she added slowly, "I think that if I had become more involved with her, I would have been hurt."

A report from Croydon says that "Mary's head was thick with lice when she arrived . . . she has hundreds of nits." Her first night there she couldn't go to sleep and was crying. She said she felt she was being strangled.

During that week at Croydon, on 16 August, Mary had a first interview with Dr. Robert Orton, specialist in psychological medicine at Newcastle Royal Victoria Infirmary. Although not specifically a child psychiatrist, Dr. Orton has had considerable experience with severely disturbed children. "Throughout the interview," he said later, "she was chirpy, bright, and a bit cheeky."

"Cheeky" was the word most people applied to her. "She called me by my first name," said Policewoman Constance U., who a few days later brought Mary back from Croydon. "I told her off and no mistake—cheeky." Policewoman U. made no bones about disliking Mary, and Mary later told someone she didn't like her

either. ("She always knew who liked her and who didn't," said
Lynn W. "It was uncanny.")

Dr. Orton was immediately aware of the complete lack in Mary
of one dimension of feeling: "I asked her of course to tell me about
the events of 31 July. 'I never done anything,' she said. 'It was
Norma. I tried to pull her off but she screamed and I didn't want
to hurt her. I says to Norma I should tell the police, but I'm
not.' When I asked her what she thought might happen to her,"
Dr. Orton continued, "she replied, 'I might get put in an Approved
School. I have been disgusted with myself,' and added immediately,
'I have been put away twice, that is enough.'

" 'What do you mean by that?' I asked. 'I was a week in Seaham in the Remand Home,' she said, 'and then two days in
Croydon, I've had enough punishment.' "

On 21 August the girls were remanded for the third time. "I
had Mary in that day," Mr. Dobson recalls. "Our investigation of
the death of Martin Brown was completed. And I put it to her
that I believed either she or Norma had killed Martin. She denied
it. Meanwhile I had also learned more about the mysterious accident to John G. in May. I had it on very good authority that Mary
and Norma had taken John for a walk that day and Mary had
thrown a sand shoe up the old bank on top of the air raid
shelter. Then—so my information went—she told John to run up
and get it, that's how she got him up there. And then she is supposed to have tripped him up and he fell the seven feet down onto
the concrete footpath. That's what I'd been told. I put it to her
that she had pushed little Johnny G. down from the air raid
shelter. But she denied that too."

In that connection it is interesting to compare Norma's statement to the police on 12 May (as quoted on pages 9–10 of this
book) and a "news" story slightly different in important details
which she wrote in her "Newsbook" at school one day later:

> On Saturday my friend Mary Bell and I decided to go for a
> walk to the carpark and we were playing on the grass for
> 15 minutes [she wrote]. Then Mary said, 'Would you like to
> go down to Vickers Armstrongs?' So I went. It is only be-
> hind the carpark. Then I said, 'Have you ever been inside

the dark passage?' May said 'yes, I always go inside.' I said
to her 'Come and we will go inside again', so then we went
in. On the floor was a little boy and his head was split wide
open. I picked him up and it was little John G. I stood John up
and then he fell down and his head began to bleed more.
He was screaming. Then I tried to speak to him but he could
not. I helped John out of the dark passage and I had to push
him up to get on to the hill he was sick all over; I said to
May are you going to help because he is your own Cousin,
so she helped him on to the grass. . . .

(John G. *is* Mary's cousin. In all fairness to Mary it should
be said that John's mother, who subsequently attended the final
day of Mary's trial, waved good-bye to her and showed considerable sorrow and affection—not the attitude of someone who
thought Mary had injured her child.)

Anthony Smith, a highly experienced solicitor who had previously acted very successfully for Norma Bell's family in an accident claim involving one of their sons, had instructed R. P.
(Roddy) Smith,* one of the youngest and brightest Q.C.s† in the
country, to act as Norma's counsel. On 26 August they applied
to Judge in Chambers (in London) for bail and stated that the
purpose of bail would be that Norma would enter a mental hospital for observation. Bail was granted with this condition, and
Norma consequently spent the three and a half months of her
remand living as a patient in the care of doctors and nurses in
the children's wing of the Prudhoe Monkton Mental Hospital five
miles from Newcastle. The superintendent of the hospital, Dr. Ian
Frazer, was to be the only psychiatrist to examine her and the

* Now Circuit Judge (February 1973).
† Queen's Counsel. This title—or King's Counsel, as the case may
be—actually has nothing to do with the Queen; it is given to senior
barristers who have applied to be appointed and have been nominated
by the Lord Chancellor. It is by no means an automatically granted
distinction: only about ten percent of the barristers who apply are
nominated. As it puts them in a different work (and considerably
higher fee) category, there are experienced barristers, who, because they are possibly already older and do not wish to change
their field or take the risks, may prefer not to apply. In a murder
case or other "serious" crime, it is normal procedure for the
accused to be defended by a Q.C. and "Junior."

only medical expert to be called to testify about her at the trial.

Mary's solicitor was a young man, David Bryson, who had originally been retained to represent her in the matter of the breaking in at the Woodland Crescent Nursery. He was a man of integrity and humility who became deeply and agonizingly involved with this case and, throughout the months of preparation, the weeks of trial, and the following year, gave unsparingly of his time and of himself.

Counsel instructed to represent Mary was J. Harvey Robson, a particularly kind and courteous man who in the 1950s served as Attorney General in the Southern Cameroons and has had a long and distinguished career as a barrister in northeast England. Perhaps more than any of the other principals Mr. Robson, in his handling of the case, was to project gentleness and sympathy for all concerned. Nothing he or anyone else could have done could have changed the eventual legal outcome for Mary.

Mary was sent to Seaham Remand Home where she spent the next three and a half months with other girls who were in trouble with the law (and among whom she figured as a star). She was therefore—if not factually, certainly psychologically—immediately in a quasi-punitive situation. The Remand Homes were at that time run not by the Children's Department but by the Prison Department.

"She was very worried about going to Seaham," Policewoman Pauline Z. remembers. She took her there on 21 August. "She kept saying 'Will I be all right there?' in that funny way she had of saying 'all right.' 'They say you have to scrub floors there and all that,' she said. 'I don't mind that, but will I be *all right?*' I never did understand what she meant by 'all right' that day."

The Seaham Remand Home is fifteen miles from Newcastle, by the sea. Standing in the midst of fields, walled in on one side, but with a view of the sea and a lovely beach two minutes away on the other, it still looks like a large comfortable farmhouse, which it was a hundred years ago when Lewis Carroll used it while writing parts of *Alice in Wonderland*. Now, too, almost the only obvious evidence of its present role is the locked entrance door which can only be opened from the inside, by a member of the staff.

A generously staffed Remand Home catering for girls between

fourteen and eighteen, it is a pleasant house with comfortable bedrooms, a big, sunny sitting room giving out onto a garden, and a large, modern kitchen, the hub of communal life where the girls help with the preparation of tea, occasional snacks, and late-night cocoa. They sleep three to five to a room, where each girl has her own chest of drawers, wardrobe space, and cuddly toys on her bed. There are no uniforms, school lessons are given on the premises, and outings for walks or shopping expeditions are in supervised groups. The girls are allowed weekly visits by their families, their correspondence is supervised and the length of their stay on average is about a month.

The matron at the time Mary came there was a former nurse, Miss D.A. A woman in her early forties, tall and tweedy, she had a sonorous voice and laugh, a ruddy complexion, and expansive movements. Totally immersed in her work, she was possessive about her position, ferociously protective of her girls, and somewhat facile in the way she discussed their problems. But she is the type of dedicated social worker on whom the social services have relied for years and without whom they would have collapsed long ago. Like many other people in the months and years to come, Miss A. appeared to feel deeply protective about Mary and was convinced that she, through the relationship she had created between the child and herself, could understand Mary and manage her perfectly well. Although an experienced housemother, she was in the formal sense untrained in dealing with seriously disturbed children. Nonetheless during those tense months she became Mary's educator, defender, and observer, and her reports on Mary's behavior and personality were taken very seriously by those who were later to decide her fate.

"She was of course very naughty," Miss A. said. "She dislikes being ignored and draws attention on herself if it appears to be concentrated on other people. She resents authority and she incites others—weaker girls, though they are frequently older than she—to behave badly. She screams and shouts and there were times when, not getting her own way, she dirtied the floor and furniture."

Miss A. said that she felt in Mary a desire—a "seeking for punishment." "One day—on advice from one of the psychiatrists who said it might do her good and certainly wouldn't hurt—

I tanned her backside for her. I don't know whether in fact it did her any good in the long run, but she was certainly as good as gold afterwards, no more trouble at all." Miss A. was very impressed with Mary's intelligence and general knowledge. "And she was very generous. She got a lot of presents from her family—chocolates, fruits, and sweets—she always shared with the other girls and us."

Miss A. felt a real resentment of what she considered "unfair" or "stupid" treatment of Mary whom she felt *she* really knew, while others did not. This feeling of defensiveness is one Mary has aroused in a wide variety of people who have been in contact with her. "It is ridiculous," the matron said, rather plaintively, "how everybody is calling her Mary. Even the child's parents have been forced into calling her Mary because the newspapers and all the officials did. Her name is May. That's what she's been called all her life."

"You have no idea how funny a child she is," she said, still chuckling at the memory. "She kept us in fits half of the time. She was a perfectly normal child, you know," she said, "if one but knew how to handle her. All this hysteria about how dangerous she is. One has to keep a sense of proportion, you know. I used to take her to the hairdresser's with me and she would sit outside reading a magazine while I was under the drier—good as gold. Of course nobody knew who she was. But—one has to understand the kind of life she's had! When I took her shopping with me she just couldn't get enough of the lights, the windows, and the decorations. But then, you see, it was the first time she had ever been Christmas shopping."

Long before this, in her "newsbooks" at school, and in several conversations with policewomen and since, Mary vividly described a number of shopping expeditions. But Miss A. can be forgiven for obeying her impulse to comfort a pathetic child: people with considerably more experience than she with very gravely disturbed children have been manipulated since into thinking or behaving the way Mary wished them to.

In October and November, Mary was seen on seven different occasions by four psychiatrists: the Home Office Forensic psychiatrist, Dr. David Westbury, who probably wrote the most complete report about her; Dr. Orton, who had been the first to see her at Croydon and with whom she then cooperated slightly more than with the others; Dr. T. M. Cuthbert, consulting psychiatrist of St. Luke's Hospital, Middlebrough, Teesside; and Dr. Monica Rowbotham of the psychiatric children's unit at the Fleming Memorial Hospital for Children in Newcastle, with whom somehow, as a woman, Mary appeared to have a different affinity.

With all of them—as on all future occasions with all the other doctors she was to see—her behavior fluctuated constantly between intelligence and indifference, frankness and evasion, pleasantness and sulkiness. With all of them she became totally uncooperative as soon as they touched upon questions she did not wish to answer—in almost every instance anything connected with her mother and her life at home. While she maintained on all these occasions her original story of Norma's guilt and her own innocence, she was ready enough to talk about the day of the murder of Brian Howe and about life, death, and feelings in abstract terms.

Both to Dr. Orton and Dr. Cuthbert she said that death was so final and murder so common that "it didn't matter any more." To Dr. Cuthbert she remarked that "Brian Howe had no mother, so he won't be missed." Dr. Orton talked to her of how someone who was strangled would suffer before he died. "Why, if you are dead, you're dead," she replied in an interested and logical sort of way, "it doesn't matter then."

"I've seen a lot of psychopathic children," Dr. Orton said later, "but I've never met one like Mary: as intelligent, as manipulative, or as dangerous. I knew a lot about her family—about her mother —from the Probation people.* But they were things I couldn't mention in Court. From Mary I found out nothing about her family at all. She simply refused to answer any questions which touched on the subject."

"To Mary," said Dr. Westbury a few months after the trial,

* It is interesting to note that "the Probation people" obviously were informed about the home circumstances of this family while the (then) Children's Department was not—an indication of the dangers inherent in not coordinating the various social services. This situation has now been much improved in Britain, as a result of the 1969 Seebohm Report.

"manipulation of people is the primary aim—it is much more important to her than what she actually achieves with it. I went to Seaham four times, but all my findings about her are based on the first two interviews. By the time of my third visit, her mother had told her to say nothing. She doesn't love in the sense we think of love. She couldn't answer any of my 'Why' questions: the way one gets an answer about this sort of thing from a child is by asking, 'Why do you like mummy?' and the child will answer, 'Because she does this and that for me.' Finally, after many 'whys,' it will turn out it isn't because of something the mother *does,* but because she *is.* Mary couldn't—or wouldn't—answer any of these questions." (And again, when Dr. Westbury asked specific questions, the answers to which might have provided a clue to her life at home, anything about her mother, or whether she had seen strange men about the house, she immediately and always said, "I won't answer" or just, "No," or, explicitly, "My Mum said for me not to say anything to you"—almost the same words she used to Dr. Orton and, in the months and even years to come, was to use to other psychiatrists.)

Both Dr. Westbury and Dr. Rowbotham—the only woman psychiatrist she saw and also the only one her mother agreed to speak with, briefly—spoke to her about "friends," and she phrased her answers to them in a very different way.

She told Dr. Westbury that she had only one friend other than Norma. And she liked those two because, "They are a good laugh and if you shout at them they take it as a joke." "She told me," said Dr. Westbury, "that she never worries about anything and is never frightened. 'I've got no feelings,' she said. She said she liked people who 'give you a good laugh and don't blabber too much.' "

To Dr. Rowbotham Mary spoke in somewhat gentler terms; she talked of the strong association there was between her and Norma, and what a close understanding they had of each other. In talking of the day of Brian's murder she said, "I was full of laughter that day."

PART TWO
THE TRIAL

A Guilty Mind

At first impression she seemed still full of laughter when the trial started at the Newcastle Assizes at 10:30 A.M. on 5 December 1968.

The Assizes are held in Moothall, an early nineteenth-century two-story natural stone building near the river and the railway line in the center of the city. Begrimed by the smoke of Tyneside factories and the soot of trains, the building is separated from the main thoroughfare by a small square. On the left, a few small shops, a pub—the "Empress"—and an iron fence outside which is space for official parking. A small gate is open, guarded by a policeman. The police constables and policewomen on duty for the trial of the two children had been carefully selected. Not because the trial was expected to arouse great public interest and attract the attention of the world press, but because the Court was determined to create an atmosphere of gentleness and compassion, with a minimum of tension and sensation. Everything was to be done to de-formalize and humanize the proceedings.

And, up to a point, it worked. For the nine days of the trial the room was always quiet, all the police officers considerate, the Court gentle, and—a secondary effect—the British press invariably discreet.

But in his summing up, Mr. Justice Cusack (who himself made every effort to make the unbearable bearable for the two children) was to say, ". . . It is an unhappy thing that the criminal courts for the most part are not concerned with the successful things of life, but are concerned with life's shadows. . . ."

A British Assize Court, with all its awesome formality, is designed to deal with these shadows, to instill fear quite as much as faith in rightful justice, and, however good the intentions to create a different atmosphere and however efficient the organization, the fearful solemnity of a murder trial cannot fail to make itself felt.

Court Two, where the trial REGINA V. MARY FLORA BELL AND NORMA JOYCE BELL took place, is a comparatively small room, with a high ceiling and three galleries—one in the center for the public and one on each side for the Jurors and "Distinguished Visitors"—the latter, in this case, reserved for additional members of the press who would not find space in the usual press seats downstairs.

The walls behind the Judge's dais were paneled in dark oak. The Jury—in this case five women and seven men—sat on three benches to his right. It was, one might say, a classic jury: the seven men included a sales representative, two managers, a schoolmaster, a photographer, a civil servant, and a wood machinist. Of the five women, two had no occupation (were presumably housewives) one was a shop assistant, one a domestic help, and one a toilet attendant.

Below the Judge sat the Clerk of Assize (the senior Court official next to the Judge) and his assistants, and on the two benches on his left the press and the Court stenographer for whom, during the children's often whispered testimony, a table was set up next to the witness stand.

The trial was originally scheduled for Court One, where Judge Cusack usually sat. At the last minute it was decided to transfer it to Court Two where, with an adjacent waiting room and lavatory, it would be easier to take proper care of the children. Also, as it had no dock, it would make it possible to make the situation less forbidding for them by seating them near their families and advisors in the second row of the court. They were placed behind their counsel, near their solicitors, and in front of their immediate families who could—and did—lean forward to touch them on occasions. In the same row further left sat several psychiatrists who observed or testified during the trial.

Yet another row of chairs further back across a small gangway from the main section was reserved for more of the children's relatives—various uncles and aunts, some of whom attended almost every day.

The public and press galleries were full for the first, the sixth, and the last two days, but the expected queues did not materialize. This was one of the most sensational trials of the century, but Newcastle did not like it. Nor did the national press, which treated it with unprecedented restraint while it went on and only gave the briefest reports and commentaries after the verdict. The "quality" papers only reported the beginning and the end, the Sunday "populars" rejected it altogether—in one instance specifically refusing the "Story of Mary Bell's Life" as offered by her parents—and only the northern dailies reported part of the trial verbatim. It was mentioned off and on in radio and television news broadcasts, but BBC-TV, in consideration of young listeners, prohibited any mention of the subject during the six o'clock news.

And yet, when the case was over, there were few adults in Britain—and many other places in the world—who were not aware that it had taken place, and who by some subtle form of self-persuasion had not arrived at the same conclusion, which was that a "little fiend," a "monster," a "bad seed" (terms which were to be used during the trial or later in the press) had been sprung upon the world and had committed these terrible deeds.

On the first day of the trial Mary and Norma were brought into town together. Later this was changed and they were kept somewhat apart.

Mary, it would appear, was chatty that day. "Driving into town," said Policewoman Margery T., "we followed a 'wagon' loaded with sheepskins."

"How do they get the sheep then?" asked Mary.

Policewoman T. felt an immediate surge of discomfort. "They catch them," she said curtly.

"But how do they get the skin then?" Mary asked. "Do they have to kill the sheep to get the skins?"

"Yes, they do."

"Oh, that's cruel," said Mary and added, "I couldn't do that. I couldn't hurt a fly."

The children were brought into Court by two of the sixteen plainclothes policewomen who were to attend them—Norma during the sessions only, Mary day and night—during the eleven days of the trial.

Norma wore a skirt and a yellow blouse with a frilled collar, and Mary a plain red dress. Both of them, their hair freshly washed, looked pink and rested, pretty and excited, even elated. Shown into the row of seats they were to occupy, both of them ran the last few steps to come level with their families.

Norma's parents, their faces desperately strained, hugged her tightly and only with difficulty managed a smile to respond to her obvious relief at seeing them. In Mary's case her mother's volubility overshadowed the quieter welcome extended by her grandmother and Billy Bell. Both girls waved gaily to other relatives in the back and friends up in the public gallery.

Norma, dark and pretty, had a face and mannerisms slightly younger than her thirteen years. During the days to come she was to be restless, constantly turning from left to right trying to meet the eyes of friends and strangers, smiling tentative and tremulous smiles which readily and often turned into tears. She was given to abrupt movements of head and body, often hid her face and eyes behind her hands, sat with her mouth open and an absent expression in her face, frequently licked her lips, looked wide-eyed, astonished, and afraid, and constantly looked around for approbation, sympathy, reactions. She smiled indiscriminately at the jury, her police escorts, and the public, allowed her face to mirror horror at the words she heard and burrowed into the arms of her escorts, violently shaking her head whenever she thought something dreadful was being said about her. Everyone became very aware of her and it was usually for her benefit that the Judge would interrupt the proceedings. Later, when she gave evidence and was asked direct questions, there was always a—still—pause before she answered, almost as if the question only registered a moment in time after it had been asked. At the same time, there were instances when her voice was curiously adult and articulate.

Norma is the third of eleven children. Her father, Thomas Bell, a good and honest man, has for the last fifteen years been unable to work because of his bad health. Her mother, now careworn, must have been very pretty not so long ago. She has an endearing quality of warmth and gaiety which she has somehow managed to impart to her family—a tribe of healthy and good-looking children, with a strong sense of family identity and loyalty. Several of them appeared every afternoon and—not actually allowed into court—waved to Norma from the doors after the end of each session. She was equally strongly supported by her parents, and various relations who attended every day of the trial. They made an excellent impression on the Court, and gained the sympathy of all those present.

Mary was a very different child from Norma. Also dark-haired, she was smaller, with brilliant blue eyes and a heart-shaped face. Exceptionally pretty, with a pert Northumberland voice, she had an agile body and a remarkably organized brain which could store up information like a sponge. Her face, intellectually very alive, had a perpetual listening quality, but, except in anger, looked emotionally blank.

During the trial she only listened and very rarely looked at anyone outside those giving evidence. If she did, then only furtively, for a mere second: she averted her glance the moment her eyes met the eyes of another person. She was only to cry, briefly, three times. She certainly never smiled during the actual proceedings. "A woman up in the gallery smiles at me," she said one day to one of her police escorts, "but I don't smile back. It isn't a smiling matter. The Jury wouldn't like it if I smiled, would they?"

In contrast to her generally small-boned frame, she had a wide, short neck and broad hands and fingers which, even when she was very quiet, were rarely still. She stroked her dress, her hair, herself, or, with a backward motion, wiped her mouth. Mary's nerves were in her hands. She flexed her fingers, spreading them wide, and constantly had a finger in her mouth, though never her thumb. One of the things noticed by many of the observers—psychiatrists, child care workers, and journalists—was that, while throughout the trial Norma was often held and petted by her various escorts and handed handkerchiefs to dry her tears, Mary's escorts' main contact with her was their instinctively corrective gesture of pulling her finger out of her mouth—as if it mattered. I only saw one single policewoman, on one single occasion—when

Mary broke down on the witness stand—put an arm around her shoulders. Partly it was because her straight back and grim attention did not admit fatigue, or compassion. Partly, however, it seemed that she provoked an unwilling and perplexed sense of distaste, not only in many of those who attended her but in many of those who watched.

Mary's parents also attended every day, but they seemed to arouse little sympathy. Her mother, Elizabeth Bell, known as Betty, wore a long straggly blond wig. The papers were to describe her as a blond: no one ever saw her long luxuriant black hair. Her face, white with strain, showed the traces of heavy make-up. She was emotional, showing frequent indignation at the accusations leveled at her child and many times during the trial went out, her wild sobs temporarily stopping the proceedings. The only visible contacts between mother and child were on the rare occasions when Mary moved and her mother, with no noticeable gentleness in the gesture, tapped her on the head.

William (Billy) Bell, Mary's father, a tall, handsome man with springy black hair and red-blond sideburns, was very quiet throughout the trial. He mostly sat hunched over, his chin cupped in his hands, showing no expression whatever was said or done. Nor did he move or turn his head at any of his wife's demonstrative exits or reappearances.

There *was* sympathy for Mary's maternal grandmother from Glasgow, who, always in hat and coat, sat between her daughter and son-in-law throughout the trial. A small, fine-boned, painfully thin woman with a deeply lined face, she was straight-backed and silent. Hardly moving at all she seemed to grow smaller day by day as she listened to every word that was said. One was aware of her all the time; her mute pain and shame were haunting to see.

These mixed reactions among the onlookers grew stronger day by day, but they began in those first minutes of the morning of 5 December, when one child clung and was hugged by her parents in quiet despair, while the other one, despite the quiet and decorous conduct of her other relatives, was immediately identified with the conspicuous conduct of her mother.

The three dull knocks behind the scenes, followed by the traditional call from the Usher, "Be upstanding in Court," brought silence to the room.

Neither Mary or Norma had been prepared for the formality of the scene. As the Judge entered in slow and measured steps, the bewigged barristers and Court officials bowing deeply and slowly while the many police officers stood stiffly to attention, Mary watched with lively interest but Norma turned around bewildered, looking from her mother to her father, her face reflecting that mixture between a nervous smile and incipient tears that was to become so familiar to us. Her mother shook her head and gently pushed her back to face the Court—another gesture we were to see a hundred times.

Mr. Justice (Sir Ralph) Cusack was appointed a High Court Judge on the Queen's Bench in 1966 and is one of the most respected judges in Britain. He is known to be meticulously fair, but at the time of the trial—which was later to be described as one of the most difficult in the annals of legal history—it was rumored that he had little experience with children, perhaps because he is a bachelor. While he was occasionally testy with counsel he never once lost patience with the children and seemed to know exactly and instinctively when to apply gentleness or discipline to help them over many difficult moments. His skill was especially apparent with Norma, who lacked Mary's astonishing poise and seeming self-containment and control during the trial.

Before the beginning of the trial proper he asked the defense lawyers whether they wished him to prohibit the girls' names from being published—in view of their ages this was within his power.

But both defense counsels said they had no objection. It was explained later that, although everybody in Scotswood already knew who was involved, unless the names *were* used a slur *could* eventually remain on other children. In view of those circumstances the Judge allowed publication.

Mr. Justice Cusack warned the Jury that the case might take several days and draw considerable attention. During adjournments —which he would permit in view of the children's ages—none of the Jury were to discuss the case with anyone or allow anyone to discuss it with them.

Mr. Rudolph Lyons, Queen's Counsel, a leading "silk" (a term

derived from the silk gowns worn by Q.C.'s) and now Circuit
Judge at Liverpool,* opened the case for the prosecution at 11:30
A.M. He was to speak for six hours.

The Jury faced an unhappy and distressing task, he said, because the girls were so young. They were charged with two
murders, within the space of little more than two months. . . . He
told the jury that in the course of the evidence they might find
certain points of similarity between the two charges. For example,
the choice of victim and perhaps also the method of killing. The
prosecution contended that such similarities tended to indicate
that both boys were killed by the same person or persons. But,
although they might find these and other links between the two
cases, that did not absolve them from considering each of the
two charges separately, but not of course in artificial isolation.

During this first hour of Mr. Lyons' presentation both girls
listened intently to every word he said. But it became apparent
very quickly, even on that first morning, that, while both of them
understood some words and phrases he used, there were others
Mary could understand but Norma could not—and some neither
could understand at all. Mary's capacity for concentration, or
possibly simulation of concentration, was so exceptional that it
was only in the course of time that one began to recognize the
mannerisms which indicated that she had temporarily stopped
listening and was daydreaming. Even then, however, she seemed
capable of two levels of awareness, for the moment anything was
mentioned that interested or puzzled her, she whispered to her
solicitor asking him to explain. Norma's face, especially at the
beginning of the sessions when she was less tired, mirrored every
degree of comprehension or bewilderment: a manifestation of
childishness everyone in Court was as aware of as of her inability
to sustain concentration for long.

After the lunch recess, Mr. Lyons began his specific description
of the two crimes. He first dealt in detail with the Crown's case
concerning Martin Brown. He described to the Jury how the little
boy's body had been found: the two girls' appearance on the
scene within minutes of the discovery of the body; their apparent

* February 1973.

eagerness to be involved as shown by their running to get Mrs. Finlay, and their subsequent approach to Mrs. Brown; the arrival of the police; the examination by the pathologist; and finally the fact that the police regarded the case as an unsolved mystery and not a possible murder until the similar death of Brian Howe, two months later. He then spoke of the breaking into the Woodlands Crescent Day Nursery (on 26 May) and the finding, by the police (on 27 May), of the four "We Murder . . ." notes (on which almost the whole case of Martin Brown's murder was going to hinge). At that time, said Mr. Lyons, the police had no idea who was responsible for the notes, or for breaking into the Nursery. . . .

. . . But after the murder of Brian Howe in July, said Mr. Lyons—and there was no doubt that he was murdered by asphyxia too—it became clear that both or one of the accused girls was responsible for that murder. They were subsequently questioned about the breaking and entering of the Nursery (on 26 May) and as a result of their answers and of comparisons made by a handwriting expert between the four notes and the undoubted handwriting of the two girls, the prosecution was submitting, Mr. Lyons said, that there could be no doubt the intruders in the Day Nursery were Norma and Mary. The handwriting expert, Mr. Page, was given a lot of other material to examine too. In due course, Mr. Lyons said, Mr. Page would produce a set of charts to show the reasons for his opinion.

The Jury were then handed photostat copies of the four notes alleged to have been written by the two girls and photostats of the specimens of their handwriting.

On the first occasion, and in the days to come, whenever photographs or photostats were examined, Mary could be observed leaning over, trying to see them over the shoulders of her counsel in front of her.

Norma not only evinced complete lack of interest in all documents, but, on several occasions—some of which were to remain in the audience's mind as some of the most poignant of the trial —desperately resisted any attempt to ask her to acknowledge or identify such photographs.

Mr. Lyons said that both girls had each written one note, and the other two were a result of their joint efforts. "If you accept the prosecution case about the handwriting on these notes," the prosecutor said, "then you have these two girls writing within hours of the death of Martin Brown that 'we murdered Martin Brown.' Maybe . . ." he went on, "they could not resist the temptation in their childish way of showing to the police how superior they were by writing about something they did not know." He proceeded with the other events that followed the death of Martin Brown; Mary's calling on Mrs. Brown to ask to see Martin's body in his coffin, the two girls' constant visits to Mrs. Finlay and their harping on Martin's death; and Mary's visit to the house of Brian Howe in July and her telling his sister and a friend that "Norma got hold of little Martin by the throat" and showing those girls how Norma allegedly throttled Martin. At this time, Mr. Lyons said, no publicity had been given to the possibility (never even officially considered by the uniformed police who would otherwise have turned the case over to the C.I.D.) that the little boy had died as the result of asphyxia.

Yet here was the suggestion, made by Mary, that Norma had seized Martin by the throat. The prosecution would therefore ask the Jury to consider that Mary knew the cause of the boy's death (long before it was made public).

Detective Chief-Inspector Dobson said he interviewed Norma on 14 August in the presence of her solicitor. He told her that he had reason to believe she and Mary broke into the Day Nursery and wrote some notes. Norma replied that she had broken into the Nursery the following weekend, but not the one Chief-Inspector Dobson was talking about; that on that second weekend she had been in the loft, but not in the school itself at all, and that she had never written any notes. She agreed to give samples of her handwriting.

When shown the four notes she said, "I'll tell you something: that is Mary's writing. I have not seen them notes before." Later she denied Mary's allegation (to Irene F.) that she had murdered Martin Brown and said, "I never." Mr. Lyons said that at this stage Norma declined to make a statement, saying she was losing [her] voice and would like to keep it. Her solicitor had intervened and said the interview was at an end.

On 2 August, Mr. Dobson had interviewed Mary in the presence of her solicitor. Mary admitted spilling disinfectant and "pink stuff" over the floor, pulling some papers from the office, and writing part of the notes. She denied having written anything about murder and said, "Me and her were at the top at the time it happened. We went to the house and went in. There were crowds of people. We saw Martin in the workman's arms. We went to tell his Auntie Rita."

Mr. Lyons pointed out to the Jury that one phrase in that statement was of particular importance—seeing Martin in the workman's arms. Asked why Norma wrote on the note, "We murdered Martin Brown" Mary replied, "For a giggle. I don't think she could have done it. She was up at the top with me."

Mr. Lyons said that fibers found on Martin Brown's clothing and the clothing of Brian Howe were found by scientific examination (evidence for which would be produced) to match exactly fibers from a gray woolen dress worn by Mary.

He said that in September of this year a teacher at Mary's school had found two of Mary's exercise books: on the cover of one of them, entitled "My Newsbook," there was a poster which said "Evening Chronicle, Saturday, 1968" and then in larger words "Boy found dead in old house." Mr. Lyons said that the important part of this document was a drawing of a little boy, the main significance of which was that Mary had told Chief-Inspector Dobson that the only time she saw the body of Martin was in the workman's arms. Yet, he said, here she was drawing what the prosecution submitted was the position in which the body was found, and this before there had been any mention in public of tablets, by either the police or the press. "Is it possible," the prosecutor asked, "that this was just some clue laying by a very clever little girl?"

There were three points Mr. Lyons' interpretation immediately raised in one's mind. The main one: even accepting in advance—as every single person the author spoke to certainly did—that Mary was probably guilty, what exactly would be so clever about drawing attention to herself in this way? Or did he mean on the contrary that she was outsmarting herself through not being able to resist showing off her superior knowledge? What had to be remembered though was that she did not do this drawing for anyone in particular, or to show to anyone in particular, but put it in her newsbook at school where, in the ordinary course of events, only her teacher would see it. Could this really be considered a clever little girl showing off, or is it not much more likely an unconscious cry for help? Secondly: Mr. Lyons' insistence (reported in the newspapers the next day and on the face of it generally accepted) that it was extraordinary for Mary to know about the bottle of tablets and the position Martin's body was found in. This was not acceptable because—always remembering that at this point of the trial her guilt had not been established —with three schoolboys and two local workmen having seen and probably described the terrible scene to a number of people, there could be little doubt at all that by the evening of 25 May a large part of the population of Scotswood knew all about the bottle of tablets and the position Martin was found in. And that therefore there was no reason why she should not have known too.

In her conversation with Mr. Dobson, Mary never claimed specifically that she didn't know what position the boy had been found in—she said "We saw Martin in the workman's arms" and (irrespective of her eventually established guilt) there is good reason to believe that, with all their running in and out of the building at the time, the two girls *would* have seen him in the workman's arms.

These points—in an effort to maintain an open mind—at the time occurred to *this* observer. There is of course no question but that it was entirely proper for the prosecution to present the case exactly as it did. However, what has emerged since as the important aspect of this and many subsequent occasions is that this emphasis on Mary's "cleverness" in instances where this "cleverness" *can* also be interpreted differently, that is as a cry for help, greatly added to the impression which seems to have been generally accepted: that, irrespective of medical evidence, what we had here was *not* a "sick" child, but a clever little MONSTER. A conviction which may be at least in part to blame for the fact that few if any questions were asked or information aired about her background and her life during the trial, and that the dispositions made for her by the authorities concerned when the trial was over were never really questioned in the sense of being unsuitable for her—only that they might cause discomfort to other people.

Mr. Lyons completed his presentation by beginning the detailed description of the events following the death of Brian Howe. Describing how Brian had been found, and the police investigation that followed the discovery of his body, Mr. Lyons said that in statements taken by the police each of the two girls told lie after lie, eventually ending up admitting that they had both been there when Brian was killed but each saying that the other had committed the act.

He said that in one of the statements, which could only be described as "cunning," Mary had tried to involve a totally innocent small boy in these events.

"This gives you some indication of the sort of girl she is," Mr. Lyons said, and that concluded the first day of the trial.

Fernwood Reception Centre, where Mary spent the nine days and two weekends of her trial (while Norma remained at the Mental Hospital throughout), is a large well-equipped Victorian house set in a lovely big garden in Jesmond, a residential district of Newcastle. Under the authority of Newcastle's excellent Children's Department, Fernwood is used for children of school age who come there primarily because of sudden family emergencies and does not need or have "special provisions for high degree security."

Mary was sent there in spite of this drawback because it was within a few minutes drive from the Court, which might make it less tiring for her; because being in Newcastle and in its own grounds it would be easier to patrol; and above all because, on the top floor, separated from the rest of the house by a lockable door, was a small flat—with bedroom, sitting room, and bath—where she could be kept in isolation from other children for the period of the trial.

The carpeted and cheery bedroom, the window looking out onto the drive and neighboring houses, like the rest of the house light and comfortable, had been equipped for her benefit with television.

In the sitting room next door, used mainly on weekends, the window looked down over gardens to a cemetery beyond.

Fourteen policewomen guarded Mary in eight-hour shifts during the days and nights of the trial, when for very good reasons she was never to be left alone for a moment, was not allowed to communicate with any other child or outsider, and was only allowed brief meetings with her family, under guard, in a waiting room off the Court. Policewomen are carefully trained to deal with women and children in times of stress. This may well be why many of the things Mary said to some of them are more revealing than anything she is known to have said at that time to anyone else. It is also a fact that many of Newcastle's policewomen happen to be exceptionally good-looking and that Mary usually responds very positively to good looks in men or women. Of course, almost everything she said—or did—during this period had significance. And, had more been known about her to begin with, her conversations, behavior, and acts during the hours she spent with these observant young women might have been accorded the importance they deserved and—if taken into account—might have helped the people who later had to decide her fate.

Policewoman Mary S. guarded her twice at weekends, from eight A.M. to four P.M. "We had been advised not to talk to Mary about the trial but I thought it couldn't possibly hurt her to talk," she said. "It would probably hurt her more *not* to talk. We talked about a great many things. One could hardly believe that this was a child of eleven—she talked more like someone of sixteen."

They were supposed to stay next to her even when she went to the lavatory. "Some of the policewomen were frightened of Mary, I never was," Mary S. said. "I trusted her and I told her so. She was very intelligent, you know. That first Saturday morning, she was watching the 'Learn French' course on television and she picked up French words, you know, and spoke them perfectly, and understood them too. The only thing, she had a funny way of staring at me, through me; that was strange. And then, she was always wanting to have baths. Both times I was with her from eight to four, she suddenly said she wanted a bath in the middle of the day. I thought that was interesting, you know. But I said no, she couldn't."

All the policewomen wrote formal reports. "But nobody ever asked us questions about her, nothing about what she said or what we thought or noticed."

"Just as if nobody *wanted* to know," said one perceptive girl. These formal reports wouldn't have included Mary's constant talk about her family, her little brother, her aunts Cath and Audrey, and, above all, her "gran," to all of whom she seemed exceptionally attached. She told many of the policewomen, "When it is all over I'll go and stay with my gran in Scotland." The reports would not have spoken of her fondness for animals or her love for her big dog. Some of the policewomen did write down that she hardly slept, but there was no place to mention her terrible restlessness in the night; her sitting "bolt upright" at the slightest sound when she finally did drop off; her mumblings in her sleep; her obviously growing anxiety as the days wore on; and finally her terror, ill-masked by the continuing cheekiness she displayed with everybody except a few of the policewomen, who, warm, pretty, and secure in themselves, offered her something she badly needed and to whom, in return, she seemed to offer a kind of affection. She tried to find points of contact with all of them, almost as if she had a compulsion to leave her "mark," even with those she did not like. Of the girls who spent time with her, there was not a single one who did not remember something special about her, positive or negative.

"She had no feelings for people," said Policewoman Hazel R. Hazel, as many others were to feel, could hardly bear to look at Mary, let alone touch her, and felt ashamed of this revulsion from a child. "She was a little horror, wasn't she?" she said defensively.

Policewoman Jean Q. was a former staff nurse in a mental hospital. She guarded Mary, either from four P.M. to midnight or midnight until eight A.M. for eight days. Mary told another policewoman she didn't like Jean Q.: "She is too bossy," she said. But Jean did not return her dislike. Having dealt widely with disturbed children, she was particularly interested in Mary and had no doubt whatever that she belonged in hospital. "If I was still at Northgate," she said, "I would have no hesitation whatever to take her on. And I think I could have helped her. . . ."

Policewoman Mary S. spoke of the only incident that made

everyone briefly sit up and take notice. "It happened that first weekend. She was bored. She was standing at the window watching a cat make her way up the drainpipe and she asked could she bring the cat in. I thought why not, poor kid. So I said all right. We opened the window and she lifted the cat in and started to play with it on the floor, with a bit of wool. I was looking at a magazine or something and then I looked up and I saw first that she was holding the cat by the skin at the back of the neck. I thought, 'Well, that's how people pick up cats.' But then I realized she was holding the cat so tight it could not breathe and its tongue was lolling. I jumped to it and tore her hands away. I said, 'You mustn't do that; you'll hurt her.' She answered, 'Oh, she doesn't feel that, and, anyway, I like hurting little things that can't fight back.' "

It made one wonder again, not so much why she did such a thing even while under guard, for this may well be a compulsion, but why should a girl described as "very intelligent" and "cunning" make such a remark, which she must have known would be reported? She said something similar to another policewoman she liked, Valerie P. "She told me she'd like to be a policewoman," Valerie said, "and I answered, 'Well, you've had that.' So she said, 'Then I'd like to be a nurse.' I asked her why. 'Because then I can stick needles into people. I like hurting people.' "

At the start of the proceedings on the second day of the trial, Mr. Justice Cusack said that he understood that some of the five women jurors had not felt very well on the opening day. (Their discomfort—it had been generally noticed—had arisen when they were handed the photographs of the dead little boys.)

"I have every sympathy with you. This is not an agreeable case for anybody," he said. "But I want to say to you, and I hope you will sympathize with me, that this is a case in which the assistance of women jurors is of very great importance. Of course women nowadays take the place of men and have the same duties to perform as citizens. If there is any lady on the Jury who really feels so ill as to be unable to discharge her duty and follow the evidence, I will reconsider the position. But I very much hope the ladies will feel they are doing a public duty in this case and will do their best to discharge it. I gather from your silence," he said a moment later, "that you are all ready and willing to serve, and I thank you."

Mr. Lyons' mention of the incident at the sandpit, which occurred two weeks before the first murder and during which the throats of three little girls were squeezed by one of the accused girls, caused the first interruption of the trial by Mary's mother, who broke down and began to sob. Norma turned around at once to watch her: Mary sat, if possible, even stiller than before and did not turn around even when a policewoman escorted her mother from the room.

Continuing after Betty Bell had left, Mr. Lyons said that the sandpit incident would be proved in the course of evidence by the prosecution but was not the subject of another charge. He said the prosecution would introduce it because it might show on the part of one of the girls an abnormal propensity to squeeze the throats of young children. A propensity of this kind, he said, could be valuable as a means of identification when there was no motive besides pleasure and excitement, or possibly the feeling of superiority and a child showing herself cleverer than the police.

From the point of view of propensity, the "sandpit incident," as it became known—and the allegation of Norma's eleven-year-old sister Susan that she too had been attacked by Mary Bell in this particular manner—were of considerable significance.

It was when children were on the witness stand—particularly of course the two accused—that one became increasingly uneasy about the incongruity of a trial where a jury was required to evaluate the words and thought processes of children in adult terms. For realizing that, on the basis of legal procedure as it exists in Britain, facts alone establish guilt or innocence, one began to question the validity of such a system with regard to children accused of capital (or any other) crime. While it was certainly possible to establish certain facts—that is: two little boys *had* been killed; several little girls *had* been attacked; a series of bizarre notes *had* been written, etc.—it did *not* follow from there that adults untrained in the ways and problems of disturbed children could possibly gauge *degrees* of guilt, or understand motives, and it began to seem indefensible to accuse or convict a child on the same terms as an adult, without understanding all the background of her life, her way of thinking, and the pressures that might have led to her crime.

It is important to remember that for young children it is not the formality of taking the oath that decides whether or not they are going to tell the truth. Their truthfulness is determined—indeed is predetermined—quite simply by whether or not they are truthful children; that is, children who are growing up in an environment where being truthful is a matter of course. To a great many children lies are not at all "lies" in the adult moral sense, but merely fantasy. This does not mean that all children—from whatever environment—do not tell lies at times. But it does mean at least that, for a child who comes from a "truth-oriented" environment, telling a lie under these particular conditions and in answer to a direct question, would be a conscious act—and not easy—while children whose immediate environment is not "truth-oriented" would not necessarily be particularly troubled by such a lie but would consider it a normal, not to say automatic, way of "getting the better" of authority, or of dramatizing themselves in a situation where their own role would otherwise seem negligible. Basically Norma Bell comes from a truth-oriented environment.

It was 2:22 P.M. on Wednesday, 11 December, the fourth day of the trial, when she was called for her examination-in-chief by her counsel. She wore a red dress and yellow cardigan and as always looked beseechingly left and right as her police escort walked her to the witness stand. The room grew silent. Her parents quietly left the Court (they were to sit silently in the snack bar while Norma gave her evidence). Her grandmother stayed.

As Norma, her policewoman escort next to her, stood (very pale and already crying) just a few feet away from the Judge in the witness box, Mr. Justice Cusack leaned forward and spoke to her quietly and gently.

"Norma, I want to say something to you before you start telling us what you have to say. When you went to school, were you taught about God?"

"School and Church," she whispered.

"You were taught about God. Do you know what the Bible is?"

"Yes."

"And if you take the Bible and say that you will promise before God to tell the truth, what does that mean?"

"I must tell the truth."

"Yes, you must tell the truth. She may be sworn. . . . Norma, you can sit down," he said, after the oath had been administered, and waited until she had been seated on the chair which had a large cushion on it so as to bring the children well up into view.

"You are going to be asked some questions," he then continued, gently. "If you feel tired and feel that you do not want to go on, or feel that you want to go outside for a few minutes, will you tell the lady who is sitting beside you? Do you understand that?"

"Yes."

"Norma, your full name is Norma Joyce Bell, is it not?" said R. P. Smith, her counsel.

"Yes." Her voice could hardly be heard.

"Is that right?"

"Yes."

"And you live at 68 Whitehouse Road, Newcastle?"

"Yes."

"Have you lived there for about two years?"

"Yes."

"And you live with your mother and father?"

"Yes."

"And five brothers, have you?"

"Yes."

"And five sisters?"

"Yes."

"All the time you lived there, has a girl called May or Mary Bell lived next door?"

"Yes."

"Number seventy?"

"Yes."

"Do you call her Mary or do you call her May?"

"Both."

"Have you played together?"

"Yes."

"And you are thirteen, Norma?"

"Yes."

"When is your birthday?"

"March thirty-first."

"You will be fourteen next March, will you?"

"Yes."

"You go to school but not the same school as May?"

"I have just left the school; I have just left Mary's."

R. P. Smith questioned her in detail about the sandpit incident, and she said that she had never touched any of the three little girls but that she had seen Mary squeeze their necks. Much later she was again questioned about the sandpit incident, this time by Mr. Lyons. He was always direct, logical, detached, and quick in his examination. Mary—one felt—at times almost enjoyed sparring with him, but Norma was terrified.

"Norma, I want to ask you about the time Mary squeezed Pauline's throat," he said. "Did she put both hands around the girl's throat?"

"Changed them, changing from one hand to two."

"Changed hands, did she?" asked Mr. Justice Cusack (to emphasize her reply for the Jury), and Mr. Lyons too repeated, "Changed from one hand to two."

"Did she ever have both hands on at the same time with Pauline?" the Judge asked again.

(These questions were put because medical evidence on Brian Howe had shown that his death was brought about by simultaneous pressure on the neck and on his nose. They were intended to establish whether there was any precedent of Mary's exerting this pressure with one hand, leaving one hand free to hold the child's nose.)

"She still used two hands, one each time," Norma answered Mr. Justice Cusack's question.

". . . Is this right," said Mr. Lyons again, "did you say Mary put both hands round the girl's throat and squeezed?"

"Changed her hands," Norma repeated, her voice a mixture of stubbornness and fatigue.

"This is in the sandpit," Mr. Justice Cusack asked again, obviously concerned lest she mixed up the different incidents which were being referred to.

"One each time," she answered again.

"It is Cindy I am thinking of now, not Pauline," said Mr. Lyons. "Do you remember when she squeezed Cindy's throat?"

"I don't know Cindy."

"What?"

"I don't know Cindy, but still a girl there." (She meant there was a girl there, but she didn't know her name.)

"A girl there. How many girls did Mary do that to in succession? Was it three different girls?"

"Two at first."

"Two at first. Then one afternoon—let's take the first one: that was Pauline, was it?"

"No, the first one was Cindy."

"Was Cindy, yes. When Mary squeezed Cindy's throat, did Mary put both hands round her throat?"

"I forget."

". . . Then, when Mary went to Pauline, did she put both hands round Pauline's throat?"

"Changes."

"Was there a time when she had both hands and was squeezing Pauline with both hands?"

Norma nodded and Mr. Justice Cusack said, "She nods."

"You nod, yes?" asked Mr. Lyons.

"Yes."

"And did Mary do the same to Susan?"

"Yes, but I was not there all the time. I was behind the shed."

"Did you know that was a wrong thing for Mary to do?"

"Yes."

"Did you think Mary was a very wicked girl for doing that? Did you?"

Mr. Justice Cusack intervened (as he did on many occasions when he felt that counsels' language was too ornate for a child's understanding or their manner too pressing). "Did you think she was very naughty to do it?" he asked.

"Yes, yes," Norma replied.

"Did Mary ever talk about killing little boys or girls?"

"She shakes her head, no," said Judge Cusack.

"No," repeated Mr. Lyons. "Did she ever show you how little boys or girls could be killed? Did she ever show you that?"

Norma didn't answer. "Did she, Norma?" asked the Judge.

"Yes," Norma murmured.

"She is murmuring yes," said the Judge.

"Well," said Mr. Lyons, "that was a very naughty thing to do, wasn't it, to think of killing little boys and girls and talk about it?"

"Did you think that was naughty?" asked the Judge. "She nods her head, yes."

"Yes," Norma said.

It had been their phrasing, not hers—but—if that was how they put it, she was obviously prepared to agree: it was naughty.

(Mary was questioned much later about the sandpit. She claimed that, not only had she never touched the children, but that she was playing behind a hut nearly all the time and saw nothing. "I'm not saying Norma did it. All . . . I'm not saying anybody did it, because I don't want nothing to do with that. . . ." she said.)

It was Norma who was questioned first about Martin Brown during the trial, and the prosecution had already made it plain that, while fibers of Mary's dress had been found on Martin's clothing, there was nothing whatever to connect Norma with Martin's death, apart from those macabre notes.

On that Saturday in May 1968 when Martin Brown was found dead he had been seen many times by a large number of people. The last time, by all accounts, not more than twenty minutes before he was found lying spreadeagled and dead on the floor of an empty room on the first floor of a derelict house two hundred yards down the street from his home. The room was up two flights of stairs. The boy looked as if untouched; no sign of violence, or struggle. . . .

(Martin's mother, June Brown, said to me later that they had never been able to understand how it would have been possible for Mary, on her own, to get Martin up to that room and kill him. "When Martin was two," she said, "we'd just moved into this house —we hadn't been here more than a few days—he stumbled on top of the stairs and fell down. I tried to catch him, but I couldn't. Ever since then he was dead frightened of stairs. He'd never go up any stairs by himself. That's why I knew that someone had to take him up them stairs in that old house that day—he wouldn't have went up of his own accord—I knew... And then you know, Martin, he was a big bairn," she said. "He wasn't the sort you could push around. He was so tall, like a six-year-old—we realized that again, when he was dead like, you know, because of the coffin. If it's small bairns up to six, they can put the coffin in a car—but we had to get the hearse, because he was too big. He was so strong, was Martin, that when he played around with his dad—he could quite often push him off.

"A child's instinct is to protect himself. Martin, he'd have kicked and screamed unless somebody sat on him to stop him. And never, never would he have ventured up them stairs ...")

Mr. Smith asked Norma about Martin almost immediately after he finished questioning her about the sandpit incident.

"... I want to ask now about the day little Martin Brown was found in one of the old houses." Norma turned her head away and covered her face. "Now don't get upset. Did you see little Martin Brown that day?" he asked quietly.

"Yes," Norma whispered after a moment.

"Was it before dinnertime or at dinnertime or after dinnertime?" Again Norma turned away. "Was it before or after?" Mr. Smith repeated.

"Yes."

"Yes?"

"Both."

"When was the last time you saw him?"

"Well, first one was in our back and once beside the workman's —that's twice."

"Once in your back?"

"Yes."

"Was that by the fence?"

"Yes."

"And the next time was by the roadwork men. Was that in St Margaret's Road?"

"Yes, but when I seen him the second time I was just by myself then, on the second time."

"Now the second time you saw him is the time I want you to tell the ladies and gentlemen of the Jury about. What were the workmen doing in St Margaret's Road, do you remember?"

"They were sitting down having a cup of tea."

"Yes?"

" 'Cos Mr. Hall asked what time Davy's shop opens and I said 'I don't know,' so I went along the street and it was still shut. . . ."

". . . And did you go back and tell the workmen?"

"Yes. It was around about something to two."

"Yes? In the afternoon?" She didn't answer. "Was Martin still there when you went back to tell the workmen?"

"Oh no, he wasn't there."

"Did you ever see him again?"

"Not until the nighttime when he was found; when he got carried into the ambulance."

"He was taken into the ambulance?"

"Yes."

"You say it was something to two?"

"Yes, Davy's shop doesn't open until around ten past or half-past [two], around about there."

"I want to ask you about something that happened a little later. Were you near your house when Mary's mother wanted Mary to do something?"

"I was there."

"About what time was this?"

"About something to three; it wasn't three o'clock yet; it was still something to three."

"What did Mary's mother want Mary to do?"

"She wanted a loaf of bread and something for the dog and a small tin of pease pudding."

"Did you go with Mary to the shop?"

"I went right there with her. Yes, I went up with her."

"Is it far from your house? How long does it take you to walk there?"

"Just a couple of minutes—about two—depends how fast you walk."

"Did it take you a couple of minutes on this day or longer or . . ."

"A good couple of minutes."

"Were you served straightaway in the shop?"

"Yes."

"Or I should say was Mary served straightaway?"

"A man was served and then it was her turn next. There wasn't very many in the shop. . . ."

". . . And then where did you go?"

"Me and her walked down the street and we got down the street 'cos she gave me the things to take home, and the corner of the street, she went down there."

"Which road was that?" asked the Judge.

"I am going to find that out." Mr. Smith turned back to Norma —"You and Mary separated?"

"Got separated."

"Now which road was it that you were in when you separated?"

"Me going down Whitehouse Road and her going down Crosshill Road . . . . She gave me the things to take home."

"And you were going to take the things home, is that right?"

"Yes."

"What did you do when you had got these things? Did you take them to Mary's home?"

"In her back was C. and D. (Mary's sisters) and I remember giving them to one of them two. . . ."

". . . And where did you go?"

"In the house, 'cos my mam was ironing. . . ."

". . . In your house?" Mr. Smith repeated—emphasizing her reply.

"Yes."

". . . How long did you stay watching your mother doing the ironing—a long time?"

"Five minutes—no, it wasn't a long time."

"No, it wasn't a long time?"

"No."

"Did someone come along?"

"Mary Bell."

"Where did you see Mary Bell, in your house or in a garden or where?"

"Well, there's a hole in a fence."

"Is that this back way down to St Margaret's Road?"

"Yes."

"You saw Mary there, did you?"

"Yes, 'cos she peeped her head through the hole."

"Did she want something?"

"She wanted me to go down to Number 85." (From Mary and Norma's houses down this way to St Margaret's Road would take less than a minute.)

"Do you remember what she said?"

"There's been an accident."

"Did she say anything more about it at that time?"

"Well, we went down. She took us down 85. Both of us went down to 85 and we went through the door and then we got out. There's a hole in the toilet. We went through there and through— no, just through the hole and up the steps. . . ." Norma began once again to twist her body to and fro, almost as if trying to get out of her own skin.

"Did she say . . ." Mr. Smith paused and waited while Norma's police escort handed her a handkerchief which in her peculiarly childish way she handed back, wet, after blowing her nose.

"Did Mary say something more to you about the accident," Mr. Smith continued, "before you went through and out into the back and through the hole in the wall?"

"No, but she knew the name, 'cos she said Martin Black."

"That is what I want you to tell the Court about." (This was the sort of detail which most people had already become convinced Norma could not possibly have invented, and it was therefore of great significance for her defense.) "She had said something, had she, before you went through the hole?"

"Yes, she said, 'It's Martin Black who has had the accident.' But I don't know who she really meant."

"Did you know any little boy called Martin Black?"

"I don't know Martin Black."

"But you knew Martin Brown, didn't you?"

"Yes, that was him."

"And you found out later that it was Martin Brown and not Martin Black, is that right?"

"Yes."

"What about going into the back and through the hole in the wall? Who was leading the way?"

"Me, 'cos we went up the steps."

"Did you say 'me' or 'May'?"

"May, 'cos me and May went up these steps."

"But who knew the way? Did you know the way?"

"Did I know the way in? No, Mary Bell."

("I felt sick and went to the window to get some air," Walter Long had said in evidence: While standing with his head out of the window which gave onto St Margaret's Road, he saw two girls coming down the street which at the time was empty. "I knew the smaller one," he said. They stopped directly underneath the window, and the one he knew, Mary, said to the other one; "Shall we go up," and the other one replied, "Howay then, let's go up.")

"Now there were some steps. What happened when you got to the steps?" (This was in the back of the house.)

"May said, 'Away up' and I said, 'Away then.' "

"So you did go up?"

"Yes."

"What happened?"

"Well, you could hear the workmen's voices and some other voices."

"Did any of them say anything to you two girls? Do you understand, Norma? You heard some voices of the workmen and some other voices. They were talking to each other, were they?"

"I could hear them talking."

"Did they talk to you?"

"Told us, Mary and me, to get away."

"They told you to go away?"

"Yes."

"Who was it that told you? Was it one of the workmen or somebody else?"

"I can't remember."

"And so did you go away?"

"Yes."

"How far into the house had you been, Norma?"

"Not the first steps, but going onto the second ones."

"We heard the other day, you see, that there were some stone steps outside and some wooden steps inside. Which steps did you get onto?"

"On the wooden ones."

"Did you ever get up to the room upstairs in Number 85?"

"I never went in."

"Well now, when you were told to get away and you went out, did you go out straightaway in the same way, that is, through the hole in the wall and back through the downstairs flat?"

"Yes."

"And out into the street?"

"Yes."

"And what happened in the street?"

"Well, when we got out there was a crowd." (This whole part of Norma's testimony differed sharply from the evidence Mary was to give the next day but, as far as the emptiness of the street is concerned until they got back out there, it coincided with Walter Long's evidence.)

"Did you talk to anybody in the crowd or did you go somewhere?"

"I was just in the crowd. I was not with Mary Bell then, not in the meantime."

"Will you just tell the Court what happened when you got into the street and there was this crowd?"

"Well, they wanted to know whose little boy it was and Mary went up—but I never went up. She went up into the room and she named the boy."

"What do you mean by 'she went up into the room'?" Mr. Smith asked. "What do you mean by that?"

"She went upstairs where little Martin was."

"How do you know she went up, Norma?"

"I saw her going through the wall and she told me 'cos those boys . . ." again Norma stopped and cried.

"You had come out into the street," R. P. Smith went on after she had composed herself, rephrasing his question to help her clarify her reply, "because the workmen or somebody had told you to go away, and there was a crowd of people and somebody wanted to know whose little boy it was. That's right, is it?"

"Workmen wanted to know."

"And you said that Mary went off and went upstairs to the room. What did you see Mary do?"

"Just go through but I never went with her."

"You saw her go through where you had just come out of?"

"Yes."

"You and Mary were told to go away by the workmen, is that right?" asked Mr. Justice Cusack.

"Yes."

"And you went away and arrived in the street, is that right?"

"Yes."

"Did Mary come with you?"

"Back in . . ."

"Did Mary come down with you," he repeated, "and arrive in the street? Do you understand?"

"Yes."

"What happened, did she come down with you?"

"She came all the way with us."

"She came all the way back with you?"

"Yes."

"And then did she go back inside again?"

"Yes."

"That is what I was not sure about," the Judge said.

"Did you see Mary come out?" Mr. Smith asked.

"Did I see her come out? No."

"Did you yourself go to Rita's house that afternoon?"

(It was part of the prosecution's contention that, after Martin Brown's death, *both* girls had taunted Martin's mother and aunt and had behaved as if the little boy's death was "a big joke.")

"I went to Rita Finlay's house with Mary Bell," Norma conceded.

"When was that?"

"After May came back again."

"So she did come out and the two of you went to Rita's house?"

"Yes."

"What for?"

"May wanted to tell Rita that there had been an accident, 'cos she said there's been an accident and Martin and something about blood all over something." Again Mr. Smith stopped for a moment when Norma—as was to happen time and again—became very agitated at the mention of death and blood.

"That's what Mary said, is it?" he finally continued.

"Yes."

"Did she say that to Rita?"

"Yes."

"Norma, I do not want to ask you anything else about that afternoon."

Mary's examination-in-chief began after the lunch recess on the sixth day of the trial. "My Lord," said Harvey Robson, her defense counsel, "I now call Mary Bell." The public and press galleries were very full, the only day when the atmosphere in the Court—unlike all the other days—was faintly tinged with that morbid fascination one associates with certain types of murder trials. As Norma the day before, Mary too was pale, her lack of color emphasized by the yellow cotton dress she wore which, she had told Policewoman Barbara O. the night before, had been made for her by her mother. That night too, Mary had asked Policewoman O. the meaning of the word "immature." "The lawyer said Norma was more immature," she'd said. "Would that mean that if I was the more intelligent I'd get all the blame?"

If it had been apparent all along that the attitude toward Mary of many of those in Court was very different from that toward Norma, this became even more obvious now when Mary took the stand. Norma's obvious bewilderment evoked the protective instincts any adult feels toward a helpless child. Mary's extraordinary self-possession, on the other hand, seemed to bar this reaction and resulted in many people—rather than showing or even feeling compassion—watching her with a horrified kind of curiosity.

"Mary," said Mr. Justice Cusack, "I want to ask you some questions." Throughout the trial whenever he addressed remarks to the children, he would alter his position in his chair so as to turn his whole body toward them, a gesture which underlined his determination to deal with them individually and personally, and which never failed to focus their entire attention on him. "Have you been taught about God?" he asked.

"Yes, sir."

Her voice was clear and distinctive, with the slightly singsong and melodious Northumberland inflection which meant that the "sir" of the always recurring "Yes, sir" of the next two days was two tones above the "Yes," which gave it a particularly childlike sound.

"And have you been taught that at school?" asked the Judge.

"Yes, sir."

"Do you go to Church at all?"

"Sometimes, sir, to the Mission."

"Sometimes to the Mission. Do you know what the Bible is?"

"Yes, sir."

"And if you take the Bible and promise before God to tell the truth, what do you think that means?"

"You must tell the truth, sir."

"You must tell the truth. Very well, she may be sworn."

The general public did not know, but the Court and several members of the press were aware that the Bible had a very special meaning in Mary's life: Norma, the day before, had with great difficulty been questioned about "a book Mary used to like to look at." But she had resisted all attempts at persuading her to pronounce the *name* of this book. The book in fact was the Bible. Billy Bell was to say later, "She had five of them, she was always reading the Bible." But he did not know that what apparently mesmerized Mary in one of the Bibles was a list of names, dates, and addresses that had been glued in—the list of relatives who had died.

Questioned about Martin at the beginning of her examination-in-chief, Mary's description differed from Norma's in several essential details. By this time of the trial—to all of which she had paid close attention—all witnesses (except one) had given their evidence: the boys who had found Martin; the workmen who had tried to revive him; the pathologist who had examined him; his mother and aunt, and Norman Lee, principal scientific officer of the Forensic Science Laboratory at Gosforth (Newcastle), who had testified that, "Five wool fibers found on Martin Brown's clothing matched exactly those from a gray dress belonging to Mary Bell." Martin's death had, of course, remained an unsolved mystery for two months, and his clothing was kept at the police station and was only examined scientifically after Chief-Inspector Dobson reopened the investigation in August.

"... I want you to tell us all here, first of all," said Harvey Robson, "about the day when Martin was found dead. Do you remember that day?"

"Yes, sir."

"Did you know Martin before that day?"

"Yes, sir."

"Do you know his full name, or just the name of Martin?"

"Martin George Brown, sir."

"You knew that at the time? Or did you only learn his full name later on?"

"I cannot remember, sir." (The examination about Martin Brown first brought out Mary's ability—phenomenal for someone of her age, education, and background—to absorb, remember, and later use the testimony she had heard and of using the technique of elaboration to deter uncomfortable or dangerous questions.)

"Where had you seen him before that day?"

"In—" this is where she began the first of her often successful attempts to throw her audience "off the scent." "I think it was Voting Day," she said thoughtfully, "because me and Pat Howe went down to June's house and they have got a dog called Pat and it has got a leash and she was saying to Martin about twiddling the leash around and that . . ."

"Was that on the same day?"

"A couple of weeks before he died, sir." she said politely. (But, as it turned out a moment later, she had already achieved her objective of getting everybody thoroughly confused.)

"Earlier than that day, during the weeks or months before that day," said Mr. Robson, "had you seen Martin about?"

"Yes, sir."

"Where?"

"He used to play around the streets with Mrs. Finlay's child."

"Now, you say you saw him on that day when something was done with the dog's lead?"

"Yes, sir."

"Where was that done?"

"In his house, sir."

"And at about what time of the day?" (All this was immaterial as "that day" was one several weeks before the day of Martin's death.)

"About half-past eleven or quarter to, sir."

"In the morning?"

"Yes, sir."

"And when that had happened, did you go to your home for dinner?"

"Well, we had to wait until June came back."

"Until what came back?"

"June, Martin's mam came back from Delaval Road because that was where the voting was being held."

Mr. Justice Cusack now intervened. "I think," he said dryly, "she said the dog leash incident was a couple of weeks before Martin died."

"Is that right?" Mr. Harvey Robson asked.

"Yes, sir," Mary replied artlessly.

"Then on that morning . . ."

This time it was the prosecutor, Mr. Lyons, who interrupted. "I thought she said on Voting Day first."

"That is certainly not what I heard," said the Judge. "We can verify it later if need be."

"On the day that he was found dead in the house," Mr. Robson specified, getting Mary firmly back to the point, "Mary, did you see Martin in the morning?"

"Yes, sir."

"Where?"

"I gave him a swing. I saw him coming out of Rita's place and gave him a swing by Fothergill's wall."

(This is a reply which, later in his address to the Jury, referring to the scientific evidence of fibers from Mary's dress being found on Martin's clothing, the prosecutor was to describe in the following terms: "One of the fibers," said Mr. Lyons, "was on his undervest. How did it get there, members of the Jury? Might it not have been when little Martin was perhaps being pushed or lifted through that window? This you may think of the utmost importance: that on 18 September when Mary was interviewed by the police in the presence of her parents and solicitor, she said that she knew nothing about the finding of the fibers. Then she was asked about having played with Martin [and] she said she had never played with him. And then she went into the witness box and said that on the very day he died she gave him a swing on Fothergill's wall. Why didn't she say that to Chief-Inspector Dobson on 18 September when she was asked if she had ever played with him? Is it not obvious that what has happened is . . . that in her evidence Mary has adapted her evidence to fit the scientific evidence . . . ?")

"You gave him a swing?" Harvey Robson continued.

"A swing by Fothergill's wall," she repeated.

". . . And was that before your dinner?"

"Yes, sir."

"Then did you go home to your dinner?"

"Yes, sir."

"And after dinner, did you see Martin again, or not until you saw him in the ruined house?"

"I cannot remember, sir, but I went up to the top with Norma for some dog's food."

"That is the shop, is it?"

"Yes, sir. . . ."

". . . Can you say about what time of the day that was when you went to the shop?"

"Er—about quarter to one or something."

"About quarter to one. What time did you have your dinner, can you remember?"

"About ten past, because I let my dinner digest."

"About ten past you say? Ten past one?"

"Twelve," she corrected.

"So that you had your dinner before going to the shop and then you went to the shop with Norma and bought those things?"

"Yes, sir." (Her replies threw all the timing that had been established into confusion.) "We doubled back down. We doubled back down to Crosshill way and then we went down Crosshill because I was going to go home the back way, and we went along . . ."

"Wait a minute. You say you went to Crosshill." (This was a completely different description from the one given by Norma.)

"Yes."

"Down Crosshill because you say you were going in the back way?"

"Yes, because the dog just barks if it hears the front gate open."

"And did you notice anything when you got down Crosshill?"

"Well, we come along St Margaret's Road and there was a crowd of people by the derelict houses."

(According to Mary's account of the time when all this happened, she and Norma would have come upon a "crowd of people by the derelict houses" long before the time when Martin really died.)

"Yes, what did you do then?"

"I think I gave the food to Norma and she gave it . . . she says she gave it to Colin or Mitchell." (Boys who were only mentioned this one time, and were never called.)

"You did not see her give it to Colin or Mitchell?"

"No."

"Where did Norma go when you gave her the food?"

"She went up the back way and through the pathway, through Maxine's house [66 Whitehouse Road—Norma's neighbor] and jumped over the wall, climbed over her fence."

"Where did you go?"

"I went along to see what happened, what had happened."

"When you got along, as you say, what did you find?"

"People were saying someone had met with an accident, somebody was dead. You know, different things. And of course, I went up."

"Yes? I think your last words were, 'Of course, I went up.'"

"Well I always . . . I always go to see what has happened if there is anything happened."

"Norma says that some time you went and called through the hole in the fence to her?"

"Er—yes, sir."

"Had you been 'up' as you say before you went to call for her?"

"When the crowd was there and I went up and there was a boy

in the workman's arms and I went to tell Norma and because there is a hole in part of her fence, in the back fence, I shouted of her."*

"When you saw the boy in the workman's arms, did you recognize him then?"

"Yes, sir."

"And who was it?"

"Martin George Brown, sir."

"And then you say you went and called Norma?"

"Yes, sir."

"Now, when you called Norma, did she come out and go with you?"

"She never come straight out, sir."

"How long do you think passed before she came out?"

"She might have got a drink of water or something, sir."

"Quite a short while?"

"Beg pardon?"

"Quite a short time?"

"Yes, sir."

"Just while she had a drink of water or something of that kind?"

"Yes, sir."

"Then did she come out?"

"Yes, sir, she come out the back door."

"And where did you go?"

"We went—I was already in the back lane, so she had to climb over her fence and come through the hole in her part and all."

"And then what?"

"We went down to where the house was and we got up the stairs and there was just the boy and he shouted, 'Go and get down' and . . ."

"Wait, I think you have gone a little too fast. You say you went down to the house?"

"Yes, and . . ."

"And then where did you go when you reached the outside of the house?"

* (The way Mary presents this here does not accord with the testimony given by Walter Long and John Southern. See pages 22–23.

"I am not sure if we went through the downstairs part, but we went up through this washhouse thing. You would think it was a washhouse because there was a hole parting the two houses and you could get through it and we went through it and we went up and up some stone stairs and the door was a little bit jammed, so Norma put her finger in the bottom and pulled it, and we got up some wooden stairs."

"And was that where the boy was?"

"No, we only got—when you get up the wooden stairs there is a scullery and then there is a sitting room and then through the sitting room there is a door and then there is a bedroom and another bedroom and stairs going down the front way and all."

"Where was the boy who told you to go out?"

"He was in the bedroom. He was coming through the sitting room, sir."

"So that you were up the wooden stairs?"

"You are going too fast for me," Judge Cusack said. He was taking down a great deal of this evidence, and on several occasions asked counsel to slow down to enable him to keep pace.

Mr. Robson waited a moment. "So that, when the boy spoke to you, were you up the wooden steps as well as the stone steps?" he finally went on.

"Yes, sir."

"And when he told you to get out, did you go down again?"

"Er—I think so, sir, I'm not sure."

"And did the boy go down about the same time?"

"No, sir, I cannot remember."

"When you went down, what did you do?"

"Someone—we went and told—er—what's her name? Rita, sir."

"Why did you go and tell Rita about it?"

"Because she was one of the nearest relations to Martin, because his mam lived right—well, not right down the bottom of St Margaret's Road, but she lived round the back, down the bank, sir."

". . . Did anyone ask you about the little boy, as to who he was or anything like that?"

"I cannot remember, sir."

"You cannot remember? Now. you went and saw Rita?"

"Yes, sir."

"And what did you say to her when you got there?"

"Er—'Martin's met with an accident.' But I cannot remember saying there was blood all over. I may have said that, sir."

"Yes, what did Rita say?"

"She never believed us, sir, but Ann Carter waved over to her. I think it was Ann Carter—Mrs. Carter."

"Somebody, at any rate, waved over. Waved from where?"

"From the outside of the crowd, sir."

"And then what did Rita do?"

"She just dropped everything and ran because she . . ."

"And what did you do?"

"I followed her, sir."

"Now, you have been talking about yourself. Was Norma with you at this time, or for part of this time?"

"Yes, sir."

"All the time?"

"Yes, sir."

"Yes, and when you say you followed Rita, did Norma go with you?"

"She went back, sir, with us."

"When you got back, what did you do?"

"I had already been upstairs, sir. I knew where Martin was and Rita never saw. I think Rita was in front of me or I was in front of Rita. I don't know, sir, but I bumped into Rita somehow and she pulled herself up on us."

After putting some more questions to her about her conversations with Rita Finlay and June Brown, Harvey Robson asked Mary directly, ". . . On that day, at any time on that day, did you take hold of Martin in any way to hurt him?"

"No, sir," she said firmly.

"Were you in the house No. 85 at all, while Martin was alive?"

"No, sir."

"Now, do you remember some time later on saying something about Martin being hurt?"

"Er . . ." she hesitated for a moment, but not for long, "yes, sir."

"To whom did you say that?"

"Irene F. and Pat Howe, sir."

"How long after Martin was found was that?"

"I cannot be certain, sir."

"Was it a matter of just a few days or two or three weeks or something of that kind?"

"I cannot remember, sir."

"Now what did you say that time?"

"I knew something that would get Norma put straight away."

"Yes, did you say what you knew?"

"Yes, sir."

"What did you say?"

"That she killed Martin."

"Why did you say that?"

"Because I had been having an argument with her that day, sir, and after that I went and apologized to her mam for saying it."

"I want to go back a little, I think. It is back to after Martin had been found but before his funeral. Did you go to his house and speak to his mother?"

"Yes, sir."

"And what did you say to her?"

"I asked if I could see Martin."

"Yes?"

"Me and Norma were daring each other . . ."

". . . You were daring each other," he repeated. "What did you want to see Martin for?"

"I don't know sir, because—er—we were daring each other and one of us did not want to be a chicken or something . . ."

The next day, toward the end of her examination, Mary gave prosecuting counsel the reasons for some of her actions and statements.

"I want you to look at the drawing you did," Mr. Lyons said. "Exhibit 51. You have drawn a little boy there, haven't you?"

"Yes." Almost always meticulously polite on the witness stand, Mary's leaving out the "sir" in a reply to a direct question was a clear indication of fatigue or anger. She was very often angry with prosecuting counsel.

"That boy is supposed to be Martin George Brown?"

"Yes."

"Is he supposed to be lying on the ground in this drawing?"

"Yes."

"And what is that behind him, is that the window?"

"Er—yes."

"How did you know he had been found lying near the window?"

"Rumors," she said laconically.

"Rumors?"

"Isabelle O'Connor and all them were saying that he fell through the attic and he died, like this way, that way, and the other way and . . ."

"Yes."

"And Mr. F. encourages us to write things."

"Did you say all the little girls were discussing exactly where he had been in the room where he was found?"

"No, people were saying different things."

"You have put him near to one end of the window, is that right?"

"Well, Isabelle was talking about that, so was I. Nearly all our table was talking, and, anyway, I saw him in the workman's arms."

"You saw him in the workman's arms?"

"Yes."

"But you have drawn him on the ground near a window?"

"Yes."

"Was it because you had seen him lying just like that?"

"No. It is because everyone was putting things in. Isabelle was saying things and that was the way—just put things down."

"Now then, near his right hand, you have put something and you have written 'tablet' near it?"

"Yes."

"Is this right—you drew a tablet on the ground near his right hand?"

"Yes."

"Yes. Why did you do that?"

"Well, it was rumors again."

"What rumors?"

"Well, people were saying—well, look, John Southern or somebody Long, went along—was up and they might have told Isabelle O'Connor. They might have told them what had happened or anything and Isabelle sits next at our table. It is just rumors, that is all."

"What was the rumor?"

"Just that some people says he had fell through the roof, come through the stairs or something and some people were saying he was found by the window and people found him."

"Why draw tablets?"

"Well, it was rumors."

"What were the rumors about tablets?"

"People were just saying there was a bottle of tablets and things spilled out of them. It was just to make it look better and that."

"How do you think he died?"

"I don't know. He might have fell through the roof and rolled into that room."

"But when you made up a nasty story about Norma to Irene F. and Pat Howe, you said that Norma took hold of him by the throat, didn't you?"

"Yes, but that was only because I had had an argument with Norma that day and I couldn't think of nothing else to say."

"You wanted to say that she had killed this little boy?"

"I could have said something else, but I never."

"But you didn't know if you were right—you didn't know that he had even been killed by somebody else?"

"No."

"And even if somebody kills a little boy, there are different ways of killing a little boy, aren't there?"

"Yes."

"What you said to those girls was that Norma had got hold of him by the throat and you showed how that had happened?"

"I cannot remember showing her."

"But you mentioned 'throat.' You didn't say, did you, that Norma had hit him on the head and killed him?"

"No."

"Why did you decide to talk about throat?"

"Well, you see . . . you see that on the television, on the 'Apache' and all that."

"Didn't you also see on television people being killed by being hit on the head with something?"

"It does not kill them, it just knocks them out."

"Had you ever played with Martin Brown?"

"Well, not played with him, but sometimes I gave him a swing."

"Do you remember Mr. Dobson asking you if you had ever . . . do you remember Mr. Dobson asking you if you ever played with Martin?"

"Yes, I think so."

"What did you tell Mr. Dobson?"

"Er—no, or yes, I'm not sure what I told him."

"Didn't you tell Mr. Dobson that you had never played with him?"

"But I *had* played with him." When she was tired and felt driven into a corner, her voice took on a querulous quality, waspish rather than childish.

"Didn't you tell Mr. Dobson that you had never played with him?" Mr. Lyons drove home his point.

"I might have done." She always seemed to know when to concede a little. The Judge searched in his papers for the relevant page. "My Lord," said Mr. Lyons, "Page 121 of the statement."

Mary tried to divert their attention. "Pat showed him that trick with the dog leash," she started in an informational tone of voice, but Mr. Lyons was not to be diverted.

"I want to ask you about the last time Mr. Dobson questioned you," he said. "Do you remember, your solicitor and your parents were there once when Mr. Dobson asked you some questions about Martin Brown?"

"Where was it, sir, please?"

"When?"

"Where?"

"At Police Headquarters on 18 September. I think the last time you were ever questioned. And your father and mother were there, and Mr. Bryson, your solicitor?"

"I cannot remember, sir."

"Well, do you remember Mr. Dobson saying this: that when he had seen you on a previous date, 21 August, you said this; 'I will tell you something. I saw Martin once that day. He was coming out of Rita's. I didn't see him again.' "

"That's when I gave him a swing, when I never saw him again."

"Didn't Mr. Dobson ask you, 'Did you play with him when he came out of Rita's'?"

"He may have done, sir."

"Didn't you say, 'No, I didn't play with Martin'?"

"Yes, I never played with him, I just gave him a swing."

"Did you say, 'The first time I met him I was at Rita's sister's June, with Pat. That . . .'?"

"Yes."

"Did Mr. Dobson ask you, 'Had you ever played with Martin'?"

"Well, I have never played with him, but I gave him a swing."

"Did you say, 'No, I've never played with him'?"

"That's right," she said coldly, "but I *have never* played with him. I have only given him a swing." She stuck firmly to her own interpretation and to those who watched, at the time, it sounded credible.

"Did you tell Mr. Dobson about the swing?"

"No."

"No. Isn't the reason you mentioned giving Martin a swing to-day because of the evidence you have heard about your gray wool dress?"

"No."

"And the fibers that were found on Martin's clothing? . . . On that occasion Mr. Dobson went on to ask you this, didn't he? 'Can you remember what you were wearing on the day Martin Brown died'?"

"Beg pardon?"

"Do you remember Mr. Dobson asking you 'Can you remember what you were wearing on the day Martin Brown died'?"

"Er—" She had not understood.

"Mr. Lyons," said Mr. Justice Cusak, "this could be approached much more directly."

"Yes, My Lord. Didn't you tell the police that you had not been wearing your gray dress on the day that Martin died?"

Mary sounded completely bewildered. "I cannot understand him," she said to the Judge.

"May," he tried to help, "didn't you pretend that you were not wearing your gray dress on the day Martin died?"

"Er . . ." she hesitated. "When my solicitor was there," she said, "I said I was not certain."

"Didn't you earlier pretend you were not wearing that dress and hadn't worn it for a long time?"

"I cannot remember, sir," she said, still sounding honestly puzzled.

"Are you sure about that?" asked the Judge.

"Yes."

"Do you remember saying to Mr. Dobson you had not worn it for a fortnight?" Mr. Lyons specified.

"No," Mary answered at once. "That was about Brian Howe, wasn't it, sir?"

"Yes," Mr. Lyons agreed, "Brian Howe."

"That was about Brian Howe," she pointed out again.

"Yes," said Mr. Lyons again, "about Brian Howe."

"I says there I had not worn it for a fortnight . . ." she stopped for a moment, and then continued, "I thought you were on about *Martin Brown*, sir."

"Sorry, you are quite right," said Mr. Lyons. "I had gone on to Brian Howe . . ."

It was neither the first nor the last time that in the charged emotional atmosphere of the court the names of the two murdered boys were mixed up.

The prosecution called four scientific witnesses: Roland Page, handwriting expert from the Forensic Science Laboratory in Cardiff, Dr. Bernard Knight, forensic pathologist and barrister, from Cardiff (both re Martin), Dr. Bernard Tomlinson, Senior Consultant Pathologist from neighboring county Durham (re Brian), and Norman Lee, principal scientific officer of the Forensic Science Laboratory, Gosforth, Newcastle.

The defense for Norma called Dr. Ian Frazer, Physician Superintendent of the Prudhoe Monkton Mental Hospital. The defense for Mary called two psychiatrists: Dr. Orton and Dr. David Westbury.

Mr. Page, questioned by Mr. Lyons about the "We Murder" notes found in the Nursery, said that he had examined four of them. He concluded that some words on these notes were written in Norma's handwriting, some in Mary's, and again in other words consecutive letters had been written by both girls.

"This case is unusual," he said in reply to a question from Mr. Smith, "insofar as I have had to compare every letter by itself in isolation and this has presented a difficulty. Therefore I cannot say looking at this word particularly that it has been done by Mary or Norma. I can just suggest and point out the difficulties I face."

The notes (to remind us) read:

1) I MURDER SO THAT I MAY COME BACK. (Exhibit 12)
2) BAS . . . FUCH OF. WE MURDER. WATCH OUT. FANNY AND FAGGOT. (Exhibit 13)
3) WE DID MURDER MARTAIN BROWN. FUCKOF YOU BASTARD. (Exhibit 14)
4) YOU ARE MICEY. Y BECUASE WE MURDERED MARTAIN GO BROWN YOU BETTER LOOK OUT. THERE ARE MURDERS ABOUT. BY FANNYAND AND AULD FAGGOT YOU SRCEWS. (Exhibit 15)

The prosecution maintained that these notes amounted to a confession by the two girls that they were the killers of Martin Brown.

The defense, for both girls, replied that, however vulgar and unpleasant the wording of these notes, they were simply childish fantasy and could not be regarded as confessions of guilt by either of the girls.

R. P. Smith, Q.C., questioned Norma about the notes after taking her through the events of the day Martin Brown was found dead. Throughout her examination, Norma's eyes, again and again, swiveled to Mary's face.

"Norma . . . I want to ask you about the next day, the Sunday. You were in May's house, is that right?"

"I was in the next day. She was playing her recorder."

". . . And when she stopped playing the recorder, what did she do? . . ."

"At first we were playing drawings."

"Whereabouts, in her bedroom or downstairs, or where?"

"Scullery." Every time Norma answered with only a single word, or an ungrammatical, confused, or unfinished sentence it was an indication of her distress and her unwillingness to speak.

"And when you had finished playing drawing, what did you do next?"

"Wrote some notes."

"What with?"

"A red Biro pen. . . ."

". . . I want you to look, Norma, please, at four notes," Mr. Smith said, "Exhibits twelve to fifteen." Norma looked around the room. "You have got the notes there, Norma, have you?" Mr. Smith tried to fix her attention.

"Yes."

"Do you see the one which reads, 'I murder so that I may come back?' Exhibit 12?"

"Yes, I wrote that one."

"You wrote that one?"

"Yes."

"Where did you write it?"

"In the scullery. . . ."

". . . You just hold it up. The original is written in red. Why did you write that, Norma?"

"Just for me and Mary."

"Whose idea was it? . . ."

". . . May wanted some notes to be written."

"May wanted some notes to be written?"

"Yes, to put in her shoe." She added something under her breath.

"I did not catch that," said Mr. Justice Cusack. "Did you say 'the brown one'? Is that right?"

"Yes."

"Did May write any notes herself?"

"Yes." Norma indicated Exhibit 15, Note No. 4 and held it up to the Court.

"That looks like Exhibit 15," said Mr. Smith. "She wrote that, did she?"

"Yes," she murmured.

". . . Can I ask you again whose idea it was to write these notes?"

"It was in her scullery, it was her idea to get the paper and her idea for the red pen," she said succinctly and angrily.

"Whose idea was it to write the words?"

"Mary's, 'cos she first got scrap paper and I was writing a different letter on it and I wrote that and she put that in her shoe. I don't know why. I didn't know what she was going to do." (Norma was never to be asked what this "different letter" was which she presumably wrote on her own initiative.)

"Norma, how did you know what to write?" asked the Judge.

" 'Cos Mary says . . ."

"Now there are four notes here, Norma," continued Mr. Justice Cusack. "I want you to look at the other two. There is one that has got a number thirteen on it which has a very naughty word on it and then says, 'We murder. Watch out Fanny.' Do you see that one?"

"Yes. . . ."

". . . But after the notes that were written in the scullery were put into May's shoes, what did she do? Did she go somewhere?"

"She went out. . . ."

". . . When May went out, did she say where she was going?"

"No, but I knew she wanted the notes for the Nursery, but I didn't know that she went."

"How did you know she wanted the notes for the Nursery?"

" 'Cos she said so. . . ."

After taking Norma through their breaking into the Nursery, Mr. Smith returned to the notes. "When you had got into the loft," he asked, "what did you do?"

"Wrote the note. . . ."

". . . Can you see the note which you wrote? Is it any of those?"

"Yes, that one. If it is any one of those, it is one of those two, 13 or 14. . . ."

". . . I want you to look at 13 first, which has the letters 'B-A-S' in capitals. Did you write those letters?"

"I don't know. I don't know what it means."

"You never mind what it means," said Mr. Smith. "Did you write them?"

"No."

"And then 'FUCK,' did you write that?"

"No. No. 'Of', I mean the 'F', not the other one, not the 'O'."

"Who wrote that?"

"Mary, because we were joining writing."

"You were joining writing?"

"Yes." Taking her then first through the words and then the individual letters of each word, Mr. Smith tried to establish which had been written by her and which by Mary.

". . . When the notes were written what did you do with them?"

"Both me and Mary went downstairs."

"Do you mean out of the loft?"

"Downstairs."

"Into the Nursery School?"

"Yes. . . ."

". . . And what happened to the notes when you got downstairs?"

"There's this kind of phone and the thing opens and one got put in there but I'm not sure whether it was one of these two. . . ."

". . . And who put the note in there," asked Mr. Smith. "You or Mary?"

"Mary. . . ."

". . . Did *you* put any notes anywhere?" asked the Judge.

"Yes, where the telephone is."

"You left a note near where the telephone is, is that right?"

"Yes, and Mary left some."

One of the main objectives of many of the questions Norma was asked at whatever momentary cost to her peace of mind was to establish her truthfulness. (By the same token, R. P. Smith's repetitive questions when examining Mary were frequently intended to show, for the benefit of the Jury, how exceptional Mary's vocabulary was in contrast to Norma.) And there was soon no doubt that, although Norma may not have quite understood why it was necessary for her to tell what were frequently unpalatable truths, the combination of honestly concerned parents, a peaceful and therapeutic environment during her months of remand, and sympathetic but authoritative preparation by her legal advisers had enabled her to give truthful answers, certainly to specific questions.

Mary's approach to answering questions was very different. First of all, there was hardly ever any doubt that she understood perfectly what she was asked. Indeed, on several occasions her capacity to keep all the complex threads of the proceedings separated and in proper order must have exceeded that of many adults.

Secondly, despite the incredible act of self-assurance she put on, and her undoubted enjoyment of the notoriety, she was terrified of the situation she found herself in: a consequence of her action which—because she was innately incapable of thinking ahead (a classical symptom of her condition)—she had never consciously envisaged. Her terror showed up increasingly clearly as the trial progressed: in the comments she made to the policewomen who guarded her, and in the nightmares she had on the rare occasions when she slept.

Mary was constantly lying. But many of her lies were embedded in a mass of extraneous information, a deliberate mixture of lies and truths, a measure which, briefly successful at times, was designed to deflect her listeners' attention from the direct questions she was asked. In a way these embellishments, which she recounted with phenomenal fluency and expression, were meant to give credence and "body" to her lies. At the same time, they doubtlessly provided her with a badly needed antidote to her own terror.

Of course she too, at times, told the truth, but one felt that it was done deliberately—because she believed that on the principle of "bend a little" it was momentarily to her advantage to speak the truth rather than lie.

"... I want to ask you ... first of all, about the notes," Harvey Robson said. "Do you understand what I am referring to?"

"Yes, sir."

"Do you remember how the notes came to be written?"

"Well, we wrote—it was a joint idea."

"Yes, where were you?"

"In our house. We only wrote—er—er... two in our house, I think."

"How did it begin? Norma, I think, has said something about you were playing a recorder?"

"Oh well ..."

"Is that right?"

"Yes," she began. "I can play a recorder. I was playing a recorder. I was playing, 'Go To Sleep, Little Brother Peter'; I was playing that or 'Three Blind Mice'. I was playing one of those tunes and I just put it back in the box because too much playing it makes the inside go rusty or something . . ."

"Well, you had been playing with that," Mr. Robson interrupted the elaboration. "And then what did you do?"

"We went into the back scullery I think—no, I had a cat upstairs which was a stray cat and it was a black one and me and Norma were trying to think of a name for it, and we were thinking of names for it and it was a black cat . . ."

". . . Did you go upstairs?"

"Yes."

"Into what room?"

"My bedroom."

"And what did you do in your bedroom?"

"We were thinking of a name for the cat."

"Yes?"

"But the dog, it was coming up and sniffing under the door because it could smell the cat."

"And how did you come to make the notes?"

"Well, the doll's pram was at the side of my bed and Norma went over to it and looked under. It has . . . has got I think it is a red hood, I'm not sure what color hood, but it has got like a thing to cover it and it has got the two studs at one end, and Norma went in because she saw, she was looking at the doll . . . and she saw there was a red Biro pen and she got it out, and she was doing some drawings and it was a joint idea to write the notes, so we both wrote them, but we never wrote them in the bedroom, we wrote them in the scullery."

(Nobody claimed they had written the notes in the bedroom; this was one of her impulsive and, as happened often, momentarily successful red herrings.)

"Do you remember how many notes altogether you wrote in the bedroom?" asked Harvey Robson.

"We never wrote notes at all in the bedroom," she repeated patiently. "We only wrote them in the scullery because you cannot do none in the bedroom because if you rest it on the bed the pen would go straight through it because the bed is soft, and there is like a sideboard thing and it has got a round thing which has a frilly thing on it."

"You did not make any of the notes in the bedroom. How many notes did you make in the scullery? . . ."

". . . Two."

"And when you had made the notes, did you stay in or did you go somewhere?"

"We went—er—Norma says, 'Are you coming to the Nursery?' I said 'Yes, howay then,' because we had broken into it before."

"Yes?"

"We had been in a week and all—the week before that."

"And how did you get into the Nursery?"

"Well, I was going to climb up first, but there was barbed wire right round the pipe, so I says, 'Norma, I cannot get up.' She says, 'Mind, I will get up' and she went up first, but there was a piece of barbed wire stuck onto her cardigan so I got up and I was pulling it off her and I got back down again and when she got up, there was like an aluminium roof or something. It is bumpy . . ."

". . . Yes." Harvey Robson continued, "And what was done about the roof?"

"Well, after that I got up and I had got up, there was some slates and it was a Sunday this I think, because there was a man working in the garden on overtime. Norma pulled a slate up which made a noise and she always lay down on the bumpy part of the roof, and so did I in case the man would see us."

"You lay down, too?"

"Yes."

"Yes?"

"And under the slates—do you know—in an attic the long bit of wood between every slate? Well, it was . . . it went fat and then it went thin in the middle and we just stood on it at this end that was barbed wire and all, because it had been broken into before, and we got through it and there is a trap door."

"And you went through the trap door?"

". . . Yes."

"And went down?"

"Yes."

"Where did you go down below?"

"We got out of the lavatory room and we went, er—up the passage. All the doors were locked excepting the swinging doors off the passage and there is this cupboard and it had like an aluminium tub in it, there was keys on top and Norma got up and got them."

"What did the two of you do with the keys?"

"We got a bunch each."

"Yes?"

"And we were opening the doors and we were being destructful."

"You were what?"

"Being destructful."

"Destructful," Mr. Justice Cusack repeated.

"What did you actually do?" asked Mr. Robson.

"Well, with them it was the Head's office we went in and we pulled some papers out and there was this bag and it had like a pinned note, signed on it, and we opened it, and we got the little— there was nothing inside except for little domino things, tiddly-winks."

"Was there a telephone?"

"Yes, that was upstairs."

"Was that in the Head's office, or where?"

"No, there was telephones all over the place but we went upstairs. We were going to see the other rooms and we went upstairs and there is a telephone and it has got like a little box thing on the bottom and you pull out, and it has got something like a mousetrap or something, not a mousetrap, but like an iron thing that keeps the papers flat."

"And did you pull off, or pull out any of those pieces of paper?"

"Norma put the piece of paper what she had wrote on in that— in that thing. I don't know if it was my bit of paper or not, or I'm not sure whose bit of paper it was."

"Were there any more notes made in the Nursery?"

"Yes."

"I am not quite sure what happened to the other piece of paper," the Judge interposed. "Norma put the piece of paper that she had written on, in the spring thing in the telephone?"

"Yes, but I'm not sure if it was. . . ."

". . . May," Mr. Robson suggested, "I think you were going on to say something about more notes written in the Nursery?"

"Yes, sir. We wrote some more because there was like a little ball-bearing thing—like a little ball-bearing thing attached to the telephone. I'm not sure if it was a spring or something. And we wrote on that because there was a notebook, a little book in."

"And can you remember exactly how many notes were written at the Nursery?"

"About four or five, or something like that, sir."

"And what happened to those notes?"

"Er—we, I think we just left them by the telephone or they were scattered around or something. I can't remember."

"Now, will you tell all of us, May, what was the object of writing the notes and leaving them in the Nursery?"

"That is two questions in one," said the Judge, "let us take it one by one."

"What was the object of writing the notes?" Mr. Robson repeated."

"For a giggle."

"Yes, and what was the object of leaving them in the Nursery?"

"I don't—I don't know. We just left them. We thought it would be a great big joke."

At the end of that morning's exhausting session—after two and a half hours of continuous questioning (the first time that no mid-morning adjournment had been called)—R. P. Smith cross-examined Mary.

". . . It was on a Sunday, was it, when the notes were written?"

"Er—yes . . ."

"Was it the day after Martin had died?"

"I think so."

"Well, was it your birthday?" (It was.)

"No."

"What day is your birthday?"

"The twenty-sixth of May."

"Was that a Sunday this year?"

"I can't remember."

"Would you remember that Martin Brown was found in the old house the day before your birthday?"

"No."

"You don't remember that. Whenever the notes were written, they were written first in your house, were they?"

"Only two."

"Two. On paper which you got from your bedroom?"

"Yes."

"With a red Biro which you had got from your bedroom?"

"Yes." (For once forgetful she had forgotten that she had originally said Norma had found the pen in the pram.)

"And it was your idea to write those notes?"

"No, it was a joint idea."

"What do you mean by 'a joint idea'?" (She wiped her forehead with the back of her hand.) "Are you all right, Mary?"

"Yes."

"What do you mean, Mary, by a joint idea?"

"Because it was."

Mr. Smith's mild manner and quiet voice were deceptive: if he did not get the answer he required he had a particularly unnerving way of repeating it over and over, in that same quiet voice, the same inflection, always waiting for the reply in perfect silence until —it rarely failed—he finally got it.

"What do you mean?" he said again. "What does a 'joint idea' mean?"

"It was both of us."

"Both of you what?"

"That wrote the notes."

"Yes, but who decided the notes should be written?"

"Her."

"She did?"

"Yes."

"What did she say?"

"She says 'We will do it for a giggle.' "

"I think I am right in saying, aren't I, that this moment is the first time you have ever said that?"

"Yes."

"Yes . . . ?"

"I says it to Mr. Dobson and all, it was both of us."

"Would the shorthand writer read that answer, please?" said the Judge.

" 'I says it to Mr. Dobson and all, it was both of us.' "

"Robson," Mary corrected.

"I beg pardon?" Mr. Smith asked.

"Mr. Robson," Mary said, sounding tired and nettled.

"You mean your barrister?"

"Yes, it was both of us. The idea, she came out with it first."

"Did you ask why she thought this would be a giggle?"

"She wanted to get put away," Mary said, sounding very angry now. . . .

". . . Is this true, what you are telling the Court?"

"Yes, because after that she asked me to run away with her."

"She asked you to run away with her?"

"Yes."

"Where to?"

"She just says, 'Run away with us.' "

"Where to?"

"Anywhere."

"What for?"

"I don't know. I have run away with her before."

"But did she say why she wanted to get put away?" asked the Judge.

"Because she could kill the little ones, that's why."

"Because *what?*" Mr. Justice Cusack asked and Mr. Smith—the words sounding all the more incongruous coming from him—dryly repeated Mary's reply. " 'Because she could kill the little ones, that's why.' "

"And run away from the police," Mary continued, unasked, her voice now shrill with suppressed hysteria. "She was going to go . . ."

The Judge interrupted her, firmly shutting his notebook. "Yes," he said and stood up, everyone immediately coming to their feet with him. "I think we will adjourn now until 2:15."

"I'll kick her mouth in," Mary shouted as, the policewoman's hand restraining her, she was taken out of the witness box and led away.

Everyone in the room had begun to talk as if to drown the sound and impression of her voice. Every time—the many times—Norma had broken down on the stand, there had been silence in the court and a strong feeling of sympathy for her distress. Now, when for the first time Mary behaved like a tired child of her age, we refused to accept it. We had allotted a certain part to her: it was out of character for her to have lost control. We looked away.

The notes were a catharsis for both children. The trial certainly confirmed what the police already knew: that both girls had written them. But the hours that were spent on trying to penetrate the childish thinking process behind them to separate fact from fantasy, lies from truth, produced no greater understanding of these two children, their relationship, their motives, or their actions. It is relevant to point out here, where we are analyzing a total situation in retrospect, that these two girls and their actions (and later reactions) cannot be seen or judged in isolation from each other. We cannot say for certain what each of them might have done—or left undone—if the other had not been there. But basing our thoughts only on facts, we *can* say, although it was never said in Court, that Mary had never run away prior to meeting Norma: they ran away together once (4 June 1968); Norma ran away alone on 11 June and was gone two days. And, since the trial, repeated acts of absconding have been Norma's pattern.

Both girls were re-examined at length about various aspects of the notes by Mr. Lyons. "I want you to look at Note 1 please, Exhibit 12," he continued with Norma after taking her through several of the details. "You wrote that, is that correct?"

"Yes, she said that." Judge Cusack was always very quickly aware of the limits of Norma's endurance.

"I said I wrote all of it; I don't know . . ."

"Do you know what it means?" Mr. Lyons asked.

She repeated her answer, in her fatigue the words beginning to sound disconnected from each other—almost as if she was speaking in her sleep.

"You don't know what it means?"

"Yes, I know what it means."

"What it says was, 'I may come back.' Does that mean to say 'I may come back to the Nursery?' "

"Norma, listen to me," the Judge said. "When you wrote that, on that piece of paper you have just been looking at, what did you mean?"

"May has wrote on one of these here," she answered, desperately.

"Yes, but I am talking about the one you say you wrote. What did that mean? Are you able to tell me?"

"I don't want to."

"Did you think that Martin's dying was a big joke?" Mr. Lyons asked.

"No."

"Would you look at Note No. 2 please, Exhibit 13. Can you see the words in the middle, 'we murder'?"

"Not by me."

"Now just think. Isn't that your writing, Norma?" (It had been established as being her writing.)

"No."

"Look at Note No. 1, Exhibit 12."

"I don't want to."

"Can you see the word 'murder' there?"

Norma by now, painful to watch, was sobbing bitterly.

"Well, Mr. Lyons," said the Judge, "this gets increasingly difficult and I appreciate your difficulties, but it is obvious that this child shows great reluctance to deal with these notes at all and really doesn't want to look at them. You must pursue the matter if you think right, but detailed examination, at any rate, may not achieve any purpose. You see, Mr. Lyons, you have your duty to discharge on behalf of the Crown. I, on the other hand, not only have to conduct the trial but to see that, in the case of a young child, not too much distress is caused."

"Yes, My Lord, I would be very grateful if Your Lordship would stop me at any time," Mr. Lyons said stiffly. "My Lord, I do have a duty. . ."

Mr. Lyons made one more try but when Norma again broke down, the Judge called a short recess. When he resumed, he addressed some of the most significant remarks of the trial to counsel and Jury:

"Mr. Lyons, before you go on, I want to say this: I have been giving thought to this matter. You have your duty to cross-examine on behalf of the Crown . . . I will not, and I hope I have not done anything to impede the defense in any way. I am justified, I believe, perhaps in taking a slightly stricter view toward the Crown. You must put, and I hope you will put briefly those matters which you think it right to put to this child. But neither I, nor I think the Jury, would be willing to sit here and have a weeping child applied with questions. We may reach a stage when it would not be right to go on. The Jury, of course, are entitled to take into consideration not only the oral evidence, but the demeanor of any particular witness. And one of the matters which in due course I shall refer them to is that sometimes children break down because they are genuinely upset; sometimes they take refuge in weeping because they don't want to face what is being put to them. That is essentially a matter for the Jury to consider and which they have to have in mind at this stage. But for whatever reason we reach that stage, if we do, I am afraid I shall not permit you to go on if I thought it was either too distressing to the child, or indeed too distressing for the Jury. Mr. Lyons, that does not involve the least personal criticism of you. Like everybody else in this case, you have a difficult duty to discharge, but it may be of some guidance to you if I tell you what I have in mind now."

By the time Mr. Lyons came to cross-examine Mary about the notes, one and a half days after Norma, she had entirely regained her composure. And her ingenious replies and behavior on this occasion were to have an equally decisive influence on the course of events.

Mr. Lyons' approach and attitude toward Mary was always exactly the same as toward Norma. "Would you look at the four notes, please, Exhibits 12 to 15. You say that these notes were your joint idea?" he asked.

"Er—yes."

He held up Note 1, the sense of which no one had ever understood. "Look at the first one which begins, 'I murder so that I may come back.' Have you got that one?"

"This one?"

"Yes, that's right. Who wrote that one?"

"I'm not sure, sir, I'm not sure who wrote any of them."

"Well, you told the police, didn't you, that Norma wrote that one?"

"I might have done, sir, but I cannot remember now. We wrote two in our scullery, sir."

"Do you know which the other one was? Is it there, the other one you wrote in the scullery?"

"That's the one, I think."

"That is one, I think. Do you know which the other one was?"

"No, sir, it is not here."

"Do you know what that one means, 'I murder so that I may come back'?"

"In what way do you mean, sir?"

"What does it mean?"

"We may come back to the Nursery, which we did."

"May come back to the Nursery: Come back to the Nursery to do a murder?"

"No."

"You see, it was at the Nursery, though outside in the grounds, [in the sandpit] that Pauline Watson's throat was hurt?"

"Er—yes."

"Yes, and this means 'I murder.' Does this mean this: 'I murder so I may come back to the Nursery?' "

"Yes, that's one of the notes we wrote in our house."

"Does it mean this," asked Mr. Lyons again, " 'so I may come back to the Nursery to do another murder'?"

"No," Mary replied, "as far as I am concerned it does not."

"Why did you pretend that you and Norma had murdered Martin Brown if it wasn't true?"

"For a giggle."

"What?"

"For a giggle."

"Which one of you was supposed to be 'Fanny' and which of you was supposed to be 'Faggot'?"

"I was supposed to be 'Faggot.' "

"Just look at Note 4, Exhibit 15. Just look at the front of it. Is that your writing?"

"I think so."

"Yes. Now, does it say, 'You are micey'? Does 'micey' mean stupid?"

"Yes."

"And who is the 'you'? Does it mean the police?"

Mary pointed at the lone "Y" on the note. (See p. 26) That's a 'Y' there," she said.

"No," Mr. Lyons said firmly. "It says, 'you are micey.' Did you mean that the police were stupid?"

"I don't know. We just put it down. Everyone."

"Well, look at the last line. Did you write, 'you screws'?"

"I think so."

"Well, who did you mean by the 'screws'?"

"That's what people call policemen."

"Yes, and weren't you saying, 'you police are stupid'?"

"I suppose so."

"Because we murder Martin George Brown."

"Er—yes, it says that," she said artlessly.

"That's right, isn't it," Mr. Lyons pressed, but Mary was not to be caught in such an easy trap.

"Yes," she went on, calmly reading from the photostated note she held in her hand, " 'And you better look out.' "

"You better look out there are murders about," Mr. Lyons continued doggedly, "and there was another murder, wasn't there, two months later?"

"Yes."

"Yes, you were showing the police how clever you were, weren't you?"

"How?" she inquired.

"What?"

"How?" she repeated.

"Well, you knew that you knew something about Martin Brown's death that the police didn't know?"

She had maneuvered neatly. "I never knew nothing about it," she said calmly. "The police knew more than me . . ."

Every day after the session ended, the girl's families were allowed to see them for a few minutes in the small waiting room off the

Court. During the first two or three days these were treated as social occasions, with laughter and chitchat on both sides. As time went on, the meetings became quieter, with an undertone of anxiety and nerves.

For Mary it was her father she was most eager to see. Once when the time came for her family to leave she said, "All of you go first and Dad go last because I love him best of all." A little later, everybody having left, her mother came back and kissed her once more.

"Oh Mam," she protested, "now you've spoilt it. Now Dad has to come and kiss me again so I can feel his lips on me till tomorrow."

All of Mary's family confirm that it was only at this period that she allowed herself to be kissed. Otherwise, as her Aunt Audrey had said, "She always turned her head away."

If until the very end of the trial, and beyond it, there was doubt in the minds of people about how Martin Brown met his death, and if both Norma and Mary steadfastly denied having had the least part in his killing, there was no such doubt about Brian Howe. Mr. Justice Cusack, in his final summing up, made this clear:

". . . As to Brian Howe's death, there is no dispute that he was killed by somebody. In that there is a difference between him and Martin Brown. . . . [But] each of the girls denies harming him and each says that it was the other one who attacked him. You will remember the evidence, not only about the marks on his throat, but how his body was marked in a way consistent with the use of a razor blade. How his body was punctured in a way consistent with the use of those scissors which you have seen. And how his hair had been cut and the cutting was left on the ground not far from him. You will also remember that there were compression marks on the lower third of his nose towards the tip, and points to where it is said his nose had been squeezed."

Dr. Bernard Tomlinson testified that he was asked to consider the possibility of what the slits might represent or suggest. "If you stand on the left-hand side of the body the marks could have been considered as crude attempts to produce capital letters. It was possible to see an 'M' or an 'N' in these marks, and standing on the other side of the body one of the letters looked rather like a 'W'." There were three similar marks on the thigh.

Chief-Inspector Dobson later confirmed that to him the marks had looked like the letter "N" to which another line, completing the letter "M", had been added by a different hand.

Forensic scientist Norman Lee had examined Brian's clothes and found eleven gray wool fibers which had many similarities with those of a dress belonging to Mary Bell. A red fiber from Brian's jumper was indistinguishable, he said, from one found on Mary's dress, and two maroon fibers from a skirt belonging to Norma matched exactly those found on each of Brian's shoes.

While both girls in their first statements to the police had denied any meeting with Brian on that day, or any knowledge of his whereabouts beyond having seen him playing in the streets, each of them, as they panicked, had abandoned a little more each day their attempt at keeping faith with each other and added a little bit of additional information in each statement. Norma had first brought in Mary's name and finally accused her of the murder. Mary had tried first to involve a completely innocent little boy and, when that failed, had accused Norma.

The first four days of the trial they were kept together during adjournments and the midday meal. "They are chatting away like two little women," said a police officer, shaking his head. "They are talking about clothes, films, pop stars." He shook his head again. "It's like a party, it's incredible." Their attitude toward each other in and outside court was as unreal, as childish, and—if one wished to acknowledge it—as sad as everything else about this trial. In some way their ability—perhaps an unconscious need—to disassociate the things they were accusing each other of having done in the past from their feelings and behavior toward each other in the present was incomprehensible to the adults who watched them.

The fact is—this being the essential unreality and anomaly of the trial—that "death," "murder," "killing" had a different connotation for Mary than it has for other people. Basically for her all of it had been a game (in the sense that an experiment can be a game to children)—a grisly game, but a game nonetheless.

For Norma, too, neither mentally nor emotionally capable of

dealing with anything except on a momentary or immediate basis, the events, far too terrible to absorb in all their horror, had probably in retrospect assumed the depersonalized quality of a film.

For Mary too, though, it was not something she had *done,* for none of Mary's actions were committed for the sake of *doing* but rather for the sake of *feeling.* Incapable of connecting her compulsive need to *feel* with the consequences of her actions, she simply could not conceive that every action *has* a consequence. It is perhaps as if a connecting link is missing in her brain and in her deepest self.

For both of these children, for different reasons, the only reality they felt as the trial progressed was fear. In the meantime, while this process took place, it was almost as if both of them—separately and together—existed on two planes, with two personalities toward each other.

In court, on innumerable occasions, their heads turned toward each other, their eyes locked, their faces suddenly bare of expression and curiously alike, they always seemed by some sort of silent and exclusive communion to reaffirm and strengthen their bond.

It was not something real, not something one could understand or interpret in so many words. What we witnessed were the intangibles in a relationship which may well have been as mysterious to them as it was to us.

The other aspect of it, much easier to accept, was exactly what one would have expected: they shook their heads incredulously or furiously at what one or the other said; they turned abruptly, glaring at each other when hearing themselves quoted as having accused the other of something outrageous; and they commented audibly—in Norma's case with tears and desperate cries of "No, no," in Mary's case with loud and furious remarks—about and against each other's evidence.

Listening to them one after the other answer the same specific questions about the events leading up to and the murder of Brian Howe, with virtually identical descriptions of each other's movements, facial expressions, actions and words, was an eerie experience.

The stage had of course been set: just as there remained no doubt as to who had squeezed the necks of the three little girls in the sandpit, so, almost even before the evidence began, there was hardly any doubt in anyone's mind that it was Mary who had actually murdered Brian Howe. The trial therefore to some of us began to take on some of the distressing characteristics of a Grand Guignol, a spectacle which was at once irresistible and intolerable.

In the case of Martin Brown we may never know quite exactly what happened. The case of Brian Howe is different. Neither Norma nor Mary denied that they, together, took Brian for a walk on the afternoon of 31 July.

". . . What happened when you saw Brian and Norman [Brian's brother] in the street?" Harvey Robson asked Mary.

"Norma says, 'Walk ahead of we,' " she answered. "And she says something about sweets, she had money or something. I says, 'Norma, where have you got money from, you haven't got none,' and she says, 'Nebby.' "

"What did you understand that to mean?"

"Keep your nose out. . . . We went down by Dixon's shop," she continued a little later, "and there is a fence there . . . and I think we got through the hole or we climbed over, I cannot remember, sir. . . . When we got to the railway fence I says to Norma, 'Where are you going?' and she says, 'Oh, you know, that little tadpole pool' . . . and I just thought she was going there. I says (to myself) oh, it's all right there because there was a frog spawn and tadpoles in it, you know, and we went over. . . ."

It all sounded so normal.

Norma presented it only a little differently: "Norma, when you first on that afternoon went with Mary and Brian Howe," she was asked by Mary's counsel in cross-examination, "was something said about going to a tadpole pool, or a frog pool on the 'Tin Lizzie'?" By this time the Judge had ordered that there should no longer be any contact between the two girls. He had directed that they were not to be in the same room at all, "and were to be kept separate from other people."

"No," said Norma, "that never got mentioned. . . . What happened," she continued a little later, "was that May and Brian and me just went down Crosshill Road and no pool was mentioned. . . ." Mr. Robson, referring to Mary's statements to the police, asked about the "sweets" with which Brian was tempted into accompanying the girls. As had happened before when questioning Norma, questions had to be repeated and clarified for her several times. ". . . Did you say this to Brian, that there was a lady coming on an 82 bus who would have some sweets with her?"

"No, I never said it," said Norma. "It was Mary Bell, but she never says she was going to come on a bus. She says the lady and she never says bus—she says the lady is coming but she never mentioned bus."

"With some sweets . . . was 'sweets' mentioned?"

"No, lollipops. . . ."

"Wasn't it you who talked about the lady and the lollipops or sweets?"

"No, Mary says it."

"And did Brian walk along with you and Mary?"

"Yes."

"When you came to the railway, there were two fences to go through, were there not?"

"There were two. One beside Dixon's shop, one fence at the top, and when you get down to the bottom, there is another fence."

"Yes, and were you able to find holes to go through both fences?"

"Hole on the top one, but we climbed over. I lifted Brian over."

"And did Mary help in lifting Brian?"

"May held his hand going down."

Mary, the next day, talked about the next fence they got through, after being asked whether they had to go across a road to get to it.

"We had to go down the bank first, sir," she said.

"Yes, down the bank, and then across the road?"

"Yes, sir. But there was—er—a big hole, a big square hole in the fence over there, Mr. Dobson could fit in," she was off on one of her embellishments, and everybody's mind (as no doubt intended) immediately veered off onto visualizing the tall Chief-Inspector Dobson getting through a hole in the fence: "So we never touched Brian getting through there," she added—as if it mattered now. And she continued her elaboration. "We went towards, like, a big round tank what had been used for the Army or something.

You would *think* it had been used for the Army. It was like a big bomb and had a round hole in it and little dots round that hole."

"Up to that time, had anything been said about sweets?"

Mary forgot what she had said herself only a few minutes before —a very rare lapse for her. "Er—no sir," she said, "it was when we got in the tank sweets were mentioned."

"Very well."

"I cannot remember who got in first."

"But all three got in?"

"Yes, sir."

"And how did Brian get in?"

"Well, one of us passed him through to the other one. I cannot remember who got in first but . . ."

"Then go on, will you, about what happened in the tank?"

"Brian started to cry and Norma says, 'Have you got a sore throat, son?' and he went 'Aye' or 'No' or something and . . ."

"Yes?"

"I cannot remember if she touched his throat with two hands or one hand, and then she says, 'Oh, this isn't where the lady comes with the sweets.' "

"Had any mention been made of a lady beforehand?"

"I am not sure, sir, but, and then—and then she says, in the tank she says, 'This isn't where the lady comes with the sweets,' she says, 'she comes over them big slabs, the concrete blocks,' she says. 'She comes on the No. 82 bus,' sir, or a 28."

Norma, during all this, had violently shaken her head and begun to cry. She had been cross-examined about this the previous day.

"When you got over the railway line," Harvey Robson had asked her, "you were near this tank were you, quite a short way away? Now when Brian got into the tank, was there somebody in already, you or Mary?"

"Mary first."

"Mary first, and then Brian had to be hauled in?"

"Yes."

"Did you actually lift him or was he able to scramble in with your help?"

"He needed help to get in."

"And Mary was helping him as he got down inside?"

"I am not sure. I have forgotten."

"And you had with you, had you, Lassie? That is Brian's dog?"

"Yes."

"What sort of dog is that? Is it a smallish dog?"

"I am not sure," she said in a tired voice. "I have not seen it for a long time."

"You don't remember anything at all about the color of it?"

"Black and white."

"Black and white. Now in the tank, did you take hold of Brian by the neck, or near his neck?"

"I never touched him inside the tank."

"Did Mary say to you, 'What are you doing?' "

"No, she never says nothing."

"And did you say 'nebby' or something like that?"

"I never says nothing because Brian never got touched in the tank not even by Mary," Norma said, and added one of those bits of information one felt could only be genuine, because it was she who said it first, "Because it was too stinky."

"We all got out," Mary recounted the next day, "and then when we got over to the concrete blocks . . ."

"Wait. When you got out of the tank, how did Brian get out?"

"Well, one of us passed him out to the other one. I cannot remember any . . . anything like that, who passed him to who, sir."

"Did you, all three of you, go to the concrete blocks?"

"Yes, sir. I thought at that time, I thought she was looking for a jar for the tadpoles," she was off again. "I never mentioned that to Mr. Bryson but I thought she was looking for a jar for the tadpoles."

"Yes."

"And when she . . ."

Harvey Robson interrupted. "Just go slowly. What happened when you got to the concrete blocks?"

"She told him to lie down. She says, 'You have got to lie down for the lady to come with the sweets,' and then I again . . ."

"Wait, yes?"

"Then again I asked her what she was talking about. I asked her what she was talking about and she just replied 'nebby' again."

Mr. Justice Cusack broke in. "Mr. Harvey Robson," he said, "do you think you could go very slowly at this stage? I don't only want to make notes, I want to be able to look up as well."

"My Lord, yes. Now, quite slowly, May, what happened after that? Don't rush on but just stop in sentences, do you see?"

The next minutes were among the most remarkable of the trial: Mary, watching the Judge and closely and carefully adjusting her rate of speech to the speed at which he was able to take notes, gave her evidence with a precision rarely achieved in court by even the most experienced witnesses. "Norma Bell," she dictated slowly, "told him to put his neck up and put his neck down . . ."

"Now stop there," said Harvey Robson. "Was he still standing up then or was he on the ground?"

"He was on the ground, sir."

"Yes?"

"And she—I cannot remember if she squeezed his neck with two hands or one hand, sir."

"Yes?"

"And there was some boys coming along and she got up and she sat on the square slab, the big one, and Brian was sitting down or something and the dog was there."

"Yes, which dog was that?"

"Lassie. And I was frightened. I never—and I was just in a kind of a trance, and I says, 'if you don't get away I will set the dog on you.' "

"To the boys?"

"Yes."

"Yes, and did the boys go away?"

"Well, they never ran straight away, they just like toddled on."

"Yes. Well, after they had toddled away, go on from there May, will you?"

"Well, she went back to him and she started to squeeze his neck again."

"Yes?"

"And I tried to pull her off but she just went mad, she just screamed at me."

"Did she say or shout or scream anything in particular, or just make a screaming noise?"

"Just made a screaming noise."

"Yes, go on?"

"And we went, and I'm not sure if she—if she banged his head off that bit of corner wood or just he might have missed it, I don't know." (This particular bit of fencing was to be pointed out later to the Jury as having some significance.) "But," she continued thoughtfully, "oh, she wasn't banging his head like that, she just let it drop or something."

"My Lord," said Harvey Robson, "when she said 'like that,' she demonstrated several times."

"Demonstrated with her hands," Mr. Justice Cusack explained to the Jury, "the motions of somebody who would actually be banging."

"More than once, My Lord."

"Yes."

"Could you see what Brian was like then?" Harvey Robson asked Mary.

"He was struggling and you could tell she was pressing hard because her fingertips, where her nails were, were going white."

"Yes?"

"And Lassie was crying—no, that was the second time it was crying, I think. I'm not sure whether it was crying the first time or the second time, but we went back and I says I don't want anything to do with this, Norma. I says, I should tell the police but I'm not going to. I think we . . ."

"You were saying, 'I think' something?"

"I don't think we went back the railway way. I think we went back the car park way."

"Now when you say you went back and you started to go back, where was Brian?"

"He was lying down."

"And did you notice anything about him?"

"He just had a bit of slavery stuff on his mouth and when we come back the second time it looked like fluff."

"Don't go back to the second time yet. Were his eyes open or shut when you left?"

"They were a little bit open, I think."

"A little open, yes. And you say you went back, you think by the car park way?"

"Yes, sir." She said she and Norma went to their respective homes. She thought she went in for a drink, or something.

The day before, R. P. Smith had examined Norma about these same events. "Where did you go," he asked, "when you got out of the tank?"

"May said, 'The blocks, howay Norma,' " Norma answered.

"May said to you, 'The blocks, howay Norma'?"

"Yes."

"All three of you went? Did you go to the blocks?" Mr. Smith's questions to Norma were always simply phrased.

"Yes."

". . . What happened when you got to the blocks?"

"May told Brian to lie down."

"Did he?"

"Yes."

"And what did May do?"

"Started to hurt him."

"How?"

Norma did not answer. "How did she hurt him, Norma?" She still did not answer and began to hide her face. "What part of him did she hurt?" Mr. Smith asked again, but still she would not reply.

"Just think a moment," Mr. Justice Cusack said quietly. "Listen to me: you say that she started to hurt him?"

"Yes," Norma murmured.

"Did he get hurt?"

"Yes, 'cos she put her hands on his neck."

"What was there about that that hurt him?"

"She used her other hand as well, but she had it across him like that," she had made a gesture with her hand.

"What was that?" asked the Judge.

"Would you do it again, Norma?" Mr. Smith requested.

Norma repeated the gesture. "She demonstrates the pinching of the nose between the thumb and fingers of her hand," Mr. Justice Cusack explained to the Jury.

"Covering the mouth with the remaining fingers," Mr. Smith added. ". . . Did that hurt Brian?" he asked.

"I don't know. I says to May, 'Leave the bairn alone.' "

"Did she?"

"Yes, she left him alone 'cos somebody was coming; some boys came."

"Some boys came, did they?"

"Yes."

"Where did they come from?"

"I think some of them from the houses above."

"What happened when the boys came?"

"Brian's dog Lassie was there, sir."

"Had Lassie come all the way with you from where you first met Brian and Norman?"

"Yes. . . ."

". . . So what happened when the boys came along and Lassie was there?"

"Well, Lassie was behind the block and May said to the boys, 'Get away or I'll set the dog after you.' "

"May said that to the boys, did she?"

"Yes."

"But did the boys go away?"

"Well, they was still around about."

"So what happened next?"

"May went back to Brian."

"What was Brian doing?"

"This time he was sitting on the block."

"Yes?"

Someone up in the gallery began to cough and Norma, immediately distracted, turned and looked, curiously—

"If somebody is going to have a coughing fit," said the Judge, "will they please kindly go out of Court."

"What happened, Norma?" Mr. Smith urged her back to the proceedings. "There is Brian sitting on the block, and what happened then? Did May do something?"

"Yes."

"What did she do?"

"She threw him on the ground 'cos she wanted him to lie down."

"Yes, and then?"

"And she went back to hurt him and this time she wouldn't let go of him when I told her to." Norma stopped and began to sob.

"I know that you get excited, Norma," Mr. Smith said gently.

"You have told me, Norma," Mr. Justice Cusack took over, speaking very quietly, "that she went back to hurt him and she wouldn't leave go?"

"Yes."

"What happened after that? Can you just tell me?"

"She went back to him."

"What did she do to him?" Mr. Smith asked.

"She started back with her hand again."

"What was she doing with her hand?" asked the Judge.

"The same as the first time but I didn't know she was going to really hurt him."

"You did not know what?"

"I didn't know that Mary was really going to hurt him."

"Did she hurt him?" asked Mr. Smith.

"I think so."

"You *think* so? Why do you *think* so?"

" 'Cos when he was on the ground he started to go purple and she wouldn't leave go of him."

"Could you hear anything—any noises?"

She started to cry again. "Little Brian was trying to shove Mary's hand—shove—shift Mary's hand."

"Which hand was he trying to shift? I mean whereabouts upon him was the hand that he was trying to shift?"

"Mary was—I mean little Brian was lying down and Mary kneeled down and she got her hand on his neck and Brian tried to shift away from her."

"Are you saying just one hand or was it two that she had on his neck?"

"One."

"What was Mary doing with her other hand?"

"I don't remember 'cos I wasn't there very long."

"Did you say anything to Mary about that?"

"No. Before, when Mary was leaning on him she said—when she was really hurting him she said, 'Norma, take over, my hands are getting thick.' "

"What did you do?"

"I went away from her. She wouldn't even leave him alone."

"Why did you go away?"

" 'Cos she wanted me to hurt him."

"Did you want to hurt him?"

"No," she shook her head vehemently.

"You are shaking your head, Norma. Do you mean that you didn't?"

"No. I don't like to."

"Did you want Brian to get hurt?"

"No."

"So you went? You went away. What was the last you saw happening? What was happening when you went away?"

"He was still alive, I know that."

"Did she still have hold of him?"

"I can't remember."

"Where did you go to?"

"Back the same way we come."

"Back over the fence, over the railway and through the hole in the fence, is that right?"

"Yes."

"And then where to?"

"Up our back lane."

"Up your back lane. What did you do?" Norma didn't answer.

"You went up your back lane?"

"Of Linda Routledge." (59 Whitehouse Road.)

"What did you do?"

"For about twenty minutes we were making pom-poms."

Later in the cross-examination she was asked about the second time she and Mary had gone to the "Tin Lizzie":

"And later," said Harvey Robson, "you went back and something was done with some scissors?"

"Yes."

"Did you use the scissors?"

"I never even used them."

"Now I just want to ask you about the scissors. You had seen the scissors with Norman [Brian's brother]. That's right, isn't it, earlier?"

Norma hesitated. "I think you told us that Norman had the scissors, didn't you?" Mr. Justice Cusack coaxed her.

"Yes."

"And you took them from him?" Mr. Robson continued.

"And gave them to Mary, yes, way down Crosshill Road." (She had already said to Mr. Smith in her examination-in-chief that she had passed the scissors to Mary on their way down to the "Tin Lizzie" with Brian, before anything had happened to him.)

"Was this when you first went with Brian?" Harvey Robson now asked.

"Yes. I'm not sure, mind."

"You are not sure?"

"But Mary still had them."

"I understand that, but you do not remember when you first gave them to her?"

"The first time."

"If you don't, say so."

"The first time," she repeated.

"The first time," the Judge repeated.

"She wanted them, as you say," said Harvey Robson. "Did she tell you what she wanted them for?"

"To make him baldy."

"To make him what?"

"Baldy."

"To make him baldy," the Judge said.

"And was that when you were going with Brian?" asked Mr. Robson.

"No."

"Toward the 'Tin Lizzie,' or later on?"

"Later on."

"When you first gave them to her and you said you did that

because she wanted them, did she tell you what she wanted them for at that time?"

"No, because it was her secret."

"Did you see what she did with the scissors at that time?"

"Start cutting some of his hair off," she was getting confused.

"Do you mean . . . ?"

Mr. Justice Cusack interrupted. "Would you allow me to intervene, because it may be I will get a response? First of all, Norman had the scissors, had he?"

"Yes," she whispered. She hated talking about the scissors and her answers concerning them were mumbled.

"And then you had them, and then you were walking along the roadway?"

"Down Crosshill Road."

"Walking across the road?"

"Crosshill."

"Yes, and then Mary had the scissors?"

"Yes."

"Where were you when you handed over the scissors to Mary in the road?"

"Crosshill. . . ."

"Crossing," said the Judge, misunderstanding her. "And when you handed them over to Mary, did she say then why she wanted them?"

"No," Norma said again. "It was a secret."

"No," the Judge repeated. "It was a secret."

"Would this be right—I think it is, Norma," said Mr. Robson, "that something was said about making him baldy only when you went back the second time?"

"I am not sure. It was second or third time."

"Second or third time. . . . And you do not remember what Mary had done with the scissors while you were at the 'Tin Lizzie' the first time?"

"No, because I never seen them when I . . ." she floundered.

"Isn't this right: that you yourself got the scissors when you were back near your home after the first time, or it may be the second time?"

"No, it was only the first time, because I gave them to May when we were going down Crosshill."

They had approached it from every side, had tried to surprise, trick, and shock her into contradicting herself. But she had come full circle; she had handed the scissors to Mary who wanted them for her own reasons on their first visit to the "Tin Lizzie"; Mary had held onto them, had then, on their way down the second time, said she wanted to make Brian "baldy" and had proceeded to cut off some of his hair.

Mary's story about the scissors was quite different. When Harvey Robson asked her whether, after having gone into her house to get a drink of water or something, she had stayed in there, or come out again, she spoke not only of the scissors:

"Come out," she said, "and Norma asked us to get a pen and I says no." (In her statement to the police, Mary had alleged that Norma told her to get a pen because she wanted to "write a note on his stomach.")

"Yes, go on," said Harvey Robson.

"Norma had a pair of scissors and a razor blade."

"When did you first see the scissors?"

"When—when we come back. When Norma asked me to get a pen."

"And when you first saw the scissors, where were they?"

"Norma was putting them down her pants. . . ."

" 'Putting them down her pants,' she said," Mr. Justice Cusack repeated.

"Pants. Yes, My Lord," said Harvey Robson. "When did you first see the razor blade?" he asked Mary.

"The same time as the scissors, sir."

"You say Norma had a razor blade. What did she do with it? Did she hold it in her hand or put it somewhere, or what?"

"I think she carried it in her hand, sir."

"And did you go somewhere?"

"We went back, sir."

"How did that come about?"

"Norma says, 'Are you coming back?' and I was—I just says yes, and I just obeyed her and I went."

(This time she had really made a mistake: when she claimed to have "obeyed" Norma, this was so highly improbable that almost for the first time since the beginning of the trial, there were smiles on many faces and even a few nervous giggles, immediately suppressed.)

"Yes?" asked Harvey Robson.

"I was all—I felt funny."

"Yes, and you went back, do you mean to the same place?"

"Yes, sir."

"And what did you find when you got to the same place, the blocks?"

"Brian, sir."

"And was he still on the ground?"

"Yes, sir."

"Yes, go on, what happened when you were back there?"

"Norma was cutting some of his hair. Cutting some of his hair with the scissors."

"Yes?"

"I never saw her cut his stomach with the razor blade," she volunteered, employing the technique of making something more credible by denying knowledge of it before it was brought up, "but I saw her cut just above his knee."

"When she was cutting the hair—before she cut the hair, did she say anything about him?"

"I can't remember, but Lassie started to whine."

"Lassie had gone back with you?"

"Lassie stopped there and Lassie started to cry, but she says, 'Don't you start or you'll get the same,' and she went for it, but it growled and she says, 'Now, now, don't be hasty.' "

"While this was going on, May, what were you doing?"

"I was just standing and looking. I couldn't, I couldn't, I couldn't move. It's as though some glue was holding us down. I just couldn't move."

"Yes, did you say anything to Norma or did she say anything to you while you were at the blocks?"

"She asked us to cut some of his hair."

"Yes, and did you answer?"

"Yes."

"What did you say?"

"Well, I never answered, but there was just—I don't think I answered, but there was just a man, well, not a man, a boy, a teenager, that was coming down over the railway, along the west part of it." She continued to tell how this young man shouted at some children who were playing some way off.

". . . When this man started shouting what did you and Norma do?" asked Harvey Robson.

"We thought he was coming over to us and so Norma dropped the scissors and put the razor blade under that big square slab, and we ran away."

After that they had walked back toward home and Mary recounted the conversation she claims to have had with Norma:

". . . Norma says, 'You should not have done that, you know, May,' she says, 'you are getting into . . .' and then she just stopped and I says, I never even done anything, because I never, and then after that she says 'Trouble,' and just after that she says, 'Trouble.' "

Her account of this conversation was curiously disconcerting, for although by this time no one underrated Mary's intelligence or power of invention, the details and the "wording" she quoted were almost too genuine for comfort.

Norma, in the course of her examination-in-chief by her counsel the previous day, had told a very confused story about the razor blade, suddenly out of the blue on the witness stand volunteering the information that she had told a lie to Chief-Inspector Dobson about seeing Mary with it.

"Do you remember," asked Mr. Smith, "when Mr. Dobson went to the blocks with you . . . and you were able to show him where the razor blade was?"

"That's 'cos Mary hid it there 'cos she said she got it out of the scullery."

"She said what?" This was completely new to Mr. Smith.

"She got it out of her scullery," Norma repeated sullenly.

"Do you remember," Mr. Smith continued, "that you told Mr. Dobson that May found the razor on the way down, on the path to the 'Tin Lizzie'?"

"Yes, I told a lie."

"Why did you tell that lie to Mr. Dobson?"

"I don't know why. I was frightened."

"Who were you frightened of?" She began to squirm. "What were you frightened of?" Mr. Smith insisted. "Norma, just think: why did you tell Mr. Dobson that May found the razor blade on the path when you tell the Court now that May had said she had got it from her scullery?"

"She did," Norma said stubbornly. "I know I told Mr. Dobson a lie."

Her capacity for thinking ahead being very limited, she had now decided that she wanted to rid herself of a lie: she didn't know why, and it would never have occurred to her that admitting to a lie would bring about a barrage of further questions. Even if it had, it is doubtful that she could have visualized this consequence sufficiently to make a decision whether to face or avoid it. All through the trial her parents had said to her again and again, "Now you tell the truth about everything: tell them everything," and, in her ineffectual and impulsive way that is what she was now trying to do. Norma was as worried about the razor blade as she had been about the scissors. What was happening in Norma's mind was that the actual killing of these two boys was finally such an enormity to her that she could not face it at all. When she talked about it, it was, in a sense, as if she was describing fiction—something impossible, certainly something she herself had nothing to do with. Her worst moments on the witness stand were when she was questioned on matters where—because the actual evidence proved it—she had to admit that she had been involved, such as the "We Murder" notes. The fact that Brian had been cut with the razor blade and made "baldy" with the scissors was in a sense more real to her than his death. And, whether true or not, it was essential to her—not from the point of view of innocence or guilt—but to her as a person, to separate herself from anything that had been done with these two objects.

Mr. Smith was in a difficult position: for, while it was his duty to protect his client's interest, at the same time, once she had publicly admitted to a lie on a vital point (never forgetting that

Mary, in her police statements, had insisted that it was Norma who had "cut" Brian with the razor blade), he could do no less than investigate her retraction. He could have requested a recess to allow him to discuss it with her in private: electing instead to question her in court was a gamble, but at the same time it was a public affirmation of his faith in his client—and it paid off.

"Why [did you tell a lie]?" he asked her.

"I don't know."

"You say, 'she found it on the path.'" He was now taking her back to her lie: again a gamble, for it could confuse her and, if it hadn't been a lie, entangle her further. On the other hand, if it was a lie, as she said, he was forcing her to deny her original statement again, to admit again to the lie and thus eventually, he must have hoped, be brought to say why she told it.

"'Cos May wanted it found on the path. If we were caught, she wanted it found on the path."

"'May wanted it found on the path if we were caught'?" the Judge repeated, but neither this nor Norma's subsequent information, equally the result of intricate childish reasoning, was ever clearly understood.

"How do you know she wanted it found on the path?" asked Mr. Smith.

"'Cos May and me were talking together."

"What did Mary say?"

"This was a few days after Martin"—she caught herself—"Brian died," she said quickly.

"After Brian died you and May were talking?"

"Yes."

"What did Mary say about the razor blade?"

"She wanted—she didn't want it to be a razor blade out of her house." (One wondered, was Mary afraid of her parents or was she trying to protect them?)

"Well, whose idea was it to say that the razor had been found on the path?" Mr. Smith asked.

"Mary told me to."

"Well now, at one stage you told Mr. Dobson that you had seen the razor blade on Brian's belly."

"That's right, that's a lie."

"Was that true?"

"No, it's a lie."

"Did you know anything about the razor blade being used on Brian's belly?"

"No."

"Did you ever see . . . ?"

Mr. Justice Cusack interrupted. "What made you say that, then, to Mr. Dobson," he asked, "that you had seen the blade being pressed on his belly? What made you say that?"

"Mary wanted to."

In her *third* statement to the police Norma had said, as she was saying now, that Mary had *told* her that she "had cut his belly." ("And she pulled up his jumper and *I saw a tiny red mark* somewhere on his belly," she had stated.) In her *fourth* and final statement she had changed her story. She said then that, on their second visit to the "Tin Lizzie," Mary had found a razor blade on the path. When they got back to where Brian was, he was lying there on his back with his arm stretched out. She, Norma, had "lifted his head and shoulders up a bit and patted his back." But his hand fell on one side and she laid him down again, she had continued. She said she had felt his pulse but "it wasn't going up and down." "Mary pressed the razor blade down on Brian's belly a few times in the same place," she had gone on. "She lifted his jersey and that's when she did it. I didn't see any blood." (The fact that a cut inflicted after death does not bleed cannot be considered common knowledge.) "That was when she [Mary] hid the razor blade and said, 'Don't tell your Dad or I'll get wrong,' " she had continued in her statement (page 43). The medical re-examination of Brian's body immediately following this fourth statement disclosed the fine lines which had previously not been noticed.

What Norma was now saying in Court was that all this had been a lie and that she had never *seen* Mary touch Brian's body with a razor blade, that therefore she hadn't been *there* when anything final was done to Brian; that, for some mysterious reason, it was Mary who wanted it to be known that she had cut his belly and *told* her so. In cross-examination to Harvey Robson, she affirmed again that she herself had been almost totally uninvolved.

"Did you do any cutting of it [Brian's hair] at all?" Mr. Robson asked.

"I was frightened," she said again, "I would not. I didn't like to because I was frightened."

". . . When you went back the first time," Mr. Robson asked a little later, "did you ask Mary to get a pen?"

"I never asked her at all, I never asked her."

"Either the first or second time?"

"I never asked her at any time. I never."

". . . Did Mary say to you, after you had gone away—after, when you were going away on the first occasion, 'Norma, I have got nothing to do with this'?"

"No, she never says nothing, because she was the leader. She was the leader of everything."

Mary, the next day, told about going back to the "Tin Lizzie" the third time—the time Norma said Mary had used the scissors to cut off some of Brian's hair to "make him baldy" and—though Norma had only mentioned this once, in her third statement to the police, but never in her examination-in-chief—"had put some purple flowers on top of the grass that was over Brian. . . ."

". . . Er—Norma had asked me if I would come back and I just says 'Yes' because at that time she was going back to cover him with those, you know, those reeds." She thought she'd been in the garden at that time and then they had gone "the car park way."

"And what did you do when you got back to the blocks?"

"Norma asked us if I would pick the reeds up with her and I did."

"Pick the what up?" asked the Judge.

"The reeds, the—like reeds, big like stocks with little purply flowery things on them," Mary *liked* explaining things to the Judge.

"And what did you do with those?"

"I was lifting them up and Norma dropped them on top of Brian and I dropped some." Once again, this had sounded credible, for in a way this manner of "burying" little Brian would have been part of the "game." But Mary, under cross-examination on the following day, also said—in a different way—that *she* had been uninvolved.

"I asked you before," Mr. Lyons said to her, "why you did not tell the boys [five boys who, both girls said, had come toward the blocks when they were there with little Brian Howe before he was dead] what Norma was doing. And you said you were frightened."

"Yes."

"But you were not frightened to shout at the boys, were you?"

"No. . . ."

". . . You shouted, 'If you don't go away I will set the dog on you.' "

"Yes."

"Why did you want the boys to go away?"

"I don't know. I was just frightened."

"So that Norma could go on with what she was doing?"

"No."

"Why didn't you shout, 'Come over here'?"

"I don't know. I was just frightened, that's all. I couldn't. I just couldn't."

"You were asked a little earlier," said the Judge, "if you were sorry that Brian was killed. Were you?"

"Yes."

Mr. Lyons continued, "You said that while Norma was killing Brian she made a screaming noise."

"She did."

"Did you think she was mad?"

"Yes."

"Did you think she ought to be in a Home?"

"No, not really, she just—I hadn't seen her like that before."

"Did there come a time when you knew that Brian was dead?"

"Yes."

"Did you think then that Norma was mad?"

"Well, I just thought she had gone out of her mind."

"If a girl can go out of her mind and kill one little boy, she might do it to another little boy? . . . Did you realize that?"

"No."

"Did you tell your mother about it?"

"No." [Her mother, as we learned later, had not been there: she was on one of her regular trips to Glasgow.]

"Did you tell anybody?"

"No."

"Why not?"

"I was frightened."

"Frightened of what?"

"I don't know. I was just frightened. I couldn't tell no one, not even if I tried I couldn't."

"You told the Court that you said to Norma, after Brian was dead, 'I should tell the police, but I'm not going to.' Is that right?"

"Yes."

"Why did you say that to Norma?"

There followed one of the many instances where the court found it impossible to follow Mary's child thought-processes. The only way in fact in which one *could* understand her reasoning on such occasions, was if, putting oneself in her shoes, lies and all, one started from her point of view.

"Because," Mary answered, "I was not going to tell the police and Norma thought I was. 'Oh, if I told the police that May done it,' she said [to herself], 'I will be on the better side of the police'— that is what *she* thought."

"I don't understand," said Justice Cusack. "Will you say that again?"

"I was not going to tell the police," Mary said, "but *Norma* says, 'Oh' she says, [or rather] she thinks to herself, 'Oh, if I tell the police, I will be on the better side of them and May will get all the backwash'—that is what she thought."

(Later in his summing up the Judge repeated that he had not really understood:

> Well, Members of the Jury, it does not make a great deal of sense to me I admit, but apparently there was some deep complicated reason in Mary's mind, according to herself, involving blame falling on one or other of them which prevented her from telling the police and made her say that she would not tell the police.)

However, what Mary was trying to tell us was that *if* it had really been Norma who had killed Brian and Mary had seen her do it, Mary's reaction out of loyalty to her friend, would have been *not* to tell the police. What she was saying to us—always on the assumption that we were accepting her presentation of the situation, rather than Norma's—was:

"*I* was not going to tell the police, and I wouldn't have told if *she* hadn't." This is basically all she meant to say. She was quite consistent in her story so far and it was finally merely a matter of semantics.

One must remember that, according to Mary's code of honor, where criminals and anyone opposing authority is someone to be lauded, people who were, as she was to say later, "in it together" owed each other loyalty.

She wasn't the only person running foul of the police to have the illusion that *if* she and Norma stuck to the story they had no doubt originally concocted together, they would win. After all, she had 'won' for two months after the killing of Martin Brown.

Mr. Lyons continued his cross-examination of Mary. "Well, did you tell the police when you were going home that Norma was acting kind of funny?"

"Yes." (She hadn't.)

"Do you mean as if she was out of her mind?" he said.

"Yes," she said again.

"What was she doing?"

"Making fingers." (Norma, when upset or excited *was* in the habit of making "faces." But it is *Mary* who, during the trial and according to the policewomen also in her sleep, constantly "spread" and "stretched" her *fingers*.)

"This was what she was doing?" Mr. Lyons asked, and Mary demonstrated with her face—making a grimace—and her fingers, spreading them out wide.

"Going like that," she said, "making funny fingers and that."

"Did you never tell anybody?"

"No," she said, "only the police when she thought she would be on the better side, that is when I told them."

"And then there came a time, the same day, when you say that Norma asked you to get a pen?"

"Yes."

This business of Norma asking her to get a pen had sounded quite credible all along. If one accepted that, to Norma, Brian's

being dead was quite unreal, and that she had unconsciously elected
to treat it as a game (as Mary did for different reasons), it was quite
within the realm of possibilities—indeed in the context of her men-
tality not only possible but very probable—that Norma would write
something on his tummy, really without meaning any harm.

"What was that for?" Mr. Lyons asked.

"I don't know," Mary answered, "she just asked us to get a
pen."

"Well, did she say what she wanted the pen for?"

"To write a note on him."

"To write a note on what part of him?"

"His stomach. But I would not get one . . ."

". . . Do you mean a note, like the one that you had both written
in the Nursery?"

"I don't know what kind of note, sir."

"Was that note a joint idea?"

"No, I asked her what for and she just says to write a note on
him."

"Why did you go back with Norma to the body of little Brian?"
Mr. Lyons continued.

"She asked us and I just—I just went with her. I don't know
what happened. I just went."

"Weren't you frightened that she might kill you?"

"No."

"Why not? She was mad. . . ."

"She would not dare," Mary said quite correctly—her self-
esteem did not permit her to allow that Norma could possibly do
her any harm.

"And she had killed a little boy?" Mr. Lyons went on.

"She would not dare," Mary repeated.

"Why would she not dare to kill you?"

"Because I would turn round and punch her one."

There was just one point—strongly in Norma's favor—which
both girls agreed on. Mr. Smith, at the end of Norma's evidence-in-
chief, asked her about the charade she and Mary had played when
they went with Brian's sister Pat to look for him:

". . . you went looking for Brian with Pat Howe?" he asked.

"And Mary Bell," Norma said.

"And Mary Bell, yes. You heard Pat Howe say—I forget which day it was—but she said that the three of you went down to the railway bridge and looked over the 'Tin Lizzie.' Do you remember that?"

"We never went in."

"I know you never went in, but do you remember going to the railway bridge and looking over the 'Tin Lizzie'?"

"Yes."

"Did Mary Bell say anything about where you should look? Where you should go? You nodded your head. Do you mean she did say something?"

Norma nodded.

". . . Yes, what did she say?"

"She says to Pat, 'He might be playing behind the blocks or he might be in between them. . . .' "

". . . Do you know why Mary Bell said that?"

"Because she wanted Pat Howe to have a shock."

"How do you know that?"

"Because she says she wanted Pat Howe to go there because she wanted Pat to see him because Pat liked Brian. . . ."

". . . How do you know Mary wanted Pat to have a shock?"

"Because she told me and I spoke back to her."

"What was the last phrase?" asked the Judge.

"Because she told me and I spoke back," Mr. Smith repeated. "What did you say when you spoke back?"

"I said, he will not be there."

This was the one place where, essentially, Mary's evidence tallied with Norma's: "How did you come to go to the 'Tin Lizzie,' toward the 'Tin Lizzie' with Pat?" Harvey Robson asked Mary.

"Norma was there with us," she answered, "and I says he might be over the 'Tin Lizzie' and Norma says, 'Oh, no, he never goes over there' and she convinced Pat that he was not over there."

Only minutes after Mary had completed her testimony, after more than three hours in the witness box, the defense called Dr. Robert Orton. He said that he had seen Mary twice: on 16 August at the Remand Home in Croydon, and again on 14 November at the Remand Home in Seaham.

"And you have heard at any rate some of the evidence?" asked Harvey Robson. "Particularly Mary's evidence?"

"I have heard the whole of Mary's evidence."

"Now first of all," said Mr. Robson, "will you tell the Court briefly to begin with what your conclusions are concerning her ... [and] then I shall ask you how you arrived at them. Do you regard her as suffering from something?"

"Yes," said Dr. Orton. "I think that this girl must be regarded as suffering from psychopathic personality, which is defined as a persistent disorder or disability of the mind which results in abnormally aggressive or seriously irresponsible conduct on the part of the patient and requires, or is susceptible to, medical treatment."

". . . Is that the statutory definition?" the Judge asked.

"That is the statutory definition, My Lord."

"What are the symptoms indicating that state of affairs?" asked Harvey Robson.

". . . The primary symptoms are: 1) a lack of feeling quality to other humans; 2) a liability to act on impulse and without forthought. And then there are secondary symptoms which really derive from the above: 3) a combination of the previous two, under suitable circumstances leading to aggression; 4) a lack of shame or remorse for what has been done; 5) an inability to profit by or use experience which includes the lack of response to punishment; and 6) with the above the presence of viciousness or wish to do damage to things or persons. And then there are negative features of the condition. . . . Lack of psychoses such as schizophrenia or depression, in other words lack of mental illness and lack of intellectual deficit . . . and lastly, My Lord, lack of criminal motivations."

Dr. Orton's meaning of "negative features" in this context was that the condition of psychopathy is not generally identified with mental retardation or any specific mental illness.

"Now, Dr. Orton," said Harvey Robson. "Did you find that Mary was suffering from some or all of those symptoms?"

"I think she shows all of them in varying degrees."

"Are you able to indicate the ones which she most markedly manifested?"

"Yes, I think I could. I think first of all I ought to dispose of [what are called] the negative features. On examination she shows no evidence of mental illness. . . . She is of average intelligence [he also told me later that she might well be much better than that], and lastly I could really, as a personal opinion, see no real criminal motivation."

". . . Does that mean that what she does is not done for gain or other personal benefit?" asked the Judge.

"Yes, I think that is what it means."

". . . Now could you come to the positive ones . . ."

"When I saw her on 16 August, she stated to me, 'I was with Norma Bell when she strangled Brian.' Now this was a statement made without any disturbance or emotion at all and I felt this was evidence of the lack of feeling quality to other humans. It was said in a completely matter-of-fact way, not as though she was talking about a human being. And she was very casual in that she went on to say, 'I am going to Whickham View School after the summer holidays,' and then asked me, 'Am I going home and then to the Court next Tuesday?' showing complete and bland disregard for the seriousness of the offense with which she was charged."

Asked about her other offenses or possible offenses, Dr. Orton continued, "She claims she was quite good at school and well behaved there but she also did admit that she had twice run away from home and again incriminated Norma Bell by saying, 'This is only since Norma Bell was up here,' and I felt these occasions when she ran away, although minimal or relatively trivial in this setting, are indications again of a tendency to act on impulse and without forethought. They really had no idea where they were going and why. . . ."

(Much later it turned out there had been a good reason for at least one of these escapades: Mary and Norma had been invited to spend Whit-weekend with Mary's aunt Cath, in the village where she lived, an hour away from Newcastle. Norma Bell's mother had even gone there, to meet Cath and see the house. But when the weekend came around, Mary's mother had said they couldn't go. When Mary then asked whether they could go instead to Rothbury, a convalescent home for eneuretic children where she had stayed in the past and whose superintendent she was particularly fond of, Billy Bell had said they couldn't go there either. When Cath asked her later why she had run away she said, "Mum wouldn't let me come to you and Dad wouldn't let me go to Rothbury, so I ran away. We were going to Rothbury. . . ." Later, however, she told another psychiatrist who tried to find out the real reason for her running away, "I thought it would be fun, and I wanted to go see my gran. . . .")

"In addition," said Dr. Orton, "she showed no remorse whatever, no tears and no anxiety. She was completely unemotional about the whole affair [of the murders] and merely resentful at her detention. That was largely the first interview. Again this shows, I thought, this lack of shame or remorse for what has been done. It's the fourth symptom. . . . She was abnormal in the way she was when discussing death and so on in this completely unemotional way, whether she be the guilty one or party to it seemed to make no difference. As party to it she was completely without remorse."

"Let us deal with the guilt of being party to it," Mr. Justice Cusack said, "because these matters are in dispute as to fact. On her evidence she knew about death?"

"She knew about it and discussed it."

"She discussed it without emotion?"

"Without emotion, without any evidence of being anxious or upset or any signs of distress for someone who had been hurt. . . ." Dr. Orton then described various incidents which occurred during Mary's stay at Seaham. "She is a trouble-maker and tends to play off one girl against another and whilst in the Remand Home she has twice absconded."

"Do you know for how long?" the Judge said.

"Well, it was only a matter of hours before she was apprehended on one occasion [the second]. She got out through the toilet window, I believe, in the middle of the night. She was returned by the police at 5:45 A.M. showing no concern, no emotion, or contrition with regard to this."

(One was tempted to wonder here why Mary should show "emotion, concern, or contrition" about running away. Do any children? Particularly as her "absconding" on these two occasions was nothing more than a gesture of defiance, or even more a way of calling attention to herself, perhaps because she feared she was ceasing to be quite the center of attention. The first time she "ran away" she had merely run across the garden and hid in a shed, within the precincts of the Remand Home. And on the second occasion she was found a mile or so away, about an hour and a half after she had left.)

"There was one further piece of information which I questioned her about," said Dr. Orton. "This question of suffering beforehand when someone was strangled.... The replies were, 'Why, if you're dead, you're dead,' and she expressed the opinion that she did not think it mattered once you were dead, implying that you were then no longer aware of previous suffering.... In addition, she discussed with me the fact, and admitted, that she and Norma had returned to Brian's body and cut the boy's hair and legs with scissors and a razor blade. This again was said without any feeling of any sort, any sign of distress or emotion.... I think it (and the breaking into the Nursery) is a fairly good example of the presence of viciousness and wish to do damage to things or persons."

"As a result of those investigations, Dr. Orton," asked Harvey Robson, "what opinion did you arrive at?"

"I came to the conclusion, sir, that I think this girl was and is suffering from such abnormality of mind, namely, psychopathic personality such as substantially impaired her mental responsibility for her acts and omissions in doing or being a party to this killing."

"And that is assuming that she was," Mr. Justice Cusack interposed. Later in his summing up to the Jury he explained the law relating to "Diminished Responsibility."

> With regard to Mary you have to consider not only her capacity to commit crime and her capacity to form a specific intent either to Murder or to cause serious bodily injury appreciating it may cause death, but you have a further problem (which does not apply to Norma). That is the question of Diminished Responsibility.... In 1957 there was an Act of Parliament and it said that ... 'where a person kills, or is a party to the killing of another, he shall not be convicted of Murder if he was suffering from such abnormality of mind

(whether arising from a condition of arrested or retarded development of mind, or any inherent causes, or induced by disease or injury) as substantially impaired his mental responsibility for his acts and omissions in doing or being a party to the killing . . . that it was up to the Defence to prove Diminished Responsibility. But that while the Prosecution has to prove things 'beyond a shadow of doubt', the Defence, in a case such as this, must only prove that it is more likely than not that there is Diminished Responsibility (which is always linked to a conviction for Manslaughter rather than Murder).

One must consider, of course, what abnormality of mind means. It includes the inability to form a sensible reasonable judgement, and as to whether a thing is right or wrong; not from immaturity; not from being a child; but because of this state of arrested or retarded development or for inherent reasons. It includes inability to exercise will power. It includes inability to exercise self-control for the same reasons.

It was with knowledge of this law that the evidence of the two psychiatrists called by the defense for Mary, Dr. Orton and shortly afterwards Dr. Westbury, was heard.

"The abnormality of mind to which you have referred," said Mr. Robson to Dr. Orton, "did it arise from a condition of arrested or retarded development of mind, or any inherent cause, or [was it] induced by disease or injury?"

"Well, psychopathic personality," said Dr. Orton, "is thought to arise from a combination probably of genetic factors, which are inherent, and there are also environmental influences. . . ."

"Environmental?" Mr. Justice Cusack repeated quickly.

"Influences," Dr. Orton repeated.

(Although no amount of additional information would have changed the legal outcome of the trial, at least an indication of the traumatic events of Mary's childhood—the environmental influences the doctors referred to—would have been of the greatest importance from the point of view of mitigating the very harsh public opinion of her that had arisen. *But no such information emerged during the trial, nor were these circumstances* [which are described later in this book] *known by the authorities, who only a few days after the trial decided Mary's future.*)

"Insofar as it [psychopathic personality] is related to genetic factors," Harvey Robson asked Dr. Orton, "would they be classed as inherent causes in your opinion?"

"Yes."

". . . It occurs to me," said the Judge, "that this may have a bearing on the capacity of a child of this age to commit crime. . . . One of the issues in connection with a child's responsibility is that of the child's ability to distinguish between right and wrong. If you are going to apply this evidence to the question of responsibility, I think subject to what you may say, you must have the opinion of this witness as to her ability to distinguish between right and wrong."

"Now, Dr. Orton, in the light of what you have been saying, in your opinion, would Mary be able to judge right and wrong?" Mr. Robson asked.

"She would."

"When you say 'wrong' are you thinking in terms of contrary to Law, or contrary to morals or doing morally wrong?"

"I would think that she would know unequivocally that it was contrary to Law."

"That what was contrary to Law?" asked the Judge.

"The acts that she was discussing with me. After all, she did admit that she was with Norma when the boy was strangled, and I think she knew these were contrary to Law."

"It comes to this," said the Judge. "Would she know that it was wrong to take another child by the neck and squeeze so that the child became unconscious? Let us take it that way."

"Yes, I think she would."

"Would she know," he continued, "that by taking a child by the neck and squeezing that she would result in [doing] injury to the child?"

"I think she would."

"Would she know that a killing was a crime?"

"Yes."

"My Lord, only one other matter," Harvey Robson said (bringing up an absolutely vital point). "Would she know that those things to which you have just answered a series of 'yes,' Dr. Orton, as being wicked?"

"I think you are trying to bring in the question of the degree of moral turpitude, a degree of wrongness from the moral aspect. Then I think one must say that only partially. I think her moral sense of virtue with her abnormality of mind is not so highly developed as the average child of eleven."

"Would she know that it ought not to be done?" the Judge asked again.

"Yes, I think so, My Lord."

It was of the utmost importance to *Norma's* defense to bring out, for the benefit of the Jury, the extent of Mary's domination over Norma and her capacity to manipulate others into doing what she wanted them to do. R. P. Smith cross-examined Dr. Orton for Norma:

". . . Is it your view of Mary that she is a dominating personality?"

"Yes, I think she is."

"And what might be called, by psychiatrists, a manipulator?"

"Yes."

The Judge, always intent on clarifying difficult technical terms for the benefit of the Jury, asked him to explain what this meant.

"I think it means this: a person who is capable of lying and deceit to gain their own ends and for instance . . . capable of playing off one girl against another . . . and so manipulating the circumstances whereby two girls [are brought to] quarrel, she really having been the instigator of the quarrel."

"She will use lies and deceit to gain her own ends?"

"Yes, sir."

"Using other people in the process?"

"If need be."

Forensic psychiatrist Dr. David Westbury was the second psychiatrist called on Mary's behalf. He saw Mary four times before her trial (and has seen her twice since).* "On the first two occasions (26 October and 2 November)," he said, "I was able to examine her fairly fully, that is to say to go through the whole procedure. But without going into it in depth, because she was

---

* His diagnosis as quoted here applies of course only to Mary's condition then.

sulky and only partly cooperative." (The other two times he went, Mary had meanwhile been visited by her mother, and refused to cooperate at all.)

"Did you form some tentative view at that time?" asked Harvey Robson.

"... I saw enough of her to form a definite view," Dr. Westbury replied. "... My opinion then was that there is no evidence of mental illness or severe subnormality, or subnormality of intelligence. But that she had however a serious disorder of personality which I called 'an unsocialized manipulative personality' that constitutes a persistent disorder of mind and has resulted in abnormal aggressive and seriously irresponsible conduct and required medical treatment. . . ."

"Did anything you say or hear subsequently alter your diagnosis?" asked the Judge.

"No, My Lord."

"You are still of the same opinion?"

"Exactly, sir."

"... You have been present throughout the trial?" asked Harvey Robson.

"I have, yes."

"Now, in your opinion, is Mary Bell now suffering from abnormality of mind?"

"Yes, sir."

"And, in your opinion, was she so suffering in May and July of this year?"

"Yes, sir."

"And, in your opinion, is that abnormality of mind attributable or arising from a condition of arrested or retarded development of mind or any inherent causes, or by disease or injury?"

"There are two parts to that, sir. It is a retarded development of mind."

"Yes."

"And this has been caused partly by genetic factors and partly by environmental factors."

"Just help me," said the Judge. "The words 'genetic factors,' what does that mean?"

"The inheritance of disease, My Lord."

"That would be inherited factors?"

"Inherited factors, yes."

"And, Doctor, in your opinion, does such abnormality as you say you consider existed substantially impair her mental responsibility for her acts?" asked Mr. Robson.

"Yes, sir, it does."

"In doing or being a party to the killing, assuming that that took place?"

"Yes, it does, sir."

"Just one matter, Doctor," Mr. Smith cross-examined on behalf of Norma. "Do you agree with Dr. Orton's view that Mary Bell is a manipulator?"

"That is my view, yes. That is my diagnosis."

". . . Did you say on page 7 of your report to the Director of Public Prosecutions that 'her social techniques are primitive and take the form of automatic denial, ingratiation, complaining, bullying, flight or violence'?"

"Yes, sir."

"From the history, you have gathered that she is a bully?"

"Yes, sir."

Both girls had been in Court throughout the whole of the trial, Norma much of the time off on thoughts of her own, but Mary listening intently. She became really agitated when the word "bully" was mentioned. This was a familiar term—and she resented it. She shook her head vehemently, whispered furiously to David Bryson, replied sharply when he told her to be still, turned around to her mother and made a furious face, and turned toward Norma mouthing angry words. It was one of her angriest moments during the trial and one to which she was to refer repeatedly in conversations with policewomen later.

Mr. Smith, ignoring Mary's behavior, continued his questions to Dr. Westbury. "She is violent?" he asked.

"Yes, sir."

"She is very dangerous?"

"Very."

"*Very* dangerous?"

"I think so, sir."

"I have no questions, My Lord," said Mr. Lyons. There was no reason for him to prolong the agony now. From the point of view of responsibility, guilt, and even degrees of guilt, the evidence of the two doctors had established and—more than was ever taken account of—explained the case.

The night following Norma's evidence, on Wednesday December 11, Policewoman Pauline Z. guarded Mary. An attractive young woman with a peculiarly Northern pugnacious kind of courage, she had made no secret of her compassion for Mary ever since she had first guarded her the night after her arrest in August. And Mary told everybody that Pauline was her favorite.

"A lot of girls never talked to her, you know," Pauline said. "They felt very uncomfortable about her. They wrote letters or read, and they talked as little as possible. Some felt in advance that she was a little horror, and they obeyed to the letter the instructions we had about not talking to her about the case and that. Except that some went further and didn't talk to her at all. Well, I felt as long as we had to spend eight hours together at a time, I might as well make them into as good eight hours for both of us as possible. She wanted to know all about you, you know; your parents, who you lived with, how you lived. If you had photographs her day was complete. I have a little dog and I have a snapshot of him and she just loved that. She loved animals."

But soon, with the relentless day-by-day accumulation of evidence, Mary was no longer able to continue her usual chatter. Norma's testimony and the compassionate and protective attitudes which Mary quite correctly sensed toward her among many in the courtroom were doubtlessly the springboard for her mounting terror.

"They won't be able to do anything to one of us without the other," she said to Pauline, half statement, half question, on that evening of 11 December. "After all, we were both . . ." She hesitated. ". . . In it. It would be unfair to punish one without the other." And later on in the sleepless night she said, "They are going to blame it all on me, because they'll say Norma's daft. . . ."

From the moment Mary had first heard herself being referred to as a psychopath, she had asked everyone of the policewomen, and some of the men, "What's a psychopath?" None of them told her, because none of them really knew. "Anyway, how can you explain it to a child?" one of them asked.

Policewoman Susan N. guarded her the night of 12 December after her first few hours in the witness stand. "I think it's all a dream," Mary said to her, "it's never happened. Do you think I'll ever go home again? I wish I was going to sleep in my own bed. Do you think I'll get thirty years? I think he is a horrible Judge if he gives me thirty years." (Thirty years were in her mind because of the sentence handed out to the "Train Robbers," a case that she often referred to.) "If I was a Judge," she continued, "and I had an eleven-year-old who'd done this, I'd give her eighteen months." The continuous tension was beginning to take its toll—her guard was down.

"Murder isn't that bad," Mary said, "we all die sometime anyway." "And then," Policewoman N. said, "she ended that sentence by saying, 'My mam gives me sweets every day.' " She shook her head. "That was funny, wasn't it? But I thought she was a canny kid. If you hadn't known what she'd done, you wouldn't have thought she could have."

The next day, Friday, 13 December, the seventh day of the trial, was devoted to the final speeches of the prosecution and defense.

Describing the case as "macabre and grotesque," Mr. Lyons told the Jury that eleven-year-old Mary had wielded over thirteen-year-old Norma "an evil and compelling influence almost like that of the fictional Svengali." "It has been a tortuous tunnel, has it not, that has led us through the grimmest and almost unfathomable recesses of juvenile thought, in which we have plumbed unprecedented depths of juvenile wickedness. In Norma you have a simple backward girl of subnormal intelligence. In Mary you have a most abnormal child, aggressive, vicious, cruel, incapable of remorse, a girl moreover possessed of a dominating personality, with a somewhat unusual intelligence and a degree of cunning that is almost terrifying."

Mr. Lyons repeated again, as he had already said in his opening address to the Jury, "I forecast that you might take the view that the younger girl—although two years and two months younger than the other—was nevertheless the cleverer and more dominating personality. . . ." He recalled that Mary had been described as a manipulator of little children and said that the Jury might think that, but for the fact that she and Norma lived next door to each other, the older girl, Norma, would never have been placed in the terrible position in which she now stood.

Mr. Lyons described again at some length the lies Mary told to the police and to the Court, and the "fiendishly cunning" way in which she tried to adapt her story to the evidence as she heard it presented in Court. He spoke of the statement to the police in which Mary had described how Norma had banged Brian Howe's head on a piece of wood and knocked him senseless. "She mentioned that in her evidence also," Mr. Lyons said, "but I am sure you will not have forgotten that she tried to play that down."

". . . Did you tell the police," Mr. Smith had asked Mary the day before, "that Norma had banged Brian's head on some wood or a corner of wood?"

"I didn't . . ." she faltered, "er . . . really mean to say 'bang.' She wasn't going like that."

"Did you say that Brian's head was banged on some wood?" Mr. Smith insisted.

"I might have done, but I never meant 'bang' really. . . ."

". . . If you had said it 'banged' on the wood, that would be a lie, would it?"

"Yes."

(Mr. Justice Cusack, in his summing up, was also to refer to these lies:

"There is reference in the statement," he said, "of banging Brian's head on a piece of wood. The prosecution say," said the Judge, "that here is another example of this remarkable child adapting her evidence by taking into account what has already been said in this court, and endeavoring to cope with it because the scientific evidence says that there was no blood, no hairs, any sign of anybody's head being banged forcibly upon that wood, and she had heard that evidence before she gave her own evidence. . . ."

Mr. Lyons then spoke of how Mary had said that it was Norma who had the Gillette blade and cut Brian's hair and ear.

("She tried to show me it was sharp," Mary had said in her statement. "She took the top of her dress where it was raggie and cut it—it made a slit.")

Mr. Smith had asked her, "Did you tell the police—Mr. Dobson —that same day that Norma had the razor blade?"

"Yes."

"And tried to cut Brian's leg and ear with it?"

"Yes."

"That wasn't true, was it?"

"It was."

"Did you tell the police that, to show you that the razor blade was sharp, Norma took the top of her dress and slit it with the razor?"

"She never slit it."

"Did you tell the police that she had?"

"I cannot remember, but . . ." She made a gesture with her arm. ". . . She went like that with it, but I . . . I don't know if it touched it or not."

"Just listen, Mary," and Mr. Smith read from her statement. "That is what you said to the police, isn't it?"

"I can't remember."

"You can, Mary, can't you?"

"No."

"If that is what you said, is it true, or a lie?"

"Well, she never slit it."

"So it would be a lie to say that she had, wouldn't it?"

"Yes."

"You have been listening very carefully to the evidence in this case, haven't you? Haven't you?" he repeated.

"Yes."

"And you understood the importance of the police evidence about Norma's clothing, didn't you? Didn't you?"

"Beg pardon?" she asked.

". . . You heard it said, didn't you, that Norma's clothing had been examined?"

"Er—yes."

"You heard it said that none of it was cut?"

"Yes."

"That is why you are saying now that you didn't tell the police that it was cut?"

"I never says that."

In his summing up, the Judge also read the Jury that part of Mary's statement: "No such slit has been found," he added, "though as you know all of Norma's clothing has been examined. And Mary, when asked about that, said she did not remember about the slit. . . ."

The lie Mr. Lyons discussed most fully was Mary's attempt (as the Judge said later) to cast the blame with regard to Brian Howe upon a totally innocent boy. "You will long remember," said Mr. Lyons, "the fiendish cunning with which she sought to lay the blame for Brian Howe's murder on a completely innocent boy of eight by saying she had seen him on the day of Brian's death and giving the police a most detailed description of the clothes the boy was wearing and by saying, 'A. was covered with grass and flowers.' . . . Of all the innocent children in the area, she picked on a little boy who, in fact, *had* played with Brian Howe. . . ."

Mr. Smith, the day before, had reminded Mary of the day after Brian had been killed—a Thursday.

"You were being asked some questions. Did you say something about a boy called A.? . . . Did you try and blame A. for Brian Howe's death?"

"Yes, sir."

"Why?"

"To get me and Norma out of trouble, sir."

"But you realized it might get A. into trouble, did you?"

"Not serious trouble."

"Some trouble. Everything you said about A. was a lie, wasn't it?"

"Not everything."

"Did you see A. on the Wednesday that Brian was killed?"

"Er—no."

"No. So when you told the police you did, that was a lie, wasn't it?"

"Yes, but all of it wasn't a lie."

"Well, I will go through it. Did you tell the police that A. was standing by himself on the Wednesday in Delaval Road?"

"Not Delaval Road—er—by Stainsbury's fence."

(It could not escape the Court's attention that she remembered sufficiently precisely the details of her own statement made five months previously—a lie though it was—to correct Mr. Smith. Mary could never resist her impulse to show how clever she was, even if it worked against her own advantage.)

"The back lane towards Delaval Road, did you say that?"

"Yes."

"That was a lie?"

"Yes."

"Did you say he was covered with grass and little purply flowers?"

"Yes."

"That was a lie?"

"Yes. . . . I don't know."

"You don't know?"

"But it is true about I saw him try to cut the cat's whiskers and that."

"Let me come to that, Mary, in a moment. I will give you every chance. You say you had seen A. playing with Brian Howe a lot?"

"Yes."

"Was that true?"

"Yes."

"That was true. Did you say that you had seen A. hit Brian for no reason at all?"

"Yes."

"Was that true?"

"Yes. . . ."

". . . Was it true that A. had hit Brian on the face and neck?" he asked again.

"Well, he always used to hit him and . . ."

"On the neck?"

"No, on the face because he always used to . . ." she faltered.

"I'm sorry—he always?"

"He was always pelting stones and that."

"If you told the police that A. hit Brian on the neck, would that be true or a lie?"

"Well, sometimes he hits him with his hand like that, not actually on the neck [but] when he goes like that to him, his hands hits his neck."

"Did you say to the police you had seen A. play with a pair of scissors?"

"Yes."

"Was that true?"

"I have seen him."

"With a pair of scissors like the ones in this box . . .?"

". . . I have saw him playing with a pair, but not like that."

"Did you try to tell the police that you had seen A. playing with a pair of scissors, like silver-colored and something wrong with the scissors, like one leg was either broken or bent?"

"Yes."

"Were you meaning to describe these scissors?"

"Yes."

"Why?"

"Because they are the scissors which Norma had used."

"Why did you say to the police that A. had been seen playing with those scissors?"

"I don't know. . . ."

". . . It was a lie, wasn't it?"

"Yes."

"Didn't you think it was very naughty indeed to tell that lie?"

"Yes."

". . . Did you tell the police that you had seen A. trying to cut a cat's tail off with those scissors?"

"Not those."

"Did you say to the police you had seen A. trying to cut a cat's tail off?"

"Yes, I have."

"Was that true?"

"Yes."
"With those scissors?"
"No."

"She admitted," said Mr. Lyons in his final speech, "most of the things she said in her statement [about this boy] were lies. But she insisted in her evidence that that little boy had been seen to cut cat's whiskers and had hurt Brian Howe in the neck. If it is true that he ever hit Brian, doesn't that make her attempt to incriminate him all the more wicked and horrible? One shudders to think of what might have happened to that eight-year-old boy if he had been in the area that afternoon instead of being, by happy chance, with other people six miles away at Newcastle Airport, where a group of people could say they saw him."

(A further tragic dimension was added to the events of the trial when, the Sunday following Mr. Lyons' final speech, and the day before the Judge's summing up, during which Mr. Justice Cusack—if this was necessary—put the final stamp on clearing that little boy A. totally of any suspicion, this child's mother died in a street accident.)

Mr. Smith, defending Norma, made an impassioned speech to the Jury, saying that, "To be an innocent bystander when a crime is committed is not to have criminal responsibility." He said Norma admitted going back to see the body of one of the murdered boys; she said it was naughty to do so, and she knew what a terrible thing had been done at the concrete blocks. But what child, he asked, would not tell a lie to get herself out of that situation? There was a difference between a childish lie and the sort told by the other accused girl who tried to get a little boy into trouble. Mary's lies were wicked and were told by a little girl, he said, who one was tempted to describe as evil. Norma had gone back to the "Tin Lizzie" because Mary had asked her to. If Mary asked her to do anything, said Mr. Smith, the probability was that she would do it.

"It is not part of my duty," he said in conclusion, "to black-guard Mary, or blacken her character. Although this is a ghastly case, and although some of the evidence may have made you ill, it is possible to feel sorry for Mary. She had a bad start in life. . . .

Her illness—psychopathic personality—is said to be the result of
genetic and environmental factors. It's not her fault she grew up
this way; it's not her fault she was born. . . ."

The last two days of the trial Mary was probably more in need
of warmth and compassion than at any other time since her arrest.
Pauline Z. and Susan N., two of the three policewomen who
guarded Mary during the weekend, were particularly sympathetic
toward her. The feelings of the third, Policewoman Brenda M.,
about Mary was more complicated: like many others, she was
curious but at the same time repelled by her and disliked herself
for having these feelings.

"I didn't like her," she said, with pretended off-handedness.
"Guarding her was just a job, like any other, except that I didn't
like it." She came on duty at eight A.M. on Sunday morning. "She
was still in bed then," Brenda said. "Then she got up, had her bath
and got dressed. I didn't want to talk to her. I started to write
letters almost as soon as I arrived. It was snowing outside. She
asked me to play a game of cards, snap. I played with her," she
shrugged her shoulders. "There wasn't any harm in it I thought, so I
played with her. I hate cards, but it was better than nothing. Then
I went back to letter writing and she went and stood at the window
and looked out at the snow."

The quiet of the scene must have accentuated Mary's isolation
and perhaps her fear. "She was talking as she stood there at the
window," said Brenda. "She said how nice it looked and that she
wished she could go for a walk in the new snow. 'Well you can't,'
I said. 'I would like to write a letter as well,' Mary said after a
while. 'Can I have paper and pencil?' "

Brenda gave it to her and she wrote, sitting on her bed and resting the paper on a comic. "She wrote for quite a long time,"
Brenda said. "Three single pages on lined paper, in her big handwriting. And then she just sat there, with the letter on her lap. I
thought to myself, 'I wonder who she wrote to, this long letter.' "

"I've written a letter as well," she finally said.

"I know," Brenda answered. "Who did you write to then?"

"I wrote to God." There was a sort of pause and then she said,
"Would you like to read my letter to God?"

"I said, 'Yes, I would,' " Brenda said. "I read the letter once and then again," she recalled, "and then once more. It seemed so funny that she should have written such a letter. It went something like this:

> Dear God,
>   I would like to thank you for the snow. I would like to thank you for the frost because it makes pretty patterns on the window. I would like to thank you for the springtime, and the pretty flowers. For the sunshine and the trees and the rain. I would like to thank you for the world being a lovely place because you have made it so nice. I would like to be a nun because nuns are good. But I don't think I will be. That is all I have to say. Thank you God for everything, love May.

"I handed it back to her," Brenda M. said. "She put it down on the bed and picked up a storybook. After half an hour or so I turned the TV on and it didn't work right—the picture was wrong. 'I can fix it,' Mary said and came across toward the TV. Then half there, she stopped, turned around, walked back to the bed, picked up the letter, and tore it up. I was sorry," said Brenda. "I'd have liked to have that letter."

On the morning of Monday, 16 December, Mr. Harvey Robson finished his final speech to the jury.

"It is . . . very easy," he said, "to revile a little girl, to liken her to Svengali without pausing even for a moment to ponder how the whole sorry situation has come about. Although you may think that this last is the most disturbing thought of all, I believe that in the course of your deliberations you, as a Jury of this city, will be able to discover some measure of pity. . . ."

Mr. Justice Cusack began his summing up, which was to take more than four hours, after the usual ten-minute mid-morning adjournment. The public and press galleries were unusually crowded. The Waiting Jurors' gallery which had been set aside for the press and V.I.P.s was occupied by a large contingent of foreign correspondents, for most of whom this was the first day spent at the trial. Nonetheless, twenty-four hours later, with the unfortunate glibness of sensational press reporting, they were to discuss it knowledgeably in headlined front-page articles all over the world and describe Mary as a "bad seed," an "evil birth," and a "child monster."

... Don't lump the two girls together in respect of any particular count [said the Judge]. It is quite open to you to find different verdicts with regard to each of the two girls, if you think that is right. But your approach must not be, and I am sure it will not be, to say either on the one hand, without really considering the evidence, 'Poor little girls, we will let them go,' or, on the other hand, 'Nasty little girls, we will convict them'. Your task, I'm afraid, is much more detailed than that: you must consider separately what is proved with regard to each girl, and with regard to each charge in the indictment. They are charged, as you know only too well, with Murder, indeed with two Murders, and the prosecution say that each girl is guilty of those Murders. The situation is this: If any unlawful killing occurs and two people participate in it, it does not matter whose hand actually does the deed. If one person commits the act which causes the death, and the other is present and knows what is intended and what is happening and is either helping or ready to help, that person is equally guilty. Help may be given, not only actively, but by keeping a look-out; heading other people off or helping to attract or to detain the victim.

If however, the person is there as a mere spectator and not there to help and not giving any help, that person cannot be held responsible. It may be wrong that a person should remain as a spectator to something that is to most people obviously repugnant, but it is not a criminal offense until they are participating in what is going on in some degree. . . . For the purpose of these two charges, and that is all you are concerned with, the prosecution must prove in each case that the boy who died was killed by a *voluntary* and *unlawful* act, and that the person who committed that act, or was party to it, intended at the time the act was committed either to kill, or, if not to kill, at least to cause serious bodily injury, realizing that that serious bodily injury could result in death. But of course, before you convict either of these two girls, the prosecution must prove that it was she who did the act, or

was party to it. . . . Pay attention to the word "voluntary" . . .
it means that what occurred was not accidental, such as might
happen if a person's hand slipped involuntarily and did injury
to somebody else. Secondly, and much more importantly, if
you find that one girl did kill, or participate in the killing, but
that at the time she may have been so under the domination
of the other girl that she had no will or mind of her own, then
she would not be acting "voluntarily" and you ought not to
convict her. I do not mean simply that she was persuaded, or
that she was reluctant. What I mean is that she had reached a
point at which she had really ceased to have an independent
existence, and ceased to have an independent will of her
own. . . .

. . . . There is an alternative to Murder open to you here on
each charge, depending on the view which you take of the
facts. The alternative is this, to acquit of Murder but to convict instead of Manslaughter. . . . Murder requires an intent to
kill or to do serious bodily injury knowing that death may
result. Manslaughter does not require that intent at all. It is
sufficient if there is a voluntary, unlawful and dangerous act
which results in death. . . .

The Law presumes that a child under the age of ten does
not know the difference between right and wrong and is incapable of committing any criminal offence. . . . These two
children are between 10 and 14. . . . The Law which applies
to them is this:

It is still presumed that the child does not know the difference between right and wrong, and it is wholly presumed that
the child is incapable of committing a criminal offence, but
that presumption instead of being absolute is rebuttable. That
is to say, it can be disproved by the prosecution and displaced
by evidence presented to you. It can be rebutted by proving
that the child, though young, has reached a state of development which enables that child to distinguish between good and
evil, between right and wrong, and to appreciate that it is
doing wrong when it is doing so.

By "wrong" I do not mean just being naughty, which all
children are at some time. I mean wicked. Something seriously
and gravely wrong. If the child does appreciate that, that
child can be convicted of a criminal offence, but not otherwise.

The degree of understanding required to make a child of this age responsible in Law is sometimes referred to as having "a guilty mind" . . . but . . . the mere fact that a child commits an act which in an adult would be a criminal offence is not evidence in itself that that child had a guilty mind. You have to look outside the act itself to see if that child had an understanding of right and wrong, an appreciation of what is good and what is bad so as to make that child responsible in the eyes of the Law. . . .

Mary had listened attentively. She had heard the Judge say at the end of the afternoon session that he was very nearly at the end of his summing up and would hand the case to the Jury certainly by eleven o'clock the next morning.

"What would be the worst that could happen to me?" she asked Pauline. "Would they hang me?"

The question made Pauline feel sick. "I know I wasn't supposed to talk about the case," she said, "but if she asked a question like that, well, it didn't seem right not to answer. You couldn't not answer, could you? I said, no, they didn't hang little girls. Yes, I liked May. I didn't know what was wrong," she said, "how it had happened. But there had to be something wrong—something had to have happened to her that made her do this. . . .

"She asked me later would they send her to prison for thirty years? I said that they didn't send little girls to prison either. But then she started talking of going home as if, you know, they'd just *have* to let her go home, and so I told her that they'd send her somewhere where she'd be safe and looked after. It was fairer to tell her the truth, to sort of prepare her, you know . . .

"I know she liked me very much. I don't know why. And I liked her. When it was all over—later—she sent me a Christmas card with a poem she wrote, but I didn't write back. There is no future in it—no future in liking her. . . ." Pauline said sadly. "It wouldn't be right."

A Christmas poem

I looked out the window one night
Oh what a beautiful sight—

There was a shrill call, it was
from the wall. Help! Help! Please
let me out a squicky voice
began to shout. I've ate an
hamburger. But you'll commite
Murder if you don't let me
out.

Tuesday, 17 December was a cold, bleak day in Newcastle. The two girls, their parents and relatives, looked pale and strained. And even Betty Bell was quiet.

Dr. David Westbury had sat in the office of the Clerk of Assize that morning and almost all of the previous day, telephoning mental hospitals all over England in an effort to find somewhere Mary could be sent, if she was convicted. "Nobody would say yes," he said. "At one moment I wasn't at all sure that I wouldn't be taking her home with me; it was incredible, quite incredible."

It wasn't only the hospitals who felt they didn't have suitable provisions or adequate security arrangements to contain this child. The Remand Centre, which Children's Officer Brian Roycroft selected as best suited to shelter her provisionally after the trial, also said it could not have her. And it was only after barrister Peter Robinson, the Clerk of Assize,* was asked by the Children's Department and the police to speak to the Remand Centre on the legal position, that preparations for her care immediately subsequent to the trial, if she was convicted, could be begun. It was not deemed necessary to make any similar inquiries for Norma Bell.

The Jury retired at 10:40 and returned at 2:15 P.M. The room was utterly silent. Norma leaned forward, her mouth as usual a little open. Mary sat straight as a rod, one finger as usual in her mouth.

The Clerk of Assize rose from his seat just below the Judge's

---

* In the recent reorganization of the administration of justice the country was divided into four circuits, each headed by a Circuit Administrator (in each case a distinguished barrister). Mr. Peter Robinson, who was responsible for much of the groundwork of this streamlining, was appointed Circuit Administrator for the North Eastern Circuit.

dais. "Members of the Jury... are you all agreed upon your verdict?"

"We are."

"On the first count of this indictment, do you find Norma Bell guilty or not guilty of the murder of Martin Brown?"

"Not guilty."

"Do you find her guilty or not guilty of Manslaughter?"

"Not guilty."

Norma began to smile and excitedly turned around to her parents. Her father laid his hand on her head and gently turned her back to face the Judge and Jury.

"Do you find Mary Flora Bell guilty or not guilty of the murder of Martin Brown?"

"Guilty of Manslaughter," said the Foreman, his next words hard to hear because of Betty Bell's immediate loud sobs, "because of diminished responsibility."

The Judge interrupted. "That is not guilty of Murder?" He emphasized the "Not" and "Murder." "But guilty of Manslaughter on the grounds of diminished responsibility?"

"Yes, sir."

"On the second count of the indictment," asked Peter Robinson, "do you find Norma Bell guilty or not guilty of the murder of Brian Howe?"

"Not guilty."

"Do you find her guilty or not guilty of Manslaughter?"

"Not guilty," the Foreman said, and this time Norma's father smiled, her mother began to cry, but with the discipline and good manners everyone had noticed throughout the trial, both of them shook their heads reprovingly when Norma turned to look at them and indicated for her to sit still.

"Do you find Mary Flora Bell guilty or not guilty of the murder of Brian Howe?" asked Mr. Robinson.

"Guilty of Manslaughter because of diminished responsibility," the Foreman said again.

Mr. Justice Cusack remarked briefly about Norma who—he said —he felt sure would still be dealt with, wisely, by the magistrates of the Juvenile Court for the offense of breaking into the Nursery.

Then—less than ten minutes after the verdict had been passed—he pronounced sentence on Mary.

Mary had begun to cry in a tentative sort of way when she heard the verdict, but no one touched her. Billy Bell sat, leaning forward, his chin cupped in his hands as he had throughout the trial. Betty Bell, her handkerchief already wet, sobbed and dabbed her eyes. Mary's grandmother, her face frozen in misery and disbelief, sat motionless. Only her Solicitor, David Bryson, sitting next to her, bent down and whispered to her when she cried. Outside of this brief contact, it seemed as if there was a gulf between her and those around her. If they cried or mourned, or suffered—it was for themselves, not for her. She seemed alone.

> The child need not stand [said Mr. Justice Cusack], and I shall adress myself to the matters without specifically addressing myself to her.
>
> On the verdict of the Jury in this case, Mary Bell has been found guilty on two counts of Manslaughter. The verdict is one of Manslaughter because the Jury found that at the material time she had Diminished Responsibility. Otherwise their verdict would have been one of Murder. In the result it means that this child, now aged only eleven, has in fact been found to have killed two other children.
>
> My difficulty is to know what order should now be made by the Court.
>
> Having regard to the medical evidence put before me, I should have been willing to make . . . a hospital order, so that she could have been taken to a mental institution to receive the appropriate treatment . . . accompanied . . . by a restriction order . . . which would have meant that she could not have been released from a hospital without . . . special . . . authority.
>
> Unhappily, I am not able to make such an order because one of the requirements of the Mental Health Act is that I must be satisfied, firstly, that there is a hospital to which she could go; secondly, that she could be admitted to that institution within twenty-eight days.
>
> Evidence has been given to me by Dr. Westbury . . . that it has been impossible to find any institution to which she can be admitted for treatment under the Mental Health Act. . . .

The responsible Government Department requires time to consider what they wish to do. No specific time is indicated.

I make no criticisms of that Department. But it is a most unhappy thing that, with all the resources of this country, whether it be the Ministry of Social Security, or the Home Office, it appears that no hospital is available which is suitable for the accommodation of this girl and to which she could be admitted.

All the requirements, apart from the one I have mentioned, of the Mental Health Act have been satisfied, and I am merely precluded from doing what I would otherwise do by the fact that no such hospital is available. No evidence has been put before me which would enable me, therefore, to make an order of the kind I would wish to make.

I must, therefore, turn to other matters.

If this had been the case of an adult, having regard to the evidence put before me, which I fully accept, that this is a child who is dangerous, I should have felt obliged to impose a life sentence for the reason that, not only did the gravity of the offences warrant it, but that there was evidence of mental disease or abnormality which made it impossible to determine the date when the person concerned could be safely released.

It is an appalling thing that, in a child as young as this, one has to determine such matter, but I am entirely satisfied that, anxious as I am to do everything for her benefit, my primary duty is to protect other people for the reasons that I have indicated.

I take the view that there is a very grave risk to other children if in fact she is not closely watched and every conceivable step taken to see that she does not do again what it has been found that she did do.

In the case of a child of this age no question of imprisonment arises, but I have the power to order a sentence of Detention, and it seems to me that no other method of dealing with her, in the circumstances, is suitable.

I therefore have to turn to what length of detention should be imposed. I say at once that, if an undeterminate period is imposed, as in the case of a life sentence of imprisonment, that does not mean that the person concerned is kept in custody indefinitely, or for the rest of their natural lives. It means that the position can be considered from time to time and, if it becomes safe to release that person, that person can be released.

For that reason the sentence of the Court concurrently in respect of these two matters upon Mary Bell is a sentence of Detention and the Detention will be for Life.

The child Mary Bell may be taken out of Court.

The feeling of relief that it was over was almost palpable in the courtroom; few had been untouched, few quite neutral, few quite objective. If there were those who felt that there was something terribly wrong, no one—aside from the few who could not and would not speak—knew what. What we felt above all was relief—a terrible gratitude that it was at last over.

PART THREE

THE PAST

"Take the Thing Away from Me"

However inured to violence we are in our time, violence done to a child causes a momentary pause—a stillness in our minds. And then we turn away, return to our daily life, thank God it wasn't us, or ours: those to whom these things happen, or who cause them, are "different," *must* be different.

Horror had dawned very slowly in Newcastle in August that year. The intolerable, the unacceptable was reduced to platitudes and pushed aside: it was "they" who were to blame. "They"—the slums. "They"—the perennial weak, the inadequate.

Unprecedented in a country famous for its murder trials and literature, the press and public not only resisted but rejected the case of Mary Bell. "I don't want to read about it," people said, "it's too horrible."

And yet, was that the reason? Was this case any more horrific than the interminably dissected and described child murders by Brady and Hindley on the Yorkshire Moors in 1965? Was it more terrible than the slaughter of the Clutter family in a small town in the Middle West of America? Was it really worse than the murderous rampage of the drug addict Manson clan, written up for months in all its details?

What was it that made the murders of these two small boys more unbearable than any of these others? What was it people did not want to know or face? Why was it that a traditionally compassionate public, a punctiliously fair court, an exceptionally enlightened city administration, and a press renowned all over the world for its sense of civic responsibility asked few questions and did not demand an inquiry or protest against outmoded legal proceedings? Why did they not reject the theories of evil birth and insist on being informed not *that* but *why* an eleven-year-old child, who had grown up in an ordinary English working-class street, in a city with all the facilities of a modern society, in a good school with well-trained teachers, and who, not at all a neglected or unloved child, was a member of a large united family, should have an irresistible compulsion to kill?

What was it, above all, that prevented Mary's many relatives from seeking advice and help when for so many years both were so manifestly needed? Could it have been foreseen? Could it have been prevented?

Mrs. McC., Mary's grandmother, her aunts Cath, Isa, Audrey, and Margaret; her uncles, Philip and Jack, are all intelligent, hard-working people who love Mary deeply. All of them could have helped. Each one could have told what combination of circumstances finally drove this girl to commit murder. "It's all of us," Mary's aunt Audrey said afterwards. "We are all to blame, aren't we?" Long before these tragic events, in an agonizing conflict of loyalties, hoping against hope that time alone could be the healer, they had made their unhappy choice of silence.

Cath remembered how "Sometime before all that trouble with May," her sister Betty had sat in her gaily wall-papered kitchen, a sunlit room in a pleasant, small house in a village north of Newcastle not far from the sea. On her lap was a book she carries with her wherever she goes. It was—they said—always within reach at home, in her handbag on her many wanderings, under her pillow wherever she slept. Her father won it at a raffle and gave it to her when she was small. It is the fairy tale of Hansel and Gretel, with pull-out pictures.

Betty ("she tells tales, one doesn't know *what* to believe") had just been telling Cath that she'd been to see "the doctors" at Newcastle General Hospital and that they'd told her she was very sick and had "only two years to live." She opened the book and pointed to a sealed and addressed envelope between the pages. "That letter is for you," she said, "if I die."

"What is it then?" Cath asked.

"It'll tell the whole story," was all Betty said.

The story started long ago, and Betty Bell, whom so many people have loved and protected and whom no one realized that *she* needed help when she was small, is the most important person in her daughter Mary's life, and always was.

Betty McC. was born in Gateshead in 1939, a beautiful child and her father's favorite. The other children in the family—all exceptionally good-looking—were Cath, the eldest, Philip, the only boy, and tender, graceful Isa, the youngest by six years. (A boy, Benjamin, born in 1940, died in infancy.)

The McC.s, living in Glasgow, were a happy family. The father, Philip, was a miner who never missed a day's work until he fell ill with T.B. in 1943. The mother, Mrs. McC., has a flashing sense of humor, is a meticulous housekeeper, and like many Scottish women gave great care to her children's education. Well-taught and well-brought up, all of them have turned out highly articulate, with a poetic turn of mind.

The family were Roman Catholics but, although they went to Mass and the children attended Sunday school, they were not fanatical about their Church and, as about the rest of their daily lives, there was a sense of humor in the way they approached religion which later enabled some of the children, without pangs of guilt and conscience, to marry happily outside the Church.

"Our Dad was a very good man," says Isa. "He was a very religious man. He never swore. He'd never stand for any man to say a swear word in front of my mother."

From 1943, when Betty was four, their father could no longer work and had to live an invalid's life. His wife, quietly competent, took over. She worked mostly in hospitals, in a variety of jobs ranging from doctor's receptionist to cleaner. Money was scarce, but in a part of Glasgow where unemployment and extreme poverty were the norm they were not desperately poor. They were "respectable." They were always clean, always warmly dressed, they always ate their fill. The children helped to look after each other, but it was their mother who did the cooking, and brushed, sewed, and polished at night and weekends. "I never made them do any housework," she says now, "perhaps that was wrong."

Betty was the light of her father's life. "She was that religious, and good, and always with the saints' pictures and rosaries all over the place," says her mother. "We all thought she was going to be a nun." But little Betty was not happy. Perhaps it was because of her father's illness, or the fact that her mother went out to work, or because, when she was just five, her mother became pregnant and Betty suddenly realized there was going to be another baby. Whatever it was, something had begun to happen to her, for around that time she began to refuse to eat with the family. They would urge, persuade, beseech, and finally punish her—"Mam would tan her bottom"—but nothing helped. The only way she would eat was if her mother put food in a corner for her, behind a chair. Then, hidden away, she would squat there and eat.

This happened toward the end of the war, when child guidance clinics would not immediately spring to mind—not even for someone like Mrs. McC. who worked in hospitals. "I suppose," she says, in a despairing voice, "the only way all this [now] could have been prevented—the only right thing would have been if *Betty* had been under a psychiatrist since she was small. But how could I know that it was wrong if a child didn't want to eat with her family?"

She was so good otherwise—they thought she'd outgrow this silliness.

"I think our Dad always favored Betty," says Isa. "Though he was always tender with both of us. I remember Betty sitting on one of his knees and me on the other." But she also remembered that fairy-tale book. "I loved that book," she said. "It was the only thing our Dad ever won in a raffle. I wanted it too, but Betty got it." Their father loved Betty's drawings. "She was so good at drawing," says Isa without envy. "But she'd always hide her drawings while she was doing them," she remembers. "They were always of religious things: she always drew nuns, and altars and graves and cemeteries."

Betty outgrew the habit of eating on the floor in corners but then would eat only if her family pretended not to see her, or if she could pretend to steal the food. Again they comforted themselves. "It's just her silly ways. Other kids don't eat properly either. She'll get over it as she did over the other business."

It was not all sweetness when the children were naughty. "Of course, now it's different," Isa says to her mother, and smiles, "but when I was small I was that afeared of you."

"Of me?" her mother asked, astonished, and it did seem extraordinary that any child should have been even momentarily afraid of this small woman whose stern exterior hides so much warmth and humor.

"If Mam promised us something," Isa said, "we could be sure as houses we'd get it—presents or hidings. Remember, Mam, when Betty and I were naughty in the streets when we were all out shopping and you'd promise us a hiding when we got home?"

They'd get their spanking two or three hours later, at home. "I couldn't very well give them a hiding in the street, could I?" Mrs. McC. said with spirit.

"Betty and I would stand in front of the mirror with our skirts up and look at our bottoms and say, 'Mine is redder'—'No, mine is.' But we were never beaten," Isa says later, "only spanked. I don't think it did us any harm." Isa is exceptionally sensitive and perceptive. "I think Betty and Cath like to think they were beaten," she said, thoughtfully, "but they weren't really. Why, my mother never had the strength for it."

"Betty was that fond of our father," Isa said, "but she loved our mother too. She was always waiting for her when she was out, the kettle on the boil and her slippers ready."

"She could be that funny," her mother said. "Remember that time," she asked Isa, "when she broke a cup over your brother's head just because I said as a joke, 'Break a cup over his head'?" Even now, they are a family who laugh a great deal. The grandmother is very much a part of each married child's family circle. There can be no doubt that they were just as gay and just as close fifteen and twenty years ago, certainly until the day Philip McC. died, finally it seems, of a heart condition, not T.B. "It was in 1953," Isa said. She was then seven, Betty going on fourteen. "They sent him home from hospital and said they could do nothing more for him." As long as he believed he could survive he fought it with equanimity. "It was so very strange," Isa said softly. "I'd never heard him say a bad word, ever. But in the last six weeks of his life he suddenly became quite different and said the most dreadful things. I remember the day he died; it was a Sunday morning. We heard a sort of croak from his room and when we went in he lay there dead. We were all terribly upset but Betty was demented. That afternoon there was a Sunday School treat and we had to go. We didn't want to, but they wanted us out of the way, so we had to. We walked two and two, Betty and me holding hands last of the crocodile, both of us crying. Then Betty sat down on the grass verge and said 'I'm not going,' and I said, 'If you aren't I am not either.' But then the Sunday School teacher came and made us go.

"The next day, Monday, my dad was lying on the bed in his room, Betty locked herself in the wardrobe and wouldn't come out. I think it took my mother an hour and a half to get her out.

"Afterwards, for a long time," Isa said, "she started going around with her shoulders pulled in and her head down, her eyes to the floor; our mum couldn't do anything about getting her to straighten up."

Isa remembers a day about a year later, when Betty was still fourteen. "She had been punished at school for doing something wrong; they said she wasn't allowed on the school bus. She had no money for the fare—so she had to walk the six miles home. To get home, she had to cross a field, or a golf course where, only a little while before that, three women had been killed. It so happened the doctor was at our house, I can't remember why—perhaps for me, or my mother. But anyway, Betty arrived in a state of collapse. It was awful. Her face was white, she was shaking all over with fear. She had picked up a stick; she was holding it in her hand; her fingers were so tight around it, the doctor had to almost break them open to get the stick away from her. He gave her pills to calm her down and we put her to bed."

"She changed," her older sister Cath said, "she'd become wild. My mother would wait up for her nights, give her a hiding when she was due home at nine and come in at two—what else could she do?"

Once the pattern—the instinct to maintain respectability at all cost, to hide family troubles from outside—is established, what is there to do for a woman trying to bring up four children on her own?

"Very soon after our dad died, Betty began to steal," Isa said.

"On one occasion she stole a purse from our aunt. Our uncle came to the house. . . . He took her to the bathroom and gave her a real hiding to make her own up. She did. And she gave the purse back."

By now Betty had begun to work, first of all in shops, later in a pickle factory.

"She stole in the shop too. But you know . . ." Isa sounds surprised even now, "she'd give all the things she stole away to other people. Slippers, bags, all that sort of thing. She never gave any to our mother because she was afraid of her, but she gave all kinds of things to our aunt, who finally got frightened and brought the lot back to our mum. Mum took the things back to the shop and Betty got the sack."

"We didn't know what it was," Cath said. "We were that worried. You know, Betty has always thought our mother doesn't like her. But it wasn't true. I sometimes thought our mum loved her more than any of us. She was that beautiful and that spoiled."

Betty's mother held her arms in front of her, in the gesture of an embrace. "I always wanted to surround Betty, to keep her safe." Mrs. McC. loves deeply but not demonstratively. The safety the family provided—perhaps the kind of safety it was—was not enough for Betty. She needed more.

When she was not quite fifteen, she fell in love with a boy, "Jimmy or Johnny." And soon she thought she was pregnant. She wrote a letter about it to somebody and her mother saw the letter. A classic situation which no doubt had the usual consequence of deep hurt, bitter recriminations, anger, and fear. But, even so, this was by no means an unenlightened or intolerant family. Betty was about to have her fifteenth birthday and anger was to be forgotten for that day.

Cath recalls the day before the birthday. "We were going out to get her a present, Mum and I. Betty carried on something terrible. But she was always jealous, always having tantrums, so we just went. . . . 'That's right,' Betty shouted, 'Go on out with your favorite, I don't care.' "

"I came home from school," Isa says—she was nine then; she knew her mother and Cath had gone out shopping to buy Betty a birthday surprise. "My mother had told Betty to give me my tea when I got in from school. I remember Betty pouring the tea, and, instead of pouring it into the cup, she poured it into the saucer, very slowly, and she had a piece of paper there which she pressed into my hand, and it said on it that she had taken fifty phenobarbitones—my mum was taking them for her nerves. She hadn't taken fifty but fifteen, but she had written in a funny way fifty, perhaps her hand had slipped . . ." Isa ran for help.

"When we got back," said Cath, "an ambulance rushed past us. We didn't know Betty was in it. She'd taken an overdose. She was very bad . . ."

Shortly after this Cath married Jack S., a miner, and the young couple moved south to a small mining town in Northumberland, an hour north of Newcastle. Perhaps Mrs. McC., deeply attached to each of her children, found it difficult to envisage being so far away from her eldest daughter who had been her chief moral support since her husband's death, or perhaps she thought a complete change of environment would help Betty—always the main worry of her life. Anyway, the family followed Cath.

They moved 250 miles south of Glasgow, to Gateshead, then an industrial overspill area on the periphery of Newcastle upon Tyne (now developed into the largest town between Newcastle and London), and found a flat at 23 Redheughbridge Road, just across Redheugh Bridge. one of the five bridges that spans the River Tyne. To the young McC.s the move must have been quite exciting. Looking left out of the front windows of their new home, they would have seen the bridge with its unceasing traffic, the railway lines next to it, the river and boats underneath. And in the distance the factory chimneys of Newcastle, many of which continued to belch smoke and flames at night when the red of the fires and the gold of the city lights were reflected in the water of the Tyne. Their immediate surroundings were anything but colorful. Across from No. 23 were the warehouses of Tait and Kelly Ltd, Builders and Contractors, Repairs to Property. To the right, on a corner building at the intersection with Redheugh Road, was a large advertisement for the *News of the World,* and beyond, straight up a steep hill, the continuation of Redheughbridge Road, the little red brick houses all exactly the same as the one their flat was in: with flimsy curtains, peeling paint, and broken hinges.

"But the flat was nice," Cath says, "my mother kept it nice."

Betty went to work as a machinist in a rope factory. "She was that 'individual,' " Isa says, her voice now too reflecting the love and admiration she always felt for Betty. "She could never wear a dress just as she bought it. She always added a bow or something."

"She was beautiful," her mother said again. "She won all the beauty competitions, she might have gone into the nationals." Photographs of Betty at that time show a spectacularly good-looking girl, with a luxuriant head of long shiny black hair, a small delicate face, huge blue eyes, a small waist, and long slim legs— very much the way Isa looks now.

"There's no telling where she might have got to," Isa says sadly.

In the familiar environment of Glasgow, surrounded by relatives and friends they had known for a lifetime, there had been some attempt to control Betty's life. In Gateshead it became almost impossible. Perhaps, had they at last sought professional advice on any level, Betty's life might have developed differently. The victories in the local beauty contests could conceivably have led on to a different, richer, and, who knows, more ordered life. But it did not happen that way. The change from one city, one street, one job to another made no difference and could not cure the trouble, or break the already established pattern: Betty's continuous and restless search for new faces and new places. . . .

On 26 May 1957 at Dilston Hall Hospital, Corbridge, Gateshead, seventeen-year-old Betty McC. had a baby. "Take the 'thing' away from me," Betty reportedly cried, jerking her body away when the baby was put into her arms minutes after it was born.

"We couldn't believe it. We just couldn't believe it," says Isa sadly.

The beginning of life for Mary Flora Bell.

But post-natal depression is a familiar phenomenon. For someone in need of love, a baby of her own is often a stabilizing influence. And irrespective of their dismay at Betty's initial reaction, this was no doubt what her family hoped and prayed for: it could not fail to happen, they thought, not when the baby was so pretty, so bouncy, and so bright.

"Oh, she was that bonny," say her aunts who, just like her

grandmother, doted on Mary from the moment they set eyes on her.

But Betty appeared to feel no joy.

Betty went back to work, Isa was at school, Cath came over often with her own baby boy, and Mrs. McC. looked after Mary. Betty was not maternal, but everybody was working, the babies were healthy, and life seemed good enough.

"Betty was that gay . . ." Cath says, "that funny . . . and she was that good a dancer . . ." Around Christmas that year, Cath and her husband Jack met Betty's boyfriend, Billy Bell, and Betty and Billy told them they were going to get married.

"Billy Bell used to be a good dancer," says Mrs. McC. "They'd clear the floor for them to dance," she adds, with an attempt at pride.

Billy Bell was twenty-one when he met Betty, a tall dark good-looking boy from a respectable working-class family. His father is blind now but has worked regularly all his life, and so did Billy, from the age of fifteen. When he met Betty he was working in a coke plant and had a room at 241 Derwentwater Road, in Gateshead not far from the McC.s.

But on 18 March 1958 Billy and Betty were married and he came to live with Betty, Isa and Mary at Mrs. McC.s flat in Redheughbridge Road.

It is seldom an ideal solution for young couples to live with their parents or parents-in-law. But flats were not easy to come by, both of them wanted to work, Betty hated housework, and there was Mary who had to be looked after.

Mrs. McC. is a very private and an intensely loyal woman who, half of her adult life, has been torn by the conflict between her love for Betty and her reluctance to seek outside help. Even now, after eleven years of intolerable pressures had driven her granddaughter into catastrophe, Mrs. McC. can hardly bear to speak about these years. Hers is a conflict that defies solution, demanding a choice no woman should be asked to make. But it is obvious that her need to surround, to protect her daughter continued even after Betty's marriage. Someone as perceptive as Mrs. McC. could not fail to see that the young Billy Bell, however decent and honest, would be hard put to deal with eighteen-year-old Betty's complex problems. No doubt the decision to live together was prompted as much by her apprehensions as by the young couple's practical considerations.

But it would seem that the tide of tragedy that started so long ago could not now be stemmed by any precautionary half-measures.

In May 1958, when Betty was pregnant with her second child, Mary, just one year old, almost died. This was to be the first of a series of inexplicable accidents and events involving her and extending over more than four years, which Mary, it appears from all accounts, remembers only too clearly.

Her grandmother took pills for her nerves ("Mum's always had them," said her daughters). But Mrs. McC. was a very responsible woman. With no lockable cupboards or drawers in the flat, she had carefully put the bottle out of reach in the back of the used needle compartment of an old gramophone and hid the knitting needle she used to extricate it in another place. Despite all these precautions, on that day in May 1958, Mary somehow got hold of a number of these acid-tasting pills and ate them. To achieve this, the baby had to find the knitting needle, get up to where the gramophone stood, open it, dig out the carefully hidden bottle, unscrew it, and take out and eat enough of the unpleasant little pills almost to kill her. As it happened she was found in time and rushed to hospital, her stomach was pumped out and she recovered.

Six months later Betty's second child was born, a boy. By this time Gateshead Council had given Mrs. McC. an excellent council house at 27 Huxley Crescent. Almost a garden community, these houses, probably nearly new at the time, spacious, with large windows, well-starched curtains, and carefully tended gardens front and back, are awarded only to the most reliable tenants. Two big rooms on the ground floor give on to the road, and a cloakroom and kitchen in the back overlook the garden. The three bedrooms upstairs and the bath and W.C. are fair sized, light, and airy. There is no traffic here, no noise, no smoking factory chimneys, no railway line, no dilapidation. Mrs. McC. must have hoped that surely now, no longer cramped for space, no longer lacking privacy, surrounded by quiet streets, trees, and flowers. Betty would settle down, be content with what she had, learn to accept love—and to love. But if Mrs. McC. permitted herself to have these hopes after the move to Huxley Drive, they were soon to be disappointed.

We can only guess at the tensions which built up between Mrs. McC. and the young couple. Billy Bell, deeply in love and instinctively protective of Betty, like most people could not fathom what lay beneath her problems. If for no other reason than for his own protection, he probably reduced them to a level he could deal with and therefore possibly chose to blame on her mother Betty's temper tantrums, her wild sobs, her extreme impatience (and perhaps what he instinctively recognized as the beginning of her rejection of him.)

Whatever the immediate grounds of the explosion, coming home late one afternoon from a day's outing, Mrs. McC. found her front door locked against her and all her possessions, her suitcases, gramophone, dishes, and furniture in a heap, in the street.

By rejecting, for good reasons or bad, this stabilizing influence in their lives, Betty and Billy had removed an important restraint. Mrs. McC. and Isa returned to live in Glasgow, and the family life of the Bells began to disintegrate before it had ever really begun.

Billy Bell, tall and well-built, has an almost classically handsome face, a wide mouth, thick black hair, and rather small blue eyes with long lashes. On his hands he has various tattoos; across the knuckles of the right hand: TRUE, underneath: PADDY and MAM; on the left hand: LOVE, underneath: BETTY. "I got up and did the bottles in the night," he said, trying to describe his life with Betty. "She couldn't be bothered. I did the cooking. She cleaned like . . ."

Eloquent enough with his family and friends, Billy Bell is embarrassed and inarticulate with outsiders. "I am thick-skinned," he says, blushing, and looks down at his hands. He means that his thoughts and words come slowly. "Billy wasn't ever good at book learning," his sister said, "but he was a good boy and a good regular worker."

Slow or not, he was unfailingly loyal to Betty, even later. Whatever she has done to him, his love for her would die hard. "She likes dancing," he said dreamily. "We . . . we danced for years." But there must have been periods without dancing. For, beginning in 1959, just about a year after they married, Betty began to go off on her own. "Yes," Billy agreed, "she left me many times. She'd just leave a note saying she couldn't settle."

The first time when Betty left home altogether was when her baby B. was six months old. Even before this, however, she had taken Mary many times to stay with various relatives and friends and already the two-year-old girl was showing the first warning symptoms of disturbance.

"I don't know where Betty had gone," says Audrey, "but she just went off. The baby went to stay with my mother, and Billy and May came here."

Audrey is devoted to her brother who in the course of a few years she saw change from a "decent hard-working lad" into someone who, as she put it, "you wouldn't have known . . . was the same man."

The three-bedroom house in Scotswood she lived in until recently was warm and welcoming, and Audrey's two boys and a girl were open-faced, bright, and happy children.

On that first occasion when Billy and Mary came to stay for several weeks, Audrey's own daughter had not yet been born and she was delighted to have a little girl about the house; "May didn't have much to wear when she came," she says. "She was that bonny, I wanted to get her some things. I went to the secondhander and got some little nylon dresses and bows for her hair. I dressed her, but you know, the moment she was out of the house—I was watching her out of the window—she tore the ribbons off and mucked the dresses all over." Audrey still sounded sad. "She was only a baby then, but she wouldn't have anything done for her. She wouldn't let anybody hug or kiss her. It was always like this. She'd turn her face away."

Just as there had been for Betty, there was a wealth of love available for Mary. But both of them seemed unable to accept it.

The people who saw perhaps most of Mary during the first critical six years were her Aunt Cath and her Uncle Jack. They are hard-working and articulate, with a special gift for bringing warmth and color into their home. If Cath, an active but delicate woman who suffers from chronic bronchitis, can be a little emotional, she is neatly balanced by her husband, a man of unfailing calm.

"When May was just two," said Cath, "you see, we'd had her so often, she was with us more than she was at home. . . . Jack and I wrote a letter to Betty and asked whether she would let us adopt May. We loved her that much. Not just me, Jack too." Jack nodded.

"You see, Cath had an operation. She has only one lung," he said. "And after our F. was born, we didn't think we could have another one. The little one came six years later. . . ." They laughed. "A surprise . . ."

"Betty came the very next day," Cath went on, "the day she got the letter, and took May away. As if she was afraid."

She took her away, only to bring her back again two weeks later and countless times after that. "I can't cope with two," she always said.

But that wasn't the real reason; considering all these events now in the context of the *whole* story, one can see how Betty wavered between her impulse to eliminate Mary from her life and her per-haps equally strong—even obsessive—attachment to her. Almost every one of the acts of rejection during the following years contain also in a strange and hapless way an element of protection of Mary and—as so often happens—a mute cry for help.

The next instance in this sequence of macabre events occurred when Mary was two and a half, in November 1959. Betty arrived distraught at Cath's house late one afternoon. Cath and her family then lived in a rather isolated place in the country, an hour or so's journey from Newcastle. Betty told Cath that Mary had had a terrible accident—a lorry had run over her. "They had to cut the clothes off her, she is that bad," she said, sobbing bitterly. Cath was so shaken by the awful news she never questioned why Betty hadn't stayed at the hospital with Mary. "They told me to come back tomorrow," Betty added, unasked. The sisters agreed that Cath would phone the hospital the next day and then go in and see Mary.

By the first post the next morning, before Cath, who didn't have a telephone at the house, had a chance to get out, a letter arrived from Betty saying that it was not true, that Mary wasn't hurt, but that she had "given May to the D.s." The D.s, old friends of Cath and Jack who lived in a small market town nearby, had taken con-siderable interest in Mary, and had also in the past repeatedly offered to adopt her.

"I didn't know what to believe any more," said Cath. But she rushed to the D.s' house, ten miles or so away, to make sure they really had Mary. When she got there, they asked her whether she had come to take Mary back. It then emerged that Betty had not actually "given" Mary to this couple—a solution which might have been a lifesaver for Mary—but, saying that "things were bad just then," had merely asked them to keep her for "a couple of weeks." Mary was returned to her mother a few days later.

It would seem that Mary remembers this incident well: In a shopping expedition with her aunt and grandmother two and a half years later, when she was five, she caught sight of Mrs. D. in the market and hid behind her granny. "Don't let that lady see me," she said. "I don't like that lady. Me mum gave me away to her when I was two, and she cut off my hair." Mrs. D., a motherly woman who had cropped Mary's hair when she was brought to her because, as was almost always the case, she had lice, gave her a present of half a crown that day. (Isa too remembers this incident well.)

The next accident happened in the spring of 1960: Cath came to visit the Bells, who—although not for much longer—were still living in Huxley Crescent. She brought a bag of "dolly mixtures" for each of the children: Mary, then three, and her eighteen-month-old brother.

The sisters went to the scullery to make tea, and when Cath returned to the room where they had left the children, she found them sitting on the floor munching sweets which had been "spilled all over." To her horror she saw among them a number of little blue pills which she recognized as being Drinamyls (Purple Hearts). "Did you eat any of them bonny little blue ones?" she questioned the little boy. He nodded twice. May said she had also eaten two. Cath shouted for Betty to come.

"I don't remember exact words any more," she said later. "It was all panic stations. But Betty said something like, 'Here, they must have taken the bottle out of my handbag.' "

"You just don't leave anything dangerous like this around for kids to get hold of," Cath retorted angrily. "I got a glass of hot water with salt in it and made the kids drink it," she says, "and they were both sick in the sink. Then I ran out to get Billy who was in the road and told him to take them quickly to the hospital. In the hospital they said they were all clear—it had all come out."

(Isa remembers this accident too—the only one any of Betty's other children were involved in. "You mean the Drinamyls Betty was taking?" she said. "That was after we'd gone back to Glasgow.")

Just after this time, Cath and Jack wrote yet another letter to Betty and Billy Bell. "We said we wouldn't ever again talk about adopting May," they said. "But would they let us have and keep her until she finished school, and then May herself could choose where she wanted to live? We said could we go and see a solicitor and make it all regular and legal?"

Their action was certainly partly prompted by their devotion to Mary, and their growing and nagging anxiety about her. But partly —and they agree now that this was so—a lot of people sought after Mary's affection, nobody knows quite why. It wasn't just because of her looks, although everyone comments on how pretty she was. ("I never felt I could reach May," said Audrey. "There was a wall between her and others. . . . It was the same for Betty," she added. "She had that wall too." Was it that, already this early in her life, Mary provoked in adults this need to prove that *they* could reach her, *they* could communicate with her, *they* could make her into an ordinary child?)

Jack and Cath say that Mary "never cried when hurt" but had temper tantrums, screamed, stamped on the floor when not given what she wanted, was never spanked at home, but stopped her tantrums at once when *they* gave her the occasional slap on her backside. They can only remember one occasion when they saw violence in her, and that was just about the time they had suggested fostering her. As usual Mary had been staying with them and they'd had a letter from Betty in the morning to say that she and Billy were coming that afternoon to pick Mary up to take her home. "Jack was sitting here," Cath said—in his usual chair in front of the fireplace in their kitchen dinette, "and May sat there," opposite him. "She was playing with a big red toy gun and Jack said, 'Your mam and dad will be here soon to pick you up.' 'I'll bash your face in,' May shouted at her uncle. And she did, with that toy gun. He still has the bump on his nose from it." They say that many times since, Mary has asked her uncle if he remembered the time she "bashed his face in."

A number of snapshots and photographs of Mary from the age

of two to when she was about five or six show her looking strained, her face "tight" as her uncle Jack puts it. In only one of them does she look like an ordinary, happy, laughing little girl. "She was stopping with us then, for a long time," Cath said.

Three months or so later, in the summer of 1960, the little boy deposited once again with his paternal grandmother in Newcastle, Betty Bell took Mary, now three and a half, to Glasgow, to stay with her mother. Mrs. McC. was working as a receptionist in a hospital at the time and had a flat on the third floor of a terraced building. The lavatories were on the ground floor and, to save taking the child downstairs, the family was in the habit of letting her "wet in the sink." One day, the window next to this sink was wide open, Philip and Isa were both in the room, sitting on the settee, about six feet away, when Philip saw Mary, whom Betty had been holding straddling the sink, falling out of the window. He lunged across the room and somehow managed to grab her ankles and pull her in. "He was off work for three weeks after that because he hurt his back catching her," the sisters say.

Betty's family had now become really anxious, and Isa was instructed by her mother not to let Betty and Mary out of her sight.

A few days later she followed Betty when she took the child out for a walk. Betty took Mary to an adoption agency. A woman came out of the interview room crying and said they would not give her a baby because of her age and because she was emigrating to Australia.

"I brought this one in to be adopted. You have her," Betty Bell said, pushing the little girl toward the stranger, and walked out.

Betty had seen Isa follow her and had shouted at her in the street in the rough language her sisters say she always used now. "I was that embarrassed," said Isa. But she had stuck to her as ordered by her mother, and Betty was perfectly aware that her sister was present when all this happened. Could she really have imagined that Isa would do nothing when she saw her apparently give Mary away? Or was this senseless act, which was surely likely to have a tremendous impact on a small girl, yet another sign of despair? Another cry for help from a very frightened woman.

Isa followed and took down the address where Mary was taken, then raced to the hospital to tell her mother. They rushed home and Mary's grandmother apparently told Betty that if the child was not back inside two hours she would notify the police. Mary was fetched with some dresses the woman had already bought her and allowed her to keep, and Betty took Mary back to Newcastle.

Only weeks after this, in Newcastle, Betty had a miscarriage. When she returned from hospital, the Bell family moved out of Huxley Crescent to a flat in the Newcastle slums. "We had a fight with some of the neighbors," Billy said. "We lived in some awful places . . . after that." Elswick Road where they moved is now gradually turning into a desirable residential neighborhood with excellent council flats. But in 1960 it was very different. And No. 28 (now boarded up and awaiting demolition), a shop of sorts on the ground floor, and upstairs the dank and dark two-rooms plus scullery, was a dreadful comedown from Huxley Crescent. It was here that a new pattern began to emerge for their lives. Betty's absences from home became more frequent. Billy stayed away from work—"Somebody had to mind the kids," he said. But he also sought companionship and escape in pubs. On Betty's returns (she was soon to be away a few days regularly every week) one must assume that the atmosphere could hardly have been peaceful. Billy seemed like a man who did not know what had hit him. But at least now he knew vaguely that Betty was sick. In the beginning he must have sought a more acceptable interpretation for her behavior. Even his far more articulate sister tried to minimize and normalize it: "Betty likes a fling," she said.

Billy said, "We had arguments like, but no fights." Even more unlikely, he claims, "We always tried not to argue in front of the kids." In fact, nothing was hidden from the Bell children. Even if they had wanted to protect them, living as they did on top of each other in Elswick Road and later, it would have been impossible to keep anything secret from them.

The boy, at two and a half was still very young. But Mary, almost four, with an awareness, everyone says now, well beyond her years, was unlikely to have remained unaffected by the tensions in those closest to her. It was about this time that Mary had her fourth and worst accident.

Newcastle General Hospital has the records. "Mary Flora Bell," the register states, "28 Elswick Road, Newcastle/Tyne, 6/3/61 to 9/3/61: under care of Consultant, Dr. Cooper."

On this occasion the police, who often help by delivering urgent messages when there is no telephone, came to Cath's house and told her that her niece was in hospital in Newcastle. It was no doubt Betty who sent for her: she always called the family for help when in trouble.

Cath left almost at once for Newcastle, but she had to dress, make arrangements for her own household and travel for more than an hour to get there. By the time she arrived, Mary's stomach had been pumped out and she had regained consciousness. Betty was standing in front of the ward. "Don't believe her," she implored, sobbing. "She says I gave her those pills."

This time apparently Mary had swallowed a number of "iron" pills her mother was taking. And it appears that when they got the four-year-old awake she immediately said to the doctor, "Me mam gave me the smarties," and kept on saying this on and off for twenty-four hours.

(Mary's best friend at this time was a girl of five who lived near her. Cath met this little girl in the street a few days later and she said, "May's mam gave her the smarties in the backyard." About five weeks later, this child was killed by a bus when out in the street with Mary.)

Mary certainly has a vivid memory of the "iron pill" incident and everything connected with it and was to mention it periodically and pointedly over the years. Even during the month of the sandpit incident and the death of Martin Brown, she was heard to mention suddenly to her mother, for no apparent reason, "Mam, do you remember them smarties you gave me to eat that made me sick?"

After this incident in 1961 there were bitter words between Betty and various members of her family who were now terrified for Mary's safety. "Once is an accident, even twice it just might be," one of the sisters said to Betty, "but three—and now even four —times is impossible." Shortly afterward, Mrs. McC. and her daughters received letters from Betty saying she never wanted to see them again. They did not see her for more than a year. But in a way the family's concern had the desired effect. For, although by no means the end of her troubles, this was to be the last of Mary's accidents at home.

In September 1961 she started school, first at a kindergarten at Westgate Hill and then the Cambridge Street Infant School where she was to stay for three years.

The headmistress and her form teachers remember her clearly—astonishingly so, considering the many hundreds of children who go through the school. The teacher remembers the first time she met Mary on a visit she paid to the school before she began to teach there. She went into the classroom where Mary (now five) was a pupil. Mary was hiding under the desk. "She was always doing this. Sometimes it wasn't really hiding; she'd go and lie under the desk on her back, stiff as a rod, and refuse to move."

"That's Mary Bell," she was told by the mistress then in charge of the class. "You'll be getting to know her soon enough." But both of these women, warm-hearted and dedicated to their profession, spoke of Mary with fondness, as a child who had interested and amused them (a reaction Mary has always provoked in people and still does).

"She was almost always naughty," they said. "But I could almost always tell in advance the days when she was going to be specially naughty," said the teacher, "because those days she would arrive at school in a 'bouncy' sort of way. The days when she was going to be good she would arrive in a 'rather withdrawn and quiet way.'"

"If a child behaves today the way Mary did then," the headmistress said, and sadly shook her head, "I automatically send them to the Child Guidance Clinic. And there *are* other children here who behave like this. But when Mary was here one did not immediately think of psychiatrists and Child Guidance. I only wish we had known more then. . . ."

The teacher told of an occasion when Mary put her hands around a smaller child's neck and pressed. "Don't do that, you mustn't do that," she had said to Mary. "That's naughty."

"Why?" Mary asked. "Can it kill him?"

Both teachers say that she was very lonely and that other children disliked her, including the boys, "even though she was so

pretty." She was always "kicking," "hitting," and "pinching" everybody ("nipping" as they call it in the North). "Once I found her
crying in the playground," the teacher remembered. "I asked her
what was the matter. 'Nobody wants to play with me,' she said. I
told her, 'You mustn't do such nasty things to them. Well, come
and walk around with me.' And she took my hand and walked
around the yard with me. She often did after that."

"She couldn't differentiate between truth and lies," both said.
"She told tall stories all the time. She had a great deal of imagination but she wouldn't work. One didn't get the feeling then that she
was all that bright—certainly not academically. But she was very
cunning, crafty. She could always get out of things. You could
never get the better of her; she always kept us going."

The teachers said that they'd had very little indication of Mary's
mother's unsettled way of life. "I don't think we ever thought anything but that she was at home," the headmistress said. "Except
once when she told me that Mary's younger brother (not Mary)
was the one she could entrust the babies to if she wasn't there. And
he was quite often absent." They remembered then that the little
boy acted strangely. "When he was away like that, he'd stay out
of school for a week or more; and when he came back he was
morose, withdrawn, and one had to start with him all over again.
It was discouraging—we'd just be getting somewhere with him,
getting him to open up and that, you know, and then he'd be taken
out of school, kept out like that, and come back in this state of
moroseness."*

But they said the Bell children were very well taken care of,
"always clean and well dressed." They thought that Betty Bell was
exceptionally involved with her children, more than most mothers.
"Mrs. Bell often came to pick them up from school," they said.
"She was aggressively protective of them. If any one of us said
something about them, she'd say, 'You are always picking on
them.'"

"But we didn't pick on Mary," they say sadly. "Of course it's
true, she was so often naughty that perhaps she did get blamed for

* This discouragement is very much a thing of the past. Mary's
brother, happily installed in an excellent small Children's Home, is
showing signs of being a very gifted child.

some things she didn't do. This happens with children who—as Mary always did—draw attention to themselves to this extent."

"She seemed to have a need to be noticed—perhaps punished too. If she couldn't get my attention any other way," one of the teachers added, "she'd come and sit under my desk and pull the hairs on my legs, you know—anything to get a reaction; I remember letting her do it; I was so determined not to give in to her craving for attention."

Both these women and the teachers at Mary's later school were more than anything else sorry and sad for her. "I often feel guilty," said the headmistress, "I don't know—perhaps I should have seen more, noticed more."

And yet, another teacher, although equally loyal to Mary and equally appalled at what eventually happened, told of the day in August 1968, when—before any names had been published—a friend who was the wife of a police officer told her that two little girls had been arrested for the murder of Brian Howe. "It really was perfectly extraordinary," said the teacher, "because the moment I heard this, the name Mary Bell shot into my mind—although by this time I hadn't seen or heard of Mary for more than three years. I thought about it for a while and then I phoned my friend back. I said, 'Look, ask your husband whether one of them is called Mary Bell? If not, don't say anything. I am just wondering. . . .' "

If Elswick Road had been a big step down for them, the Bells' next move, in early 1963, to 147 Westmoreland Road, meant that they had reached the bottom of the ladder. "Everything became so much worse six years ago," said Isa in 1969. Westmoreland Road, also now in the process of redevelopment, was then one of the worst streets in Newcastle. Although there were a couple of small stores near the house where they lived, one of them dating back to 1887 when this had been a respectable neighborhood, Westmoreland Road by 1963 was a district of dilapidated, rat-ridden housing, used car lots, petrol stations, warehouses, and billboards adorned with crude graffiti. It was the sort of dark district which the police patrolled regularly, but always in cars, never on foot.

Betty now had her third child, followed by a nervous breakdown and one of her stays in hospital. "Even before this," Billy Bell was to say later, "she was in and out of hospitals with her nerves and stomach."

The pattern, already established in Elswick Road, continued and intensified; Billy moved in when Betty went away, and regularly departed when she returned. When she was there, the flat was filthy. After none of the family had seen Betty for more than a year, Cath, too worried about her to allow the friction to continue, went to see her. "I was prepared for anything," she says. But all Betty said was, "Hello, stranger," and that was that. Betty's need for her family has always prevailed over her resentments, as indeed their anxiety about her has always outweighed their condemnation of her conduct.

"But it was so dirty," Cath says, "I used to bring a kettle and a cup when I went to tea." This split reaction exists in all of Betty's relatives except for her mother, who cannot bring herself to speak a word against her. Devoted to her, they have protected her with singular determination for years. On the other hand, most of them understandably feel that need to reassure themselves and their families by occasionally—and pointedly—disassociating themselves from the way she lives. But any critical remark any of them make is almost immediately—and frequently irrelevantly—followed by some sort of praise. "She is a much better baker than I am," Cath had added immediately on that particular occasion.

In Westmoreland Road the two rooms were separated by the scullery. Betty used the front room—the three children slept in the back. It would have been impossible for the children—especially Mary, as the eldest and most tuned in—to be unaware of her mother's activities. "I ask myself sometimes whether I did her harm, whether I did something to Mary," Betty, crying bitterly, was to say over and over later to a number of people, with reference to her life (and no doubt the degree of Mary's knowledge or understanding of it) during that period.

Outside her home, too, Mary's life was not peaceful. The children of Westmoreland Road had no park or playground—they played in the streets. When Mary was almost six, a fourteen-year-old boy stabbed her in the back with a broken bottle. The splinters had to be removed, the wound stitched, and she was left with a bad scar. Was it an attack on her, or was it the result of a fight she had initiated? No one would tell, she least of all. It is certain that she often fought. Billy Bell said later that she was "never violent but a kid has to stand up for herself or they'll walk all over her."

"May's afraid of nothing," said Cath, "except to be thought afraid. She never, never cries when hurt."

Mary later told Dr. Westbury that she never worried about anything and was never frightened. "I've got no feelings," she said, "I'm like me dad. Can't cry."

Billy Bell, a man sometimes bewildered by his own feelings, and events, *can* cry. Much later, in the course of several long conversations about his feelings for Mary and his life with Betty (now— four years later—a thing of the past for him), Billy Bell cried repeatedly and was near tears almost all the time. Not a man accustomed to talk about feelings, it takes him a long time to find the appropriate words. He spoke in single words—not sentences— with long pauses between words.

"Did you used to eat together, you and Betty and the kids?"

"She never ate with anybody," Billy said, "she'd feed the kids, she'd bring me something. She never ate anything . . . never even finished a cup of tea . . ."

"You used to dance together, you and Betty, didn't you?"

"We have danced for years."

"You love her, don't you, Billy?"

"Ay."

"If she came back tomorrow, would you take her back?"

"Yes, I'd have her back."

"Did you know she was sick? For a long long time? Since she was a child?"

"I suppose so," once again a long pause. "During the trial," he finally said, "we still . . . you know . . . together. But it wasn't any good." Another long pause. "But we had happy times," he said then, softly.

If they had happy times, they must have been well before West-moreland Road. "Billy used to dress beautiful," said his sister, "he was so careful of himself. And then something happened—about six years ago (1962–63), I don't know what." After that his clothes were untidy, his eyes bleary, his chin stubbly and he lived a seemingly aimless life between his home, the street, and his favorite pub of the moment. By no means a criminal, he has been at times on the edge of small crime. "But he isn't really a hard lad," said a perceptive police officer.

"If you didn't *know* you wouldn't believe he is the same man," is all Audrey could say.

"I suppose Billy Bell has been telling you that he is a knight in shining armor," his mother-in-law said later, bitterly, and referred to many occasions when Billy had "knocked Betty about." "I feel arguments are all right," she said, "but when a man starts knocking a woman about, then it's time for her to leave, take her children and leave."

Betty's mother does not blame the tragedy on anyone. (She said it was the slums they lived in, fate, God's will.) Understandably, she has a great need to "explain away" the troubles in her family in "conventional" terms. From where she stands, paradoxically enough, the break-up of a family and even a degree of violence is "socially" acceptable if it can be explained by a husband's instability, brutality, infidelity, and drink.

"Billy did do the housework, Mam," Isa had put in shyly. And everybody else affirmed that before this mysterious event in 1962 or 1963 which caused a complete personality change in Billy, he had been a regular worker, always a "natty dresser" who would rather not sit down than crease his trousers and that, if he liked his brown ale, so do all workingmen in this part of the world, and he had always drunk in moderation.

Billy himself admits that he gets rough when he is drunk. "I get drunk as often as I can," he says and laughs, "but only on weekends. I haven't got the"—he rubs two fingers together in the familiar gesture signifying money—"to go to the pub more often. I wish I *could* go every night."

Whatever the reason for the change in Billy, the relationship between him and Betty—although complex, tortured, and increasingly venal in various ways—continued.

In 1965 Betty even had another baby—the third girl—as beautiful as all her other children. "After that she first said the doctor suspected she had cancer," one of her sisters said. Later, she said it was confirmed, and later still she said she had a hysterectomy. True? False? They don't even know now. Nor does Billy. And her mother says she had vaguely heard about all this and knew that Betty had "an operation" but that Betty had never confided in her, never told her anything precise. What was known however is that she went as an outpatient "for treatments—regular like."

Somehow Betty and Billy had worked out some kind of "modus vivendi." Their children until the events in 1968 were never "in care" and, in a haphazard sort of way, the Bells were a family unit— which cannot fail to make us question, once again, the validity of the social work theory which claims that "any family is better than none" and that "keeping the family together at all costs" is the best guard against maladjustment and delinquency in children.

The year 1966 was a new turning point in the Bells' lives. They moved to 70 Whitehouse Road, where a few months later Thomas Bell and family were to become their neighbors at No. 68 and where Mary, then nine, and Norma, eleven, became friends.

"When May was eight," her grandmother said, "Betty came up [to Glasgow] and asked me to have her. She said, 'We could get you a bigger flat and May could stop with you, run your messages and all that.' But I said I couldn't do it, I felt too old to take on a child." She shook her head despairingly. "If only I'd said yes . . ."

It may well have been during the same visit that Mary had a talk with Isa which Isa remembers particularly vividly. "I was pregnant with our little boy," she said, "and Mary asked me about my big tummy. 'That's the baby in there,' I answered, and her whole face looked astonished. 'You mean it's really in there?' she asked, 'under your dress? In your tummy?' I took her hand and slipped it under my sweater and said, 'Feel.' She came and sat on my lap and for half an hour she just didn't say anything, just kept her hand on my tummy and felt the baby move. Later, after he was born, she used to lean over him and say, 'I felt you with my hand up your mam's kilt when you were in her tummy.' Does that sound like a cold, unloving child?" Isa asked.

In the autumn of that year Mary entered Delaval Road Junior School. The headmistress and Mary's teacher at this school were again warm and concerned people. "Mary was charming," the headmistress said, several times, obviously at a loss what to say about a child they had seen daily for three years and in whom they had failed to observe the pressures which finally drove her to kill. "I always felt there was a lot of depth in Mary," said Mr. F., who taught Mary for three years. But if he felt anything suspicious about these hidden depths, he didn't think it prudent to touch or to expose them. "There are other [troubled] children like this in the school," both teachers said. "It is better just not to poke too deeply into their lives and circumstances." "We really thought there wasn't any father in this family," the headmistress said. Mary's teacher said he had known "there was a father because Mary once wrote about him—some story of an excursion or an outing where the father had taken them somewhere."

But there was a good reason why the school did not know much about Billy Bell. For when the Bells—Billy too—moved to White-house Road ("They had a real home there," Audrey said, "the only real home they ever had.") the children were instructed to call their father "uncle" whenever anyone else was within hearing, and Betty Bell notified the council that her husband had abandoned her and proceeded to claim the relevant social security benefits.

Billy said later, with disarming frankness, "Nobody *wants* to work." He is young, fit, and strong and could earn between £25 and £30 a week. But, "as long as I have my pint," he said, "I don't need money." After Mary's trial and conviction, when Betty Bell disappeared altogether, he set up house with the three remaining children and an old friend, Harry Bury, in a house the council gave him in another part of town. Obviously then feeling morally justified in not working he said, "I can't work—somebody has to mind the kids now that Betty's walked out—she's left us." He got £10 a week from social security. "What about clothes and shoes for the children?" he was asked. "There are grants," he answered, logically enough.

Harry Bury, a sixty-year-old rag and bone man, toothless, quiet, and kind, has known the Bell children since they were born. He has often lived with Billy when he took care of them alone and they call him "uncle." He is known to have given Mary many generous presents. A fragile-looking man who suffers from stomach trouble, Mr. Bury begins to cry as soon as the conversation turns to Mary. "She was the best friend anyone ever had," he said, and one had to remind oneself that he was talking about a little girl.

"Do you write to her?"

"Sometimes, not often." He speaks very slowly with pauses between sentences. "It's different you see," he said with dignity. "I am not a relative . . . I'd always be saying the same . . . same words like, you know. When Billy goes to see her, he takes messages from me and . . . I don't need to say anything . . . it isn't necessary—May knows, I am here . . . I'm . . ."

"Her friend?"

"Yes."

"How do you think it happened—whatever it is that happened to her?"

"When she was very small," he said quickly, "that was when it started like . . ."

Billy certainly is very attached to his children and always has been. There was always ample evidence of Mary's affection for him—and his for her. But if she was able to develop some sort of feminine child-father-cum-pal relationship with Billy (and if this endures to the present), there was nothing like this between Mary and Betty.

"She and her mother had no relationship like we have with our children," Audrey said. "Rather perhaps like two sisters. But they never *said* anything to each other." (A psychiatrist who observed them together later said, in almost the same words someone had used earlier describing Mary with Norma, "They chat away about clothes, TV, pop stars and, you know—nothing—like two teenagers on the telephone.")

Even so, Mary's relationship with her mother did have its normal moments as another of Mary's entries in her school notebook proved:

> On Saturday I had to stop in bed all day I was bad and I got up and tried to sneak downstairs but the dog came running up the stairs and it barked and my mum came up to see what was the matter and I shut the door and ran back to bed but mum heard me and brought me downstairs with some blankets to lie on the sete.

Animals—her Alsatian most of all—were always important to Mary. "She had her room full of animals," Billy Bell said (everybody always spoke of Mary in the past tense, after the trial), "budgies, kitten."

"She brought animals home from school for the holidays," Audrey said, "she loved plants too."

"She talked a lot about some horses on an uncle's farm," one of the policewomen said later, "especially about one she loved and said she owned, 'a beautiful black stallion.' I thought to myself, 'What a little liar she is.'" One of the psychiatrists who examined Mary also remarked on her "fantasy life" and mentioned how she "stated with conviction that she owned a beautiful black stallion."

Cath later explained about that stallion. "One day during her remand, Mary was so miserable and homesick—she kept talking about her dog, a ferocious Alsatian nobody could touch but who'd do anything for her, and about the horses on her uncle's farm . . . she obviously missed it all so much, it broke my heart. And suddenly I heard myself saying, 'You know, your uncle's given you that great big stallion. He's yours now,' and she was that happy. But later I said to myself, 'What came over me to tell a lie like that?'"

Billy Bell said that "I've given the dog away now, he was a wild one, he was May's dog. No, I haven't told her. I won't. She loves him. He slept in the passage. She could do anything with him."

The psychiatrist who commented on Mary's "fantasy" about the stallion also mentioned that she spun a yarn about "owning a police-dog." It throws an interesting sidelight on how the best-trained specialists can jump to wrong conclusions if they are given insufficient information.

On 15 November 1967 Mary wrote in her "newsbook" under the title "On Saturday":

> On Saturday I was coming from the park with susan and the was loads of police cars. I went over. There had been a baby found dead in a polthene bag.

Underneath there is a competent drawing of a police car parked on grass. But would that have been particularly remarkable? Perhaps other children wrote about this too. They were, after all, supposed to write about interesting things that happened.

None of the people who lived close to Mary during the last two years—or months—before May 1968 noticed any significant changes in her even when, desperately wanting to help by remembering, they searched their memories. She was left-eyed, left-handed, and left-footed. This was only discovered when she was examined while she was on remand; even if those close to her *had* noticed it before, does it matter?

She was a bedwetter, but she always had been and had even on two occasions been sent for short periods to a convalescent home for eneuretic children—a place she loved and even ran away to later, with Norma. Equally, bedwetting is common enough and by no means necessarily indicative of serious trouble.

She did not sleep much, but she has never needed much sleep, nor do many perfectly normal children. She was "always reading the Bible" but who, without realizing what she was dwelling upon, could find fault with that?

And of course, there was that wall between her and others which Audrey had spoken of and had added, "Betty has that same wall." That wall had almost always been there since she was a baby. And if it did get worse—perhaps it did—no one noticed. Mary had always been conspicuous: she had for years hit, kicked, scratched, and "nipped" other children, done everything to attract her teachers' attention; lied so much that one of her aunts said "one always felt she was deceiving one." Nobody paid attention to her. On the contrary, they were resolved to ignore her. So she went further, she killed pigeons by throttling them. "You stop that, May Bell," they said. She put her hands around the throat of a newborn baby lying in his pram. "May—leave him be," somebody shouted. She allegedly pushed her little cousin off an old air-raid shelter seven feet onto a concrete floor—but no one reported her. And one day later she pressed the necks of three little girls in a playground: "The girls . . . have been warned as to their future conduct," wrote the police who had statements about *that* event, as they had taken statements from the same two girls at the same addresses one day before.

So finally a small boy died: less than twenty-four hours later, having meanwhile put her hands around the throat of yet another child, this time one of her own age whose father "clipped" her for it, Mary announced in writing that they had killed. "I murdered," she said. Still no one paid attention, so she began to shout it out in the playground, and in the street. She behaved morbidly and offensively to the dead child's relatives. A week after having broken into the Nursery to leave the "We Murder" notes, she broke into it again, in the same way; she was caught, questioned by the police—and released.

A week later, on 2 June, Mary and Norma ran away—and again twelve days later on 14 June. Again they had come to official notice. Again not enough.

Six weeks after the death of the first little boy Mary went to the house of what was to be the next victim and (though she was accusing someone else) actually demonstrated how it was done.

The two girls to whom she had shown this shrugged their shoulders, just as, six weeks before, a boy had laughed when she had *told* him she'd murdered Martin. Policemen had not taken her behavior too seriously. Teachers had not wanted to probe; neighbors did not want to meddle, and loving relatives did not choose to see. Surely the classic "cry for help" can never have been more pronounced, and never more ignored; and that is why, on 31 July 1968, Brian Howe died.

PART FOUR

THE PRESENT

"The Guilty One Is You Not Me"

As I was writing this book, almost three years had passed since the events and the trial of 1968.

June and George Brown were still living at 140 St Margaret's Road, the only family directly involved in the tragedy who have kept their original home. (Newcastle Council immediately offered new housing to all the families involved.) "It's our home," said June; "moving wouldn't have changed anything." In the sitting room there are two pictures of Martin on the mantelpiece. In one he is a baby, the other was apparently taken not long before he died. June is outgoing and tender to Linda, who at the time I saw them was three, a small, compact child with smooth, golden hair and a face startlingly like Martin's. "Like two peas in the pod they are," Mrs. Brown says. Linda is a happy child with bright eyes, glowing cheeks, and a chuckling voice; without being urged she recites poetry and sings nursery rhymes for the visitor.

"After it happened," June Brown says, "I couldna believe it. All I did was cry. I couldna stand Linda; just look at her, to think I couldna stand her. The doctor told me it would be all right, that I was bound to feel like that for a while. I kept thinking I was seeing Martin, you know, in the streets. Every morning at six or so I was standing in front of the old houses and calling him. I was real crazy, you know. Every time I saw a small blond lad in a blue anorak, I'd run and shout, 'Martin'—there were so many little lads in blue anoraks. I couldn't stand seeing any other little lads. I said, 'Rita's got five—why couldn't one of *hers* have been taken, or some of them neglected kids.'. . . George, my husband, he cried after it happened—he misses him something terrible. But he'll never talk about it now. He won't have anybody talk about it in front of him. I think he just can't bear to. Linda, she was real bad afterwards . . ." A photograph of the family at the time, taken by an Italian news photographer, shows George—whom both children resemble—sitting with a pale, closed face; June, looking ten, fifteen years older than now, gray-faced with deep shadows under her eyes, her figure bloated, sagging, and exhausted; and Linda, with a long, tiny face, her hair short and curly, her eyes huge, also with big shadows underneath.

"No, we shan't have any more kids," said June. "I don't think one can replace a kid that's dead. And we've got Linda—she is everything to us. We don't want anybody else now. It would be wrong."*

Rita Finlay has moved, but not far away. Rita is less meticulous than her sister, but there was a bright fire with children's clothes hanging from the mantelpiece to dry and a pot of tea appeared in minutes. The place was crowded with children—her own and others. They were no sooner shooed outside than they shot in again. "It's cold outside, Mam," one little boy protested.

"Out," said Rita and he disappeared, quick as a flash, before retribution could reach him.

"Won't they be cold?"

"They're used to it," Rita said and laughed—she always laughs and it probably makes the smacks she can hand out less painful. Rita talked for a long time about Martin—and then Brian. There had been no indication whatever during the trial that there was any connection between these two children. Nor had we known that Mary and Norma really *knew* them. "Oh, both of them—them two girls were always around here," she said. "Martin," she said, "I loved him like my own. I must have loved him nearly as much as June did." June is there and nods, there is no jealousy. "I've got his clothes," says Rita, "in the plastic bag they'd kept them in. One day I'll wash them, but not yet. I can't touch them like—not yet."

"That Norma," she suddenly says, "she came up to us some months after the trial and says, 'Can I take your John for a walk?' I didn't even know what to say. I just stared at her and then I walked away."

* Happily, June and George Brown have now (1972) had another baby.

"We used to hate each other, Rita and I," June says. "Well, not hate like, you know—we spoke. But we never really talked, you know, until Martin died and then Brian. Now we are that close; we are real sisters now—so close we are. . . ."

June and Rita are essentially strong and George and June Brown have a good marriage. Martin is sorely missed and lovingly remembered. But the memory of violence and death has given way to their natural ebullience and to the demands and compensations of life.

Not so for the Howes, who used to live next to Norma Bell's family, and who moved to a tree-lined street where the houses look pleasant and well-cared for.

In 1971 Eric Howe lived there with his then sixteen-year-old married daughter Pat, her husband, and their one-year-old baby boy. Mr. Howe is a small, wide-chested stocky man who began to cry the moment Brian was mentioned.

"I miss him," he said, "he was my life. He was only a bairn, but we used to talk like, you know, really talk. I think of nothing but him."

Albert, the oldest boy, had meanwhile married and moved into a flat of his own. Norman, ten, was in hospital. "They say he is slow," his father says, "but it isn't so. He is very intelligent. When we are alone together we talk about Brian. He talks about him all the time. He's sad, that's what he is, not slow."

Pat, who comes in with her baby, is pale and tense. She is profoundly uncomfortable the moment Brian is mentioned, and terribly bitter. When she undresses her baby she is so young it seems she could be undressing a dearly loved doll. She speaks of having very little money; her husband, she says, must get a better job. "How can we manage on £11 a week?" she asks, her young voice becoming querulous when she wants it to sound grown up and wifely. There is no money but she has bought her tiny baby toys: a beautiful doll, a shiny plastic car, both far too big and old for him.

"It's destroyed us," said the father, his eyes red, tears trickling down his cheeks. "All I can do is . . ." and he makes the gesture of lifting up and emptying a bottle. "Can't you fight it if you know it's bad for you?" He shakes his head. "It's the only way I can stop the depression. I can't stand it. I think of nothing except him. We aren't a family any longer. We were before. Pat will tell you. It's true, isn't it, Pat?"

Pat's face was tight, she didn't want to talk about the past. It was her private grief. "We aren't a family any longer," she agreed, "we talk, but we don't say anything." Both Pat and her father were perfectly aware of what was happening to them. But there seemed to be nothing they could do to control or limit their own despair. Brian, even though he's never been there, was in that house and that room with them. And life itself, the fact of their being alive while he was dead, appeared to be a constant reminder of the horror and the injustice of their fate.

Norma Bell's family have also moved now, although they tried for quite a while to stick it out in Whitehouse Road. For a family with eleven children it isn't easy to find a decent council house and at the time of the trial they had only lived at No. 68 for two years.

Norma, acquitted at the Assizes, was put on three years' probation when she appeared later in Juvenile Court on the long-standing charge of breaking and entering the Woodlands Crescent Nursery. The recommendation of the Juvenile Bench stipulated that she should be under regular psychiatric supervision. After a brief holiday with her sixteen-year-old brother, she returned to Whitehouse Road and her normal school.

By the following spring, five months later, she was quiet and withdrawn. She had seen her psychiatrist once, the same who had testified about her in court. Her parents, concerned and gentle as ever, stated emphatically that the whole nightmarish business was all over for her: that they never talked to her about it; that she never thought about it; that they were very aware how bad it was for her to be reminded of it; that she was now once again a perfectly ordinary child, close to her family. "She doesn't want to go out," Mrs. Bell assured me, "she doesn't even want to go to the films. She says, 'I want to stay with Mam; I don't want to go to the cinema; I only want to stay at home.'" She loved looking after the babies in the family, they said, was anxious to help with the housework and was infinitely considerate. "I have these terrible varicose veins," her mother said, "and in the evening Norma comes and lifts up my leg and puts it up on a chair for me. She's that good. . . ."

In spite of her acquittal she did have some problems at school. "Just the other day when she came from school, a boy stepped out in front of her and shouted, 'Murderer.' When she got home—I had had her coat cleaned just the day before and there it was full of mud. I didn't ask how she got it, whether they pushed her, or she fell when she ran away, and she never said. She doesn't complain. She tells me these things, but she doesn't say anything else."

All of the children except the oldest boy had been sent out of the room while we talked. When Norma, shy but friendly, came back, Mrs. Bell told her to show us her "letters." She brought over a big old handbag bulging with fan mail, most of it in response to an article that appeared in the German magazine *Der Stern*, with photographs of the family and some remarkably evocative poems she had written, one of them about Vietnam, which she recited to us—it was an extraordinary effort for a girl diagnosed as retarded by five years. The fan letters, most of them in German, were primarily outpourings of sick minds. "You are a beautiful girl, petite chérie, Norma darling," one of them said—this particular correspondent wrote four poems to her, all of them highly suggestive. One boy, "Franzl," "son of a doctor from Düsseldorf," wrote her an admiring letter in English. "He came to stay with us," the Bell family said. "Slept on the settee down here in the sitting room. He and Norma got on very well, chatted for hours, and went for walks. The other kids liked him too. He was very nice, was Franzl."

The story in *Der Stern* had brought Norma a kind of fame, and her mother seemed proud of it: "So many people writing to her," she said, "and she's even been invited to come and stay abroad."

The letters were worn thin from being handled, from being read and re-read.

"When she's home—after school and at weekends," said a neighbor across the street, "she stands for hours at her bedroom window, stands and looks out into the street."

For Mary's relatives, her Scottish grandmother and her aunts and uncles, disaster continued.

During Mary's trial they had learned that Isa's baby was in hospital with leukemia. "We kept going to the telephone to learn about her. The baby so ill in Glasgow, Mary on trial for these terrible things in Newcastle—the baby died in February; we feel as if we are being punished for something, but we don't know for what."

It is difficult to identify oneself with a family so pursued by catastrophe; it is difficult to imagine how one would act and behave in their place. As for Betty Bell, one can only guess at what went on in her beleaguered mind. During the months of Mary's remand, and the days of the trial, she was constantly writing notes, letters, poems, and prayers to her dead father. "Nobody knows how I miss you Dad, how I need you, how I love you . . ." She fluctuated between wild extremes of gaiety and depression.

"We were always dying for her to get rid of that horrible wig," Cath said. "I offered to wash it for her in the spin drier—I so hoped it would get torn. But it came out beautiful. She set it— she had the boy (their youngest) sitting here in the middle of the room with it on, and put the curls into it with it on his head. . . . It was that funny but . . ." she stopped.

One cannot—and does not even wish to—doubt that both Betty and Billy Bell were frantically unhappy about what had happened to Mary. And yet, there was the other side of the coin.

"A man phoned me one day," said Sidney Foxcroft, Newcastle reporter for *The People* and *The Sun,* who wrote several perceptive pieces at the time of the trial. "He said he was a friend of the Bells and that they wanted to come and talk to me about something. I got a friend of mine to sit in on this meeting. You know, I could hardly believe it myself. They came along, Betty and Billy Bell and their pal, and they said they wanted to sell us the story of Mary's life. Their kid was on trial for murder over there in Moot Hall and they sat here and said, 'We tried to teach her right, but we couldn't do a thing with her. . . .' Well, it was my job to listen to them— but I've never been so sickened in my life. I rang through to the office in London afterwards and told them. They said they wouldn't touch it with a ten-foot pole."

But then, sometime during that period—it was not quite clear exactly when—Betty tried once again to kill herself; she had tried several times before (and repeatedly since). On that particular occasion, late one night, she climbed up on one of the Tyne bridges, deserted at that hour. "But there was a man came up in a car," said one of her sisters, "he jumped out and pulled her back. He talked to her and asked whether she was a Catholic. When she said yes, he said he'd take her to a church; he thought she needed to talk it out with somebody trained to deal with terrible problems, and that's one of the jobs of a priest, he said. He drove her to a Catholic church and took her in. He made quite sure the priest was there before he left her. He was a good man. The priest was there all right," Betty's sister said bitterly, "but when she began to talk to him—I suppose she was very upset and crying like she does—he said, 'Are you a member of this parish?' Well of course she wasn't. So she said no, she wasn't. So he told her to go away. He said for her to go to her own priest in her own parish. And she left. . . ."

"We were that worried," said Cath, "about May, about Betty, about what was being said in court. When . . . you know, when the psychiatrists said that about 'genetic influences,' we tried and tried to remember what possible illnesses there had been in the family. My mam and I—she was staying with us—we sat up all night, with pencil and paper trying to retrace people and events." Her mother would often just drop off to sleep in her chair. "And I'd go to sleep for two hours and then up again. We couldn't find anything."

In the morning they would meet Betty somewhere in town on the way to court, "so that we'd arrive together." Betty was officially also staying with them (Billy, loyal as ever, claimed she stayed with *him*), but mostly she was somewhere else altogether. "My mother and I talked for days and nights about Betty's way of life," Cath said, "trying to understand why and how . . ."

Viewed in retrospect, how is it that some of Mary's relatives, faced with the awful certainty of her guilt, did not immediately tell more about the circumstances of her tragic life to the people who might have helped her?

The truth of the matter is that in their hearts none of them could believe that the law—even in its most formal sense—could be anything but merciful to an eleven-year-old child. A psychiatrist was to write later in his report that he encountered "a conspiracy of silence." It is doubtful whether what happened was at all deliberate. It was merely the result of an intolerable and really insurmountable conflict of loyalties.

Mrs. McC. has tried desperately to avoid saying anything that might be detrimental to Betty, even when her children, younger, more resilient, and perhaps at this point more aware of the implications, tried to persuade her. "All I want," she said, "is that May be left alone. Nothing can help now. She is paying the penalty to society."

Her children, however, like a great many other people who were involved, as time went on groped toward some means to help, to make amends. "I hope my mother talks to you," said Betty's only brother Philip, a quiet and thoughtful man. "It's terribly hard for her—she's caught between Betty and Mary. But I think she should. It would be better."

"She hugged me when I left," said Isa on another occasion when we met. "She said, 'You are old enough. You must decide yourself what you want to say and do. How can I do anything? They can't expect me to choose between Betty and May.' "

After the trial Betty disappeared. No one in her family knew where she was. Cath, tidying up some shelves a few months later, found Betty's letters to her father and all her papers: wedding certificate, the children's birth certificates, and various mementos.

"She must have put them there one day when I wasn't looking," Cath said. "In case they were needed any time." There were rumors that she'd been seen in Glasgow and working in this or that pub in Whitley Bay. Even while their apprehensions grew about Mary, all of them wondered if Betty would ever come back.

She returned three months later, for a few days. She saw her mother and her sisters, all of whom, as always, succumbed to her need for their love and support. She saw Billy and the three children who were living with him, and she and Billy went to see Mary. After that she vanished again, this time for almost a year.

Mary had been sent for a period of observation to Cumberlow Lodge, a (strictly short-term) Remand Home for girls in London, which serves as a classifying center for the metropolis and adjacent counties. A model institution of its kind, it has an exceptionally large staff, the best medical facilities, and—essential for Mary— "special provisions for high-degree security."

Mary spent over two months there, during which, by far the youngest girl there, she needed a great deal of special care and attention. Interestingly enough—an encouraging note in a sad tale —she provoked in the other girls "nothing but compassion."

She was seen by several psychiatrists. Those who were later put in charge of her said bitterly and incorrectly, with the possessiveness Mary always brings out in those charged with her care, "At Cumberlow Lodge she was seen by countless psychiatrists—every student in London was unleashed on her . . ." Actually she was examined above all by Professor Trevor Gibbens, one of the leading child psychiatrists in Britain, who concurred with all those who had seen her previously, that she needed and could benefit from medical treatment.

The Home Office, uncomfortably exposed to a wave of public concern and criticism, not so much over Mary's fate as over the danger she represented to others, was now confronted with the great problem of what to do with her.

There are a number of mental hospitals in Britain, some with excellent provisions for children and young people. There are also a number of first-rate homes for maladjusted children (more and better provisions than exist in any other country in Europe and possibly the world). The trouble was that none of them have security provisions adequate to contain children as dangerous as Mary, nor do the Approved Schools for Girls, although one or two of them have good arrangements for psychiatric treatment.

"Secure" hospital provisions, on the other hand, which do exist within the penal system, are only for those over fifteen, and tend to be restrictive rather than therapeutic.

"There was conference after conference about her," said someone who attended many of the Home Office meetings at the time. "Nobody could think what to do."

The authorities were faced with a barrage of newspaper comments and questions in Parliament emphasizing that—with the hysteria created by the outcome of the trial—the public would object to her presence wherever she was sent. It was a difficult atmosphere in which to make a decision that required courage and imagination, as well as an unemotional, level-headed approach.

It was clear that what was needed was something new to meet all the requirements: security, social environment (companionship, educational and recreational facilities, the potential for building relationships), and psychiatric treatment.

The ideal solution (valiantly supported by a few lone voices at the time) would have been to accept the challenge and accelerate a long-standing project for the creation of a "secure" psychiatric unit for severely disturbed younger children. But such a course presented—quite legitimate—practical difficulties of organization, staffing, and above all cost, and furthermore was resisted by some almost as a point of principle on the basis that Mary was a unique case whose special needs could not justify such an effort or expense.*

The belief that Mary was a unique case was certainly shared by the press and public. Fostered first by the universal revulsion against her crime, it was reinforced by the almost complete lack of background information of her life and the "extreme stress" which presumably led to these crimes, and exacerbated by the extravagant epithets—"monster," "fiend," "Svengali"—which were so readily applied to her.

The basic misunderstanding about Mary—which appears to persist today—was that insufficient mental separation was made between her *condition* and her *crime*.

Her crime—the "motive-less" murder of two small boys—is, if not unique, certainly very rare. Children who kill—and there are a surprising number of them, although usually much younger or somewhat older than eleven—are more often than not driven by "normal" (if excessive) emotions such as jealousy or fear. Murder without motive, other than perhaps a desire to *feel something,* is the epitome of psychopathy—Mary's condition as diagnosed. Although, again, very few psychopathic children commit murder, the condition itself is not rare. According to London University sociologist Professor Terence Morris, there were in the late 1960s about 200 psychopathic children within the child-care system

* But see footnote, page 242.

of England and Wales alone. Many of these are unsuitably cared for in adult wards of mental institutions, in Children's Homes or even worse, for lack of other possibilities, are prematurely returned to their homes, in many cases the very root of their troubles. In many others the condition is not even diagnosed.

A renowned child psychiatrist in an English university town said, "I could find them twenty children [like this] just in this area, tomorrow."

Intensive research into psychopathic children is being carried out in many cities in the United States, and also in Sweden, Switzerland, Austria, France, Germany, Canada, and of course Britain. In one major project alone, at Bellevue Hospital in New York City, psychiatrist Laurette Bender examined 800 children who had been diagnosed as psychopathic.

What is a psychopath? Sociologists William and Joan McCord of Stanford University, California, supply a very clear description in their book *The Psychopath** which has become an essential textbook for any student of the subject:

> The psychopath is asocial. His conduct often brings him into conflict with society. The psychopath is driven by primitive desires and an exaggerated craving for excitement. In his self-centered search for pleasure, he ignores restrictions of his culture. The psychopath is highly impulsive. He is a man for whom the moment is a segment of time detached from all others. His actions are unplanned and guided by his whims. The psychopath is aggressive. He has learned few socialized ways of coping with frustration. The psychopath feels little, if any guilt. He can commit the most appalling acts, yet view them without remorse. The psychopath has a warped capacity for love. His emotional relationships, when they exist, are meager, fleeting, and designed to satisfy his own desires. These last two traits, guiltlessness and lovelessness, conspicuously mark the psychopath as different from other men.

The McCords describe child psychopaths as follows:

* *The Psychopath*, by William and Joan McCord, published by the Van Nostrand Reinhold Company, copyright 1964 by Litton Educational Publishing, Inc.

The child psychopath has the embryonic personality traits of the adult psychopath. His tantrums and delinquencies betray his aggressiveness. His truancies reflect his impulsivity, his cruelties to animals and children reveal his asociality. The child psychopath has little, if any remorse for his diffuse, brutal, usually purposeless activities, and he seems unable to affiliate with other human beings.

Although the condition has been described—in different terms —by psychiatrists for more than 150 years, we still do not know today what causes it. Some scientists believe in hereditary factors, others in neurological ones, others again are certain that environmental reasons are more likely to blame. Of these three, the hereditary approach has now been the most discredited, and the environmental offers the most hope. A feeling of rejection in childhood, although not the sole explanation and certainly not inevitably causing psychopathy, does appear to be a common factor in many psychopaths and research has tended to confirm that the greater the feeling of deprivation, the more psychopathic the child's personality.

It is certainly on this concept of the unloved child that the Austrain psychoanalyst August Aichhorn conceived in 1907 his "milieu therapy" theory. To explore this technique he opened after World War I, in Oberhollabrunn, Austria, a home for delinquent boys, probably the most enlightened institution of its kind in the first half of the century. This became the model for a whole series of bold experiments, such as the Children's Village at Ska in Sweden; Warrendale in Canada; and in the United States—the most ambitious programs—Hawthorne Cedar Knoll, Fritz Redl's Pioneer House in Detroit, Bruno Bettelheim's Orthogenic School in Chicago and Wiltwyck in New York: all schools concentrating on giving close therapy through affection to asocial children, a considerable number of them psychopaths.* Even so, it is generally

---

* Professor T. C. N. Gibbens, one of Britain's leading child psychiatrists and Consultant to the Home Office Children's Department (now Ministry of Health and Social Services), was to say later, in a television debate following the publication of this book, that the treatment for a girl such as Mary *must* include educators and social workers quite as much as medical personnel.

agreed that very little is really known or scientifically certain about so-called psychopathic children. Psychiatrists readily concede that it is a term applied fairly loosely to people with certain character deficiencies and showing certain behavior patterns. But the same characteristics and patterns have also been noticed in children with mental subnormalities or quite specific mental illnesses, such as schizophrenia. "Psychopath" has in fact become almost a cliché—an emotive term used far too readily even by specialists, and far too often by the media. What we tend to forget—perhaps because we do not want to face it—is that psychiatry, far from being capable of performing miracles, is only at the dawn of knowledge. The fact that a few progressive experiments dealing with these problems exist in the United States (and Europe) should not be interpreted as indicating that the problem is solved —or even only marginally less acute there. On the contrary, America's violent—or disturbed—society perhaps not unnaturally produces more violent—or disturbed—children than any other place in the world. And the few amongst them who, instead of being sent to mental hospitals or even prisons, end up being treated at the two milieu therapy centers which have survived America's recession of the past few years, are very lucky indeed.*

To repeat then: Mary's *crime* was rare—her *condition* is not. And it was her condition which required specific treatment.

The final decision the Home Office made about Mary was a compromise.

On 2 February 1969, Mary was sent to the "Special Unit" of Red Bank Approved School in Newton-le-Willows, Lancashire. Until then operated exclusively for boys, it was to be transformed for her benefit into a coeducational establishment.

There are four of these experimental units in Britain, all for boys, all operated *loosely* on Aichhorn's "milieu therapy." They are designed to provide for persistently "asocial" children primarily between the ages of fourteen and eighteen, a secure environment with the constant supervision of an exceptionally numerous and sympathetic staff. Under these controlled but benign conditions, it

* The Orthogenic School in Chicago and Wiltwyck.

is hoped that the children, encouraged by a graduated reward system, may learn that it is possible to live peacefully with other people. The aim of the establishment is to return them as rapidly as possible into normal society, albeit on probation or under supervision. Few of these children are diagnosed psychopaths (also described as "dissocial children *without* neurosis"). Most of them would come into the category of "asocial children with neurosis."

Red Bank Approved School is a big, purpose-built, modern complex containing a classifying center which can take two hundred and fifty boys and a Vocational School (teaching farming, carpentry, and other skills) catering for the same numbers. They live in groups in separate houses which, colorful, spacious, and comfortable, are influenced by Scandinavian design and bear no resemblance to the traditional Dickensian English "institution."

The "Special Unit," although specifically for children requiring high-degree security provisions and therefore locked at all times, looks if anything even less forbidding. Much thought has gone into the interior design, which abounds with light, the warmth of natural wood, the color of vivid wall panels, and good, modern furniture. Although it stands right in the middle of "Red Bank" (thereby wisely reducing the feeling of isolation or segregation from which children under such restraint often suffer) it exists as a separate entity from the rest of the school. The Unit can take twenty-six children and has its own headmaster, staff, teaching and recreational facilities, and garden. Four of the senior boys sleep in a dormitory, the others in individual bedrooms along a corridor on the second floor. Each bedroom door, locked at night and during after-lunch rest periods, has an observation window, and staff are on duty day and night. While the children are given as much freedom as possible within this enclosed life, they are theoretically under constant supervision and not even allowed to go to a bathroom on their own, measures which are taken both for their own protection and as part of the Unit's concentrated process of social re-education. Sitting rooms are furnished with comfortable armchairs (and TV), the dining room where children and staff eat together in small groups is light and airy, the classrooms where they are taught in groups of three to six are warm and relaxed. An exceptionally well-equipped art room (including a

pottery kiln) allows wide scope for any artistic bent—or release for
pent-up frustration. Everything is provided that might enlarge
their horizon and add to their emotional balance: books, music,
exercise, good food, gardening, a shed for pets, and, above all,
a large number of adults who are there for the sole purpose of
helping them. The eighteen teachers and supervisors are supple-
mented by a domestic staff of twelve, all of whom form an important part of the children's lives.

It is in many ways a sophisticated and beneficial set-up for a
large number of disturbed children. Physically and materially it
offered a child like Mary, too, everything one could wish for. But
medically it did not.

This is not a reflection on the dedicated people who work
there, who were—as some of them put it—"landed with the job."
It is a reflection on our system. It seems that we refuse to admit
the inadequacy of the available provisions (by no means only for
Mary Bell but many other children too) and content ourselves
with half-way measures which jeopardize not only this one unhappy
girl, and others similarly affected, but all of their surroundings.

A sentence from the aims set out in the *Description of the
Special Units* says, "Our aim is the social re-education of each
boy through the development of affectionate and understanding
attachments between boys and staff and between the boys themselves."

This—put very simply—is the basic tenet of Dr. Aichhorn's
theory. But like many basically simple ideas, which can affect the
emotional safety of individuals, its application is very complex and
needs to be approached with restraint and care. Every one of the
establishments in the United States, Sweden, and Canada which
have so far done serious work in milieu therapy provided a
superbly staffed part Children's Home, part medical environment, and combined all available means to inquire into and to
treat the often sharply differing needs of, on the one hand, severely
disturbed, on the other, psychopathic children. While in these places
"relationships" between children and staff are also considered
of primary importance, more seriously afflicted children are also
treated by psychiatrists, educational psychologists, psychothera-
pists, and, if necessary, drugs. Even so, few of these schools have

claimed any great success with psychopathic children—all they are willing to say is that milieu therapy combined with all these other disciplines offers reason for hope.

Among the eighteen members of staff at the Special Unit at Red Bank there were, at the time of writing, five people trained in child care, some with prison experience, some with teaching certificates, some with infant training. Several of the staff had attended the excellent special courses on disturbed children run by the Home Office. But none of the resident staff had any other formal medical or academic qualifications. None of them were university graduates.

This does not mean that as far as natural gifts are concerned the staff at this and similar institutions in Britain is not of a high caliber. Generally speaking, if they were not of more than average intelligence and moral character, it is unlikely that they would either choose or be accepted for this work. Equally, some of them, whether specifically trained or not, have a special gift and the emotional strength to work with such children—which is a difficult task at best, and it is certainly essential to use these rare gifts. It is fair to say that even without formal qualifications such people can work effectively with quite a number of the children the units now deal with and their willingness to involve themselves emotionally with these children—most of whom have been emotionally deprived in one or another way—is of inestimable value. It is very much the same type of teachers or counselors who—trained on and by the job—work in places like Wiltwyck in America. The significant difference being, however, that *there* the counseling staff is trained and supervised by doctors, and therapists with formal degrees, who are in permanent attendance.

It is in my view insufficiently recognized here that, for children as deeply disturbed as Mary, those who supply this emotional involvement the children so desperately need must above all exercise considerable detachment and a sense of perspective. Detachment of this sort, essential not only for the children but for the therapist's own sake, is however infinitely difficult to achieve, and can only be found through a most careful, deliberate process of emotional and intellectual discipline. Any student in this field will confirm that this is the most difficult quality to acquire.

"In all relations with adults," said one of the most perceptive people at Red Bank, "it is Mary who decides events. She even persuades them into believing that they feel no differently about her than about the other children." Another said (mid-1970), "She has so far had four 'counselors' since she has been here. The children have the right to choose their own counselors amongst the staff—they don't have to answer to anyone about their choice. In the case of most boys—if one of them requests a change of counselor, the staff just shrug it off—it doesn't matter. But every time Mary has asked to change, people become worried about it, introspective. They feel it is a reflection on themselves, they feel guilty. Two members of the staff have left, solely because they felt themselves becoming too involved with Mary. The third still sometimes broods on why Mary didn't stay with him. And the fourth—who has also now left the school—became convinced that Mary is innocent of killing those little boys."

These problems, indicative as they are of lack of detachment in some of the staff, are of course important. But they are not the only, or even the main, reasons why I think the Special Unit at Red Bank in its present form was the wrong choice for Mary. There are three others:

First, when she came to Red Bank in February 1969 she was the only girl among twenty-three boys and this situation was to continue for about three months. Since June 1969 a few girls, all at least three years older than Mary, have come and gone, but up to the time of writing never more than three at a time, and none for more than a few months. Children's authorities around the country (who are autonomous in their areas) have been understandably reluctant to send their girls into this ill-balanced group and during the last two years* Mary—now fourteen—has again repeatedly been the only girl with over twenty-two boys for many weeks at a time. Although she is now coming nearer in age to the others, for probably the three most important years of her "treatment" she has almost entirely lacked a true peer group.

Second, the aims of the Unit state: ". . . The need for psychiatric help and guidance is essential. The psychiatrist is integrated as a member of the team and he sees all [boys] soon after their ad-

* As of 1971.

mission. He assesses the boy's symptoms and the emotional disturbances he displays. Our psychologist, who is also a member of the team, assesses the level of a boy's intelligence, personality traits, special aptitudes and school progress. The training staff provide a full picture of the boy's background and family. Having made their enquiries, the team hold a 'case conference' from which we derive the following benefits:

"An early diagnosis of the basic factors contributing to a boy's difficulties.

"Individual treatment for each boy.

"Treatment by all staff on an agreed policy.

"Guidance and the development of staff confidence in dealing with difficult boys . . ."

When Mary arrived, the staff knew little about her background. But then, at that point, neither did anyone else outside her immediate family. The original research for a series of articles which appeared in the *Daily Telegraph Magazine* in December 1969, and for this book, was done in the spring of 1969. In June of that year, the Home Office was informed of everything this initial inquiry had revealed. This was done in agreement with Mary's legal advisers, who were preparing an Appeal, the Newcastle Children's Department, and the psychiatrists interested in her, who all thought that this information was essential to the further disposition of her case. In spite of this, neither the principal of Red Bank School, the headmaster of the Special Unit, the consultant doctors, or of course any members of the staff who were working with Mary were given any of this information until months after the articles—with parts of this material in them—had appeared. "They told us in the very beginning," said a member of staff, "it's in writing: that her background was unimportant for the staff to know about."

And yet: "When you open Mary's file," said another, "on the first page, encircled in red, is a copy of a letter from Mr. Justice Cusack to the Home Office, saying she *must have psychiatric treatment*."

Third, a psychiatrist and a psychologist, both highly qualified, are, it is true, "members of the team." Their main function, however, is to consult once a week with the staff. They can give no direct treatment. Psychiatric treatment of any kind is not within the concept of the Unit, nor is the Unit equipped to function for this purpose.

The consulting psychiatrist, desperately concerned about Mary and no less about the effect she has on the other children, has several times in the past two years* recommended various methods of psychiatric treatment which would have to be carried out in a medical environment. He also recommended stringent control on which members of her family should be allowed to visit her, and, finally, has repeatedly urged that she be transferred to a more suitable—and medically oriented—environment.

On 21 July 1969, a hearing for leave to appeal was held before the Lord Chief Justice, Lord Parker,

Mr. Harvey Robson, Mary's defending counsel, in explaining the intended action, said that the application for leave to appeal against Mary's sentence was entered on the assumption that by the time it was heard arrangements would have been made (by the Home Office) enabling the Court to make the (hospital) order (it had intended) but things had not turned out that way. Unfortunately there was still no hospital suitable to receive the child.

Mr. Robson then said that, as far as could be ascertained, the Home Office had (in fact) decided that, at any rate for a considerable time to come, "the child was not in need of treatment of the kind that would be given in a special hospital. . . ." He said that Mary's legal and medical advisers were not (altogether) satisfied as to the degree of psychiatric treatment she was receiving and was likely to receive but, no hospital being available, it had been decided that the correct course was to withdraw the application for leave to apeal.

Now it was no longer just that appropriate facilities did not exist: despite emphatic professional opinion to the contrary, the authorities had apparently managed to convince themselves that Mary *needed* no other treatment.

Legally, this was the end of her case. No further steps could be taken. The only person who possibly welcomed this development was Betty Bell, who, on repeated occasions during the two

---

* And continuously since then (1973).

months preceding that day, had telephoned Mary's solicitor, David Bryson, from wherever she was and said, "I don't want her to go to a mental hospital" and then rung off. Betty Bell has of course been in psychiatric wards herself and knows well that psychiatric treatment consists of questions and—however long delayed—eventual replies.

I visited the school at the invitation of the principal and headmaster in March 1970. Mary's room—as all the bedrooms—was pleasantly light and cheerful. But I was struck that—unlike the other rooms which, aside from the odd photograph or toilet article, were comparatively bare of possession—it was -chock-ful of things. "She is still so showered with presents from her relatives," said the headmaster, "we can't give her all of them." The presents —dolls; soap in all colors, shapes, and forms; bath powder and salts, bottles of toilet water and scents; diaries and greeting cards— filled every inch of every surface in the room and were even stacked up in the corners and against the walls. Strangest of all, perhaps three-quarters of these gifts, carefully set up as for a window display, were still in their original cellophane or plastic covers. "It's like an exhibition," said one of the consultants who walked around with me. "She doesn't *use* any of them," said a member of staff, "she just looks at them."

Was that it? Was Mary looking at them, or did she set them up for others to look at? Can it have been right for her to receive so many presents when other children there had so few? What must this have meant to the other children? And can it really have been good for Mary herself? Was it not a continuation of the material "spoiling"—the hapless compensation for rejection —she got at home, particularly from her mother?

For the first ten months of Mary's stay at Red Bank, Billy Bell was her most regular visitor. (Both the Home Office and the Newcastle Children's Department are exceptionally generous about paying trips and *per diems* for Mary's relatives to enable them to visit her.) Billy Bell said that Mary liked the school. "She has a nice room," he said.

But, as of 10 December 1969, Billy could no longer go to see her. For on that day, just about one year after Mary's trial, he stood in the Newcastle Court—where Mary had been tried—accused of robbery with force, was found guilty and jailed for fifteen months.

Mr. Rudolph Lyons, Q.C., who had prosecuted in the case against Mary, sat as Commissioner of the Court and gave Billy Bell a comparatively light sentence. "I am reducing the sentence I would normally have passed," he said "because of the tragedy surrounding this man's family life."

"I'll take the kids if he's sent down," said Billy's ever-loyal sister Audrey, once more waiting in Court.

Billy Bell's defending counsel, Mr. James Chadwin, had made an eloquent—and as it turned out successful—plea for him. He had also told the Court that, while Billy visited his daughter regularly in the place where she is in custody, "his wife, I am instructed, takes no interest in the child."

However, Billy no sooner out of the way (her sources of information obviously intact) Betty presented herself at the Newcastle Children's Department and said that she would now be visiting Mary. Her first visit took place on 20 December 1969.

"Mary was told to await her mother in her room but got impatient and came downstairs," the staff say. "When her mother came, she ran towards her, and embraced and kissed her. Later they sat in the library, with Mary on Betty's lap, and both cried."

Betty now went to visit Mary regularly—by the end of January 1970 she had been to see her three times. (Between the summer of 1971 and Christmas 1972 she went at least once a month.) Mary seemed to look forward to these visits, though she was always unsettled afterwards.

"Of course," said one teacher, "with Mary one always tends to read something into every reaction." Nevertheless, the staff felt that Betty, much of the time, was as if play-acting with Mary—"She *acted* being the mother." She "played" with her—inventing things and stories. She seemed, say the staff, to "bewilder" Mary who said once that she did not think Betty *was* her mother—she "just wasn't like a mother." As time went on, the teachers (many of them, as can be seen, very perceptive) noticed the ambivalence in Mary's feelings: at one moment she seemed to idolize her mother, mostly for being "so smartly turned out." At other times she said she hated her—as she put it, for leaving her "father and the bairns" (i.e., herself).

On 21 April 1970 Mary herself decided to stop her mother's visits. She told her counselor and Mr. Dixon, the headmaster of the Unit, a fatherly man to whom she appears very attached, that she didn't want to see her again, and Betty was written to and asked to stop her visits.*

Just about that time the people in charge of the Special Unit decided (correctly enough) that it would be good for Mary to see her father who was in prison not too far away. Unfortunately, instead of arranging a meeting somewhere on "neutral ground," which doubtless—the Home Office having always shown their willingness to help—could have been organized, Mary was taken to visit Billy in prison.

In the early hours of the morning following this visit the night-watchman called the housemaster on duty and told him that Mary was lying on her bed, crying bitterly.

"I saw my dad in that place," she sobbed. "It isn't a nice place at all." She was inconsolable and the master called the headmaster. "He came over in his pajamas and sat with her for more than two hours. He finally got her to go back to sleep. She'll do anything for Mr. Dixon," he said later.

Mary's relatives felt that the solution that had been found for her—the Special Unit—was the best under the circumstances.

"May's probably getting better schooling than ours ever will," said one of her aunts.

"She writes to us every two weeks," says Isa. "She sounds that ordinary in her letters. . . ."

In some of her letters she does sound like any child away at school:

"Dear Auntie, Uncle, bairns, Dog," reads one of the early ones, "How's everything with you? . . . I am feeling low today, homesick I guess. Ten, eleven months is a long time, but time passes quickly. I think I feel sad when there is a slow record on.

---

* It is interesting to note that—although the Home Office has stated time and time again that "in law" no one has a right to stop a mother from seeing her child—this *can* in fact be done (see Postscript).

Now there's a fast one and I am better. I got fifty-two points today for good behaviour . . . lots and lots and lots of love, Mary."

When she gets lots of "points" she gets a reward; in the case of the other children the "points" automatically get them closer to the time when they are allowed outside the Unit, and even weekend and holiday visits home. In Mary's case this was impossible for a long time. Her reward would be a visit to the headmaster's home, the opportunity to play there with ordinary children, or, on very rare occasions, a drive in a carefully locked car. Slowly the manifestations of her condition became less immediately obvious. "We are doing miracles with her," some of the young staff exulted.

"My mother went to see her," said Billy Bell's sister. "She says she's lovely; she says she is so grown up and well-behaved and calm."

"She used to fight other children, used bad language, lied, bit, and scratched," said one teacher, "but she doesn't any more. She never attacked the adults, only children." But the trouble was still there—underneath. A visitor who played a game with her remonstrated when he saw her blatantly cheating. "You can't do that," he said. "Oh yes," she replied, "*I* can."

Early in her detention, on at least two occasions she was involved in the more or less mysterious demise of some hamsters which died of neck injuries.

"But she has a budgerigar," said a teacher, anxious to prove how well she was doing. "She hasn't killed *that,* has she?"

Some members of the staff are naturally glad to point to things which tend to prove how normal she really is—or has become. Sometimes, too, she is "tried out."

"Not long after our baby was born," said a member of staff, "I said to my wife, 'Let's show it to Mary; let's see what she makes of it.' We did. She wasn't at all happy—she felt very uncomfortable—you could see it. . . ."

Somebody else talked about the young woman teacher who, while she was Mary's counselor, became convinced of Mary's innocence. "Miss H . . . has tried all kinds of things with Mary."

"What kind of things?"

"Oh—psychiatric drama and that."

"Psychodrama? Is she trained in that?"

"Well, she trained in drama." (Psychodrama, frequently very effective with disturbed children and adolescents, *can* in fact be used by lay therapists, who however need to be carefully instructed in its applications, effects and above all evaluation; and therefore —as with all therapy—need themselves to be stable and mature individuals.)

When the case of Mary Bell arose there was manifestly no suitable provision for her. The simplest, most direct and constructive way to deal with the situation would have been—and still is—to turn the existing superb facilities at Red Bank into a Unit that *can* deal, medically as well as environmentally, with psychopathic children or adolescents in need of special security provisions. This would require comparatively minimal changes and could be done with comparatively minimal resources. It could even be expanded to include something like a hostel which would make it possible—if necessary—to extend treatment for young people as seriously ill as Mary, to a time when a modicum of liberty should be offered.

A psychiatric treatment Unit for severely disturbed children between eight and fifteen *has* now opened in Southern England (and three more are planned for the country as a whole). But for obvious reasons, treatment, to be effective, must start as early in the child's life as possible.* And a number of children, including Mary, are presumably now too old for this particular place.

The attractive surroundings, the orderly way of life of the present Unit, and above all the concentrated attention and affection Mary has been receiving have no doubt helped her to some extent. She has learned to want the approval of the other children, talks far more about herself, discusses at times her greatest problem, her relationship with her mother, and she does now cry. These *are* steps forward for her.

In the spring of 1970, during or just before the renewed separation from her mother she had herself requested, she wrote

---

* It is worth saying here that since the case of Mary Bell received such wide publicity in 1968, five not unsimilar cases, all involving children under fifteen killing or attempting to kill younger children, have occurred in Britain. In all these cases the names of the children were withheld.

Betty a letter in the form of a poem. This letter, an extremely important step in Mary's development whichever way one looks at it, has necessarily been seen by a number of people (and has, since the publication of the book in England, been printed in several newspapers and recited on a BBC TV program).

> 'MAM' [it said],
> I know that in my heart
> From you once was not apart
> My love for you grows
> More each day
> When you visit me mam
> I'd weep once your away
> I look into your eyes, so blue and
> they're very sad. you try to be very
> cheery. But I know you think IM Bad so Bad
> though I really dont know If you
> feel the same,
> and treat it as a silly game
> a child who has made criminal fame
> Please mam put my tiny mind at ease
> tell Judge and Jury on your knees
> they will LISTEN to your cry of PLEAS
> THE GUILTY ONE IS you not me
> I sorry it HAS to BE this way
> We'll both cry and you will go away
> to other gates were you are free
> locked up in prison cells.
> Your famley are wee,
> these last words I speak, on behalf
> of dad . . . and me
> tell them you are guilty
> Please, so then mam, Ill be free, Daughter
>
>   May

It is inconceivable that Mary—at thirteen—could have had any real understanding of the concept "freedom through atonement." One must therefore assume that—at least as far as that extraordinary sentence is concerned—her way of expressing herself was the result of instinct rather than intellect. But anyway, it is very

difficult to interpret Mary's motives for doing anything.* She may
also have written it as a result of learning about the content
of the articles which had appeared the previous December in the
Daily Telegraph Magazine, which dealt in some detail with the
problems of her mother. Although efforts were made by the
magazine and others to keep her from this knowledge at that
time, in the final analysis it may not have been possible to do
so. "All the children know everything that goes on," said one of
the teachers. "They know on the one hand by some sort of
osmosis and, on the other, there are those who believe that they
should be told everything as a matter of principle."

It is unfortunately only too possible that those who hold such
opinions would take it upon themselves even to *show* Mary—as
an experiment in honesty they might think—such published material. And it is equally possible that boys from the Unit, returning
after Christmas spent with their families, brought back copies of
the magazine. Reading this could well have prompted her to write
this letter.

There is still a third possible explanation: she must know that
letters from children in the Unit are read by the staff, more often
than not by each child's particular counselor.

It was also just about this time that Mary had requested a
young woman teacher to be her new counselor. As almost everything Mary does is done for immediate effect, it also could be
that this letter—although addressed to her mother—was really
written to influence the attitude of this teacher whose affection
and sympathy she was very anxious to have. This young teacher
was also involved in the next dramatic episode in Mary's life.

On the early evening of Monday, 15 June 1970, Mary told her
that during the weekend just past, one of the housemasters, a
thirty-five-year-old married man who had been at the Special
Unit since its inception four years before and was about to emi-
grate to a similar job in Canada, had indecently assaulted her.

"When she told me about it, it was not in the nature of a com-

* On October 5, 1972, after the book's publication in England, Professor T. C. N. Gibbens, the child psychiatrist who had examined
Mary at the request of the Home Office after she was convicted, was
quoted in the (London) *Times:* "She is really impenetrable; no one
knows what goes on in her head."

plaint," the teacher was to testify later, "she was just upset about it. It was not a complaint, in the sense that she was not asking for anything to be done about it. She was saying that she was distressed by what had happened."

Mary too, much later, was to say, "I wasn't trying to accuse him. I told Miss H. 'Don't tell anybody,' but she did anyway."

It is not likely that this was pathetically true? That Mary, in her need for her counselor's affection and attention, had built up this story on the flimsiest pretext? Is this not a classic manifestation of an emotionally deprived girl? And might it not have been treated with more skepticism at the outset?

Mary's counselor, when confronted with this tale, did what she had to do: she told her superior, who in turn informed the headmaster and the principal of Red Bank.

Although it was known that three months earlier Mary and a boy had already plotted to accuse another master of assaulting her and although—quite aside from similar incidents—it was known that three days before this alleged "assault" Mary had, by invitation, watched a boy masturbate in the pigeon shed ("She told someone, who told the headmaster and the boy got a thrashing"), Mary's allegations were taken seriously without any attempt to seek psychiatric advice. The Unit's consultant psychiatrist was not told although he paid three of his weekly visits to the Unit during the initial investigation. He finally read about it in the *Guardian*.

The police were called, the housemaster, whose name was subsequently widely published, was taken off his duties, and the result was a committal hearing and a trial.*

The committal hearing was held in the small Magistrate's Court at Newton-le-Willows on a hot day in August (1970). The slim, blond housemaster, pink and embarrassed, sat next to his counsel, Mr. John Stannard, and tried to look as if he was certain that no one could possibly take the proceedings seriously. His attractive wife, seven months pregnant, pale but with a determined smile, sat in the back row of the public seats next to her mother. The

---

* Approximately three months after she had been asked to stop her visits Mary's mother appeared at the school. "She was sobbing," said a teacher, "and said she just had to see Mary again so she was allowed in. Mary seemed glad enough to see her. They both cried."

case having received some advance publicity, with Mary's name mentioned in one or two papers, there were quite a number of reporters.

Mary's grandmother, sitting next to Betty, looked thinner and more worn than ever. Betty, with a new white-blond long and smooth wig, wore a crimson jacket, a miniskirt and white shiny boots. Her face ravaged and ashen, she affirmed in a low voice that Mary was Mary Flora Bell and was born on 26 May 1957.

Mary, tremendously changed even in the four months since I had seen her last, seemed heavy and tired. Brought in holding the hand of the Unit headmaster, Mr. Dixon, she walked with a defeated shambling sort of gait. Her face pasty and white, her eyes flickering uncertainly from wall to wall, she was a long way from the chirpy, self-assured eleven-year-old who had dominated the nine-day trial at the Newcastle Assizes eighteen months before.

Mary was on the witness stand for two hours. The first five minutes consisted of innocuous questions which she answered readily enough. She said that the housemaster had allowed her to come to the "duty-room" with him during the rest period after lunch, when she asked him to. Why had she asked him? Because she didn't like to be locked in alone. Had she done this before? No. She was asked what they had talked about in the duty-room, but she said she wouldn't answer in front of all these people. There was a commotion in the back row when her mother called out, "But you must—she must answer that" and began to cry. The magistrates consulted briefly and the Court was cleared.*

Mary then claimed that the housemaster had said to her "Are you getting any hair down there yet?" and that he had then begun "to mess about."

The rest of her story was haltingly told, with many instances of what appeared to be desperate embarrassment at having to pronounce sexual words. Her twisting, turning, and hiding her tensely pale and frozen face in her hands was incredibly convincing. In view of the circumstances of her life these terms can hardly have been new to her, and her show of distress was certainly perturbing. She made the allegation that the housemaster, pre-

---

* The author, by permission of the Magistrates, remained in Court throughout Mary's testimony.

THE PRESENT: "THE GUILTY ONE IS YOU NOT ME"

paratory to visiting her and masturbating on her bed early the following morning, had given her a book called *Oral Love* with instructions to read it before he came back to see her. Her palm-prints had been found on page 18 of this book, and cross-examination was directed at discovering how it could have come into her posession other than the way she had described. A tastelessly written book with over a hundred tawdry, pseudo-sex-education photographs, it was—it turned out—the property of the house-master who (so the evidence continued), aside from lending it to his mother-in-law, had also passed it on, over a period of several months, to at least two other teachers, one of them Mary's then counselor. But it was they—not he—who had taken it in and out of this closed unit for disturbed children.* When Mary's own testimony was over (and had been read out to the press, who were readmitted before the general public), the Magistrates called a short recess. Mary, sitting momentarily on a bench at one side of the near-empty room, looked now, the ordeal over, pink and excited. "Miss H. . . . is next," she said to me, referring to her counselor. "You like her best, do you?" "Oh yes," she answered, her eyes darting from one door of the courtroom to the other, so as not to miss the young teacher's entrance. She was out of luck because she was then taken out and back to the Unit and wasn't allowed to listen to the rest of the hearing. The testimony that followed—the public now readmitted—finally revealed that the book had on at least one occasion been left unattended in a staff duty-room in which, although it was off limits, children had in the past been found. This was by no means conclusive proof one way or another, but it did establish another possibility where Mary could have seen and touched it. Even so, the magistrates felt the allegation had neither been proved nor disproved and sent the case to trial. (Someone close to the Court said later, "I think they felt that there is something so terribly wrong at the school, something had to be done.")

Six weeks later, after four months of waiting for the house-master whose Canadian job had meanwhile been filled, the trial began at Liverpool Quarter Sessions—and ended within hours.

* It was later claimed, though not at the trial, that one of the teachers felt this book "should be read by all adolescents."

Once again the press benches were full. Once again Betty Bell, her mother next to her, attended. But the Mary who entered this courtroom was a very different girl from the one who had faced the Newton-le-Willows magistrates in such a manifestly troubled state of mind. Rosy-cheeked and clear-eyed she was dressed in what looked like a new outfit and strode up pertly, smiling hello at her relatives. She seemed entirely unconcerned about the much larger audience and undaunted by the far more formal Court. This Mary had evidently overcome her apprehensions about the unexpected consequences of an impulsive act or decision and, delivering a more than fluent recitation of the alleged events, seemed confident of victory. Far from having any compunctions now about describing all the details, she seemed to relish the occasion. She got testy once or twice at probing questions, but when asked by counsel whether she had hated and protested against what she claimed the housemaster had done to her, her reply—sadly honest under the circumstances—was "I wasn't fussy."

After listening to Mary's testimony and a few minutes of Mr. John Stannard's cross-examination which pointed out glaring discrepancies in her different statements, the Court adjourned and the prosecution withdrew to consult the Director of Public Prosecutions in London. The next morning, Judge William Openshaw, who had shown impeccable concern for Mary throughout, directed the Jury to find the defendant not guilty—a fact which, the sensation evaporated and the court almost empty, was barely mentioned in the press next day.

"She has told four stories," the Judge said, "and having told four stories, it is inconceivable that the Jury would believe any one of them. She has fabricated," he continues. "She is a very sick child. One can only hope that she can be given treatment to help her. . . ."

This unhappy episode is included in this account, not in an effort to use tawdry events for whetting tawdry appetites, but to point out the damage that can be done through misguided zeal. No one knows exactly what combination of circumstances or events produced this particular crisis. It is perfectly possible that Mary genuinely believed—perhaps because she wanted or needed to believe it—that the housemaster had made advances to her; she is after all now of an age when this kind of fantasy is not at all unusual.

It is also possible that she manipulated him into a situation which in line with her usual pattern, she could use for her own ends. Or again, he might have made some perfectly innocent gesture which was open to misinterpretation. Whichever the explanation, and in full appreciation of how vulnerable such children are and how necessary it is to protect them, there can be little doubt that the police intervention and the court case were a result of a most ill-advised overreaction. The damage that was done to the man Mary accused and his family, the upset to the school and to Mary herself is hardly compensated for by the facts that—as has been said since—"Mary is much more pleasant company since [that] court case," and that the housemaster later got his Canadian job.

The greatest danger for Mary has always been that, with the manipulative traits in her personality unaltered, and by intelligently cooperating much of the time with a program she knows is designed to get children out into normal life as soon as possible, she may succeed in persuading those around her that she *has* changed, that they *have* succeeded with her, long before such an assumption is safe for her and others.

Several of the staff of the Special Unit have been heard to use this phrase, "We are doing miracles with her," again and again. It has been suggested that she is now ready to participate fully in "school activities," which means her being allowed to take part in supervised excursions and outings. Even more recently it was suggested that it was time to begin thinking about a release date for her.

Miracles are of course always possible. And no one would want Mary—or any other sick child—to be locked away from normal life a moment longer than need be. But the problem of psychopathic children requires compassion, not sentimentality. It also requires a realistic assessment of everything the future might hold. In the light of the limitation of present knowledge about psychopathic children this realism must necessarily—if sadly—veer toward extreme caution. For however essential it is to give individual sympathetic consideration to each child, yet such children can no more than any other human being be seen in isolation from the rest of society: *that* is sentimentality, not compassion. The question in Mary's case—as in that of many other such children in many other places—cannot be "Should they be locked up or free?" but "What represents the least risk to themselves and to society? What can be done to equip them to live as good, as useful, *and* as inoffensive lives as possible—whether this be under restraint or freedom?"

As I come to the end of writing this book I remember a conversation I had with Mary's grandmother some time ago. She said that she could see no good coming from anything that was written about Mary. "Not even a serious book?" I asked, "one that just might help her now and other children later?" "No," she said, "it could not help but ruin her future. . . ." When Mary did get out, she added, such writing would surely be available for her to read and "also for her bairns one day."

I have thought of this time and again as I wrote.

But in the light of the *whole* of this unhappy story, I have wondered too: if years ago family or friends, teachers or priests, social workers or police—all of us—had known more, understood more about such deeply troubled children, need there ever have been a "Case of Mary Bell"?

This is why this book was written.

POSTSCRIPT

I revised the British edition of this book for the last time in February 1972 and it was published in England on the following September 28. As must always happen with books concerned with present-day events, the lives of the people I have written about here have been subject to development and change.

Billy Bell is completely separated with Betty. He has since made a new home with a young woman and a child in Newcastle; his two younger children from the marriage to Betty live with them and are doing well. He occasionally sees his now fourteen-year-old son who, since the events of 1968, has been in the care of a particularly good small Children's Home in the country and has developed a great enthusiasm for ornithology: it is thought that he may well make a career in that field. Betty, by her own decision, has seen none of the children except Mary, whom she continues to visit regularly. She told someone (and recently also the press) that she had given it a lot of thought and come to the conclusion it would be better for the others if she didn't see them and "disturb their [new] happiness": a decision that required courage and I think merits respect.

Betty's mother—Mary's grandmother—although ever more fragile, continues to come to Betty's aid whenever called and the same applies, as it always did, to the rest of Betty's family. All of them were deeply disturbed when the book appeared but, in several cases, are known to have remarked to friends that they were "just glad it has all come out."

The hope of Norma Bell's family that they—and Norma—with the trial over and Norma acquitted, could forget about these awful events, was not fulfilled. The world is not that forgetful and perhaps, if the truth be told, nor can they be themselves.

After several changes of school and residence, and after repeatedly running away, sometimes remaining missing for days on end, Norma went to work at fifteen, but has been unable to hold on to a job for any length of time. Now eighteen (and therefore no longer under the legal protection system o fthe Children's Act) she has, it is said, become obsessed with the past and her association with Mary: to such a degree that she has been heard to say time and again "Mary is dead, isn't she? They are just hiding it from me, aren't they?" And on the other hand she has—even lately—lost job after job because of her apparently compulsive need to describe in detail, to whomever will listen, all the events of 1968.

We can only guess at Norma's problems. Is she merely reflecting (or rejecting) the determination of those around her to protect her from a reality she was part of and which therefore, whether one likes it or not, is now part of her? Or could it be merely that, having once been in the limelight, she now, still rather immature, wishes to be again a center of attention? Or is it something else altogether that so desperately troubles her?

I have always felt that one of the most disturbing and significant things I learned during the research for this book—significant not only in the case of these particular young girls but in a much wider context—was when I was told that the staff of the Special Unit at Red Bank had been instructed that Mary's background (i.e., her past) was "unimportant for the staff to know about" (see page 236).

Is this really possible? Can anyone severely disturbed ever be effectively helped without understanding of the background—the root causes of the disturbance? If—in this mysterious domain of human behavior—we deny the relevance of past experiences, what are we left with? What is there to build on but a shell? All of us are surely aware by now of the inadequacy of psychiatric knowledge; of the imprecision of diagnosis in a field where diagnostic terms—such as for example "psychopath"—cover a multitude of symptoms and end up by defining very little. But, leaving aside theories and polemics and considering human behavior and its consequences only in terms of common sense and compassion: how *can* any individual—whether child or adult—who has been subjected to traumatic events which have affected his development and behavior, be expected to come to terms with them, with his fears, with his actions and with himself unless he be permitted and helped to face up to these memories?

The most basic fallacy in official thinking about Mary Bell remains this claim that she is a "unique case." In the light of overwhelming proof that what she represents is, on the contrary, a severe manifestation of widely and indeed universally existing problems, this attitude begins to look like an almost deliberate act of self-persuasion. Is this, one begins to wonder, something we all are tempted to do: to hide from that which is too difficult to face? To obliterate that which is too stark? To confine the existence of weaknesses to those few who can be comfortably and comfortingly "slotted" into easily definable categories?

This case—it seems to me—confronts us with some very fundamental questions concerning the responsibility of society for the individual and its willingness and capacity to discharge it. How important is this one girl? How important is any one individual, above all those who—weaker than others—paradoxically require so much of the community's collective energy and resources? How far can the theoretical (and ideal of) responsibility of the state "from the cradle to the grave" be translated into a reality that will not become an albatross and throttle the very system that—so enlightened—has created it?

More than ever, since the reactions to this book after its publication in England, I am convinced that the story told here is relevant to a multitude of unresolved problems which faces every one of us.

Mary Bell, as of this writing (March 1973)—now fifteen years old, is still in the Special Unit of Red Bank School, still on her own with twenty-two boys; there have been no other girls there in the last nine months.

The book, widely discussed in press, radio and television, focused new attention on her situation and, the school having asked for her to be moved, several alternatives for her care are now apparently under consideration.

A reportage by the highly responsible BBC TV program *Mid-Week* and a report by the equally serious London *Sunday Times* "Insight" team, following the publication of the book, brought to light various aspects of Mary's recent life which caused a furor in the national press and led to questions in Parliament.

The fact, as indicated in the book and picked up by the media (and many reviewers), that the school had no resident psychiatric staff, was first repeatedly denied and finally admitted by the Department of Health. The consultant psychiatrist who visits the Special Unit once a week to advise the staff, when interviewed, confirmed these facts and added that he had "no doubt that . . . any . . . school would need very considerable psychiatric help to know how to handle [a child like] Mary Bell."

Betty Bell was also interviewed on *Mid-Week:* she presumably agreed in an understandable effort to counteract the effect the publication of extracts from the book (in a Newcastle Sunday paper for the three previous weeks) had by then already had in her home territory. Although the TV team felt considerable sympathy for her—she always appears very vulnerable and people generally respond by coming to feel protective of her—they were staggered when, unasked, she produced a group of recent photographs of Mary, several of which were described later on the program as "candid and provocative poses [of Mary] wearing scanty underclothes." The program also mentioned the "sexual" incidents Mary had reputedly been involved in; her accusation of a housemaster of indecent assault; and the fact that a copy of the crude pornographic book *Oral Love* had been brought repeatedly into the school somehow and that Mary had been able to get hold of it. All this and the program's statement—given to them by the Department of Health—that a member of the staff had been present when Mary was photographed by her mother in her undies, raised a storm in the press which continued for almost ten days. Although the banner headlines all over the country, proclaiming "Scandal of Child Killer: Mary Bell in sex incidents at jail home," "Child Killer in Porn Scandal," etc., seemed somewhat disproportionate, it was perhaps not altogether surprising. An investigation ordered by the Home Office claimed to ascertain that the three snapshots referred to by the media were merely part of "a group of about fifty harmless family snapshots" and had in fact been taken "in the presence of the child's grandmother and a teacher."

I must admit that my own first reaction had been to say in interviews that I thought it unlikely that Mary's sensitive grandmother could possibly have had anything to do with this and equally improbable that any teacher could have been present at such silly goings-on. But when a statement by the Minister for Social Affairs, read two weeks later to the House of Commons, confirmed that this had been the situation, one could only agree with the press that, however harmless perhaps the intention, however fervent the disclaimer of the school and the Ministry, the facts remained that Mary's mother—whatever her motives—*had* taken such photographs within the precincts of this Special Unit for severely disturbed children, mostly boys, and in a room with a glass observation window in the door; the grandmother, however haplessly, *had* in fact watched it being done; and a teacher, present while the photographs were taken, had not tried in any way to interfere. The whole regrettable incident yet another example of—to put it mildly —the lack of judgment displayed continuously concerning this highly vulnerable and now adolescent girl.

The *Sunday Times,* the week following the TV broadcast, published extracts from a Report on Mary Bell, written by a Newcastle psychiatrist who had examined her at the request of the Home Office in July 1971. He says in his paper that he "had a long talk with Mary while she showed [me] around the school." The *Sunday Times* said that, in the 2,700 word document, the psychiatrist had found Mary "remarkably improved" with "a loss of nearly all of her aggressive tendencies," a "modification of her inclination to manipulate people" and "an improvement in her relations with others and of her capacity to think about the future." He also felt that she had gained insight into her mother's emotional and social instability, and added that her mother could "hinder her progress [he said, significantly enough] even in her present situation."

Nonetheless, he concluded by suggesting that "one should begin to consider 1975 as a possible release date [one could not help but notice that he made this suggestion without mentioning that Mary's sharply improved behavior in the artificial and highly controlled environment of the school was no guarantee whatever as to her possible conduct outside it] . . . She will be old enough [he said at the end] to stand on her own feet, with some support, and, if she progresses as she has, be capable of a life of her own."

Both the suggested 1975 release and the fact that Mary's mother, despite all warning signs, has continued to be allowed to visit her, drew renewed critical—indeed dismayed—comments from the press.

But there was, alas, worse to come: on 15 October 1972 Mary's mother gave yet another interview, which appeared on the front page of the Newcastle *Sunday Sun*. "It is," the paper announced, "the interview other major newspapers have tried to get and failed. For better or worse, Mary Bell is the most controversial child in Britain. And in the debates and arguments a lot of criticism— direct and indirect—has been levelled at her mother. Last week Mrs. Bell asked . . . to put her point of view . . ."

In this interview Betty Bell said that she was determined that if and when her daughter was released, they would change their names and move to another part of the country and make a fresh start together. What was even more disturbing though than Mrs. Bell's plans for a future with Mary was a letter she said she had received from Mary that very morning.

"No matter what happens mam," Mary wrote "we'll go it together. These past five years have been hard for us and everyone. I can only hope and pray things turn out for the best, mam. I love you and shall always love you. As long as you are there I'll be ok because I want you and need you . . ." Another cry for help, another plea for love, one is tempted to say quickly.

But, seen in the context of the letter-poem Mary had written to her mother in the spring of 1970 (see page 243) and the psychiatrist's optimistic remarks in the summer of 1971 about the new "insight" he thought she had gained, what she was writing now to her mother was a distressing indication of retrogression, a contra-indication of the ability the psychiatrist believed to have detected in her to stand on her own two feet: a return to an involuted kind of dependence on and need for her mother which, we know so well now from the whole history, Betty Bell out of her own need has always known how to engender, can never satisfy, and which, time and again, has had fatal consequences.

"What right have we," said a Children's Department official to me once in a meeting I was invited to attend at the Home Office, "to separate a mother from her child?"

When are we going to learn that no relationship can hold darker dangers than the one between mother and child gone wrong? When are we going to have the courage to discard the tired principle of the absolute sacredness of family and parental ties? When are we going to allow parents to be free of children they for some reason cannot love, and help children to be free of the catastrophic handicap of parents who cannot love them? When indeed will we be mature enough to accept, for ourselves and our children, that there is no *obligation* to love, there is no *guilt* in not loving, and that the only valid basis for relationships between parents and children, sisters and brothers, husbands and wives, women and men, women and women, men and men—between any human beings—is love freely given from both sides.

MARY BELL – DOCUMENTS

Photo of Mary Bell, age eleven

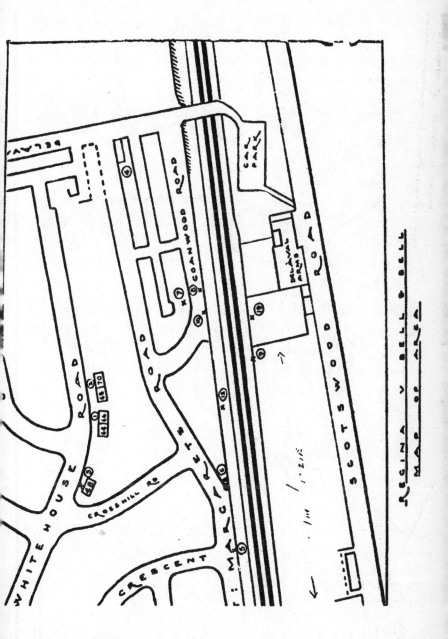

REGINA v BELL & BELL
MAP OF AREA

I murder
So That
I may come
back,

fuck off

we murder

watch art

FANNY

and FAGGOT

WE did

murer

MORtain

brown

FUCKof

you Bastard

Y YOU ARE MIKEY
BECAUSE

MART-MURDERd
BROWN YOU PETER
LOOK OUT THERE
ARE MURDERS ABOUT

BY FANNY AND

and AULD F____
YOU SREEWS___

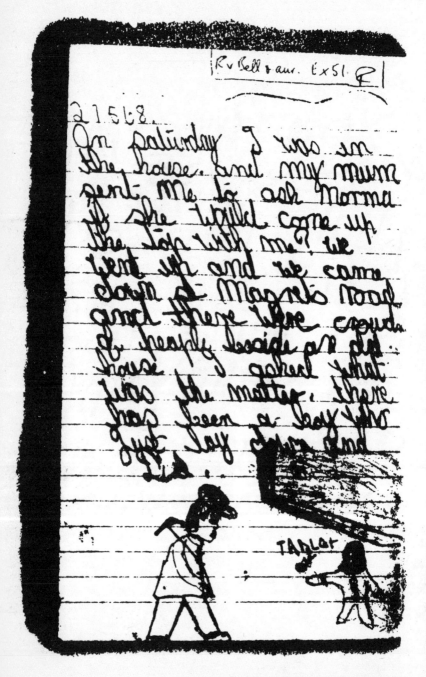

27.5.68.

On saturday I was in the house. and my mum sent me to ask Norma if she would come up the toll with me, we went up and we came down Magnis road and there were crowds of people beside pt. d. house. I asked what was the matter. there has been a boy who just lay down and

TAYLOR

Page from Mary Bell's school "Newsbook"
(See page 27)

Letter from Mary Bell to her mother, Spring
1970 (See page 243)

THE MURDER OF
JAMES BULGER

[*Note: The names of all children, except those of James Bulger, Robert Thompson and Jonathan Venables, have been changed.*]

Liverpool, a year after the murder of little Jamie Bulger, had forgotten nothing. The fact that Denise and Ralph Bulger had a new baby; that Jonathan Venables and Robert Thompson, the two ten-year-olds who killed James, were locked away in secure units; that their families—Neil and Susan Venables and their other two children; Anne Thompson and her six boys—had been given new names and "relocated" to the anonymity of distant council estates, meant nothing.

The particularly endearing face of that little blond toddler, and the fluttering video images of three apparently playful children, which in February 1993 were on every front page and TV screen in Britain and the world, appeared to have been engraved in the minds and hearts of this hugely emotional English city.

The days I spent there will remain among the saddest I have lived. But though Jamie continues to be mourned by thousands, I think the sadness one finds in almost everyone one speaks to there is less now for his terrible death than for the total inexplicability of it, which the trial in November 1993 did nothing to dispel. The most important thing I was reminded of in Liverpool a year after the murder was that in order for human beings to come to terms with such a tragedy, they need to understand why it happened.

Where do we begin to look for understanding? What was it in these children's lives that gave them the need to abduct and batter to death the unknown "Baby James", as Liverpudlians, unfailingly tender, refer to the not-yet three-year-old who died?

Certainly nothing was done to answer this question during the eight months preceding the trial, or, of course, since. One hundred and twenty police officers worked with exceptional commitment on the investigation; there is no doubt that every member of the two boys' families, every friend, every neighbour, was questioned. But except for their teachers' statements about their conduct at school, some information about the two families' circumstances, and, in connection with these, various bits of gossip which allowed speculation but not knowledge, nothing emerged which might have provided some insight into these two children's minds and inner lives. Many of the police officers I spoke to were deeply interested in the children's backgrounds, but it was not their job to go into them. As far as the law is concerned, the primary function of the police is to prepare the evidence for the prosecution.

What is astonishing is that in cases of children accused of serious crime in this country, the law forbids any therapeutic involvement by psychiatrists before the trial. So, although three psychiatrists did enter the picture in the months preceding the trial of Robert Thompson and Jon Venables in November, their job was only to establish, first, that the two boys were capable of distinguishing right from serious wrong and, secondly, that they were mentally responsible for their acts at the time they committed them.

Any psychiatric attention other than this before a trial is held to "adulterate" the evidence.

This, then, is the first question we need to ask: how effective is our judicial system in relation to children who kill? Britain is the only country in Western Europe where children may be considered criminally responsible as of the age of ten (eight in Scotland) and where, for cases of capital crime, they are tried by judge and jury, as adults.

In every other Western country (excepting a few archaically inclined states in the USA), children are brought before Juvenile or Family Courts after social and psychiatric investigations which can take years. During this process, depending on the severity of their acts, and on their social situation, they may remain at home under supervision, in care in a children's home, or in special psychiatric children's centres considerably more medically and therapeutically oriented than our "Special Units". Their cases are finally decided, usually in camera, by boards of specially trained judges and magistrates.

The British legal system, by comparison, seems both hypocritical and anachronistic. The two principles on which it bases its need to try children with the full formality of the law have, in the last few decades, changed so radically, that they have, essentially, lost their meaning. The first is that if a child is capable of understanding the difference between right and wrong, then it knows that it is "wrong" to lie, to steal, and to kill. This may have been valid for generations whose moral precepts rested securely on family, church and country. But many if not most of today's children—as we can see from the latest figures collected since the Bulger case—get their secondary moral grounding largely from the TV screen, with its confusing sense of values and constant emphasis on violence. (Their primary grounding, in my opinion, is the instinct for good all children are born with.) Whatever children might overhear or witness in their own environment can rarely compensate them for this confusion. Whatever class of society they belong to, many forms of "wrong"—such as cheating and lying, about taxes, business or social security—have become a matter of survival. Under modern-day pressures family discord is almost the rule rather than exception.

This does not, of course, mean that most children are without a sense of right and wrong, but that their moral priorities have been unbalanced. Instead of a universal acceptance of "right" contributing to the child's sense of security, a general acceptance of "wrong" adds to its confusion. The second principle is that justice must be seen to be done: the child must have the same right as an adult defendant to the presentation of evidence, an advocate to plead his or her case and a jury to decide over guilt or innocence.

But in our glasshouse existence, the meaning of this, too, has changed. I can hardly think of anything more harmful to child defendants, their families and the families of victims, than to have the crime and the suffering unroll in the greedy public arena the modern media can create. Of course, evidence must be presented and the child must be defended, but this can be done—and is in juvenile courts—in camera.

As for the jury, anyone who watched those twelve men and women in Preston is unlikely to forget either their pain when they were forced to examine the photographs of the dead child or their bewilderment as they tried to resist normal feelings of sympathy for crying child defendants or make sense of their manipulations and lies under interrogations. This jury knew just as well as the Judge, the lawyers, and the police that the brutal murder of a small child by two little boys could not be adequately explained, either with the forensic evidence of the crime, or with advocacy, however brilliantly presented, claiming that one boy was more guilty than another.

Of course the formal requirements of the law could be satisfied: James had been killed; the two boys had killed him; the two boys were guilty; the two boys had to be punished.

In the case of crimes committed by young children, can punishment be the only purpose of legal proceedings? Is it morally right that, at the end of eight months of investigation by 120 police officers and a 17-day trial involving some of the cleverest men at the Bar and three child psychiatrists, nobody knows what made these two boys commit this deed? What made them so ferocious and so cruel? I suggest that every member of that jury, that Court and the public could not have failed to ask themselves those questions during the trial. And the case should never have ended, or, more to the point, begun, without the answers being known.

We do not live in a time when whipping and hanging is seen to be the punishment for "wicked" children. We know now about the relationship of violence *in* children to violence done *to* children. We know the cause-and-effect sequence of childhood trauma; we thus know that children who hurt others have almost invariably been hurt themselves. Many in the Court and beyond suspected that something terrible must have happened in these boys that finally drove them to this frenzy. But the legal system not only precluded the possibility of delving into their lives, it led to the suppression of evidence. The intention was kind: to do everything possible to avoid adding to the suffering of James Bulger's parents. Thus an agreement was struck between prosecution and defence to the effect that, the forensic evidence entirely proving the case against the two defendants, certain injuries the child suffered would not be mentioned to the jury.

Under the system as it stands, it was a reasonable decision: this evidence, which certainly would have led to prurience in the media, was not necessary to the case. The prosecution had all they needed to prove murder. The fact that it was necessary in order to indicate the two boys' disturbance was, as we will see, not part of the case. The police, although perhaps more anxious than anyone else to protect the Bulgers' feelings, did their duty: their careful interrogations of the two boys, almost all of which were played to the court on tape, repeatedly touched upon the suspected sexual element of the crime. James's shoes and stockings, trousers and underpants had been taken off. And the pathologist's report read out in court recorded that the child's foreskin had been manipulated.

That this information remained in the report was already beyond the agreement that had been reached. Detective Superintendent Albert Kirby, who led the investigation, knew about the agreement: "But I felt that the jury had a right to know at least that much," he told me.

Knowing only "that much", however, was not enough. Even though nobody who listened to the interrogations could fail to notice both boys' desperate discomfort when questioned both about handling Jamie's private parts and about some batteries found near the toddler's body, here the tapes and the official record stopped.

Because this is the second murder of a small child by young children I have worked on at length, I have inevitably been driven to compare what happened in Liverpool and Preston in 1993, with the case of eleven-year-old Mary Bell, who killed two small boys in Newcastle in 1968. The horror people felt was the same, as was the fear of the unknown. The words which were used—"monster", "evil fiend"—were the same in 1968 to describe Mary, as in 1993 to describe Jonathan and Robert. And the supposed reasons—though twenty-five years later perhaps expressed by more commentators in more pseudo-scientific terms—were equally facile.

In 1968 in Newcastle, already in the grip of economic depression, it was the word "Scotswood" that conveyed the sense not only of the deprived area of the city where such crimes could happen, but the class which produced such killers. In 1993, in unemployment-ridden Liverpool, Scotswood was replaced by "Walton", and somehow the contrast between the modern Bootle shopping centre with its electronic miracle of security videos and the violence of the act in a deserted railway yard made the horror worse.

Yet the underlying suggestion—that this was a case of "them", the children of the poor, drunk and inadequate, and therefore could never be "us"—was the same last year in Liverpool as 25 years ago in Newcastle, and just as wrong.

Children who kill are not produced by a class, but unhappiness. Unhappiness in children is never innate, it is created by the adults they "belong to": there are adults in all classes of society who are immature, confused, inadequate or sick, and, under given and unfortunate circumstances, their children will reflect, reproduce and often pay for the miseries of the adults they need and love. Children are not evil.

In Preston Crown Court last November there was an invisible wall between Jonathan's parents, Susan and Neil Venables, and Robert's mother, Anne Thompson. Each parent was convinced that the other's child had both initiated the crime and carried it out; to a degree, therefore, each parent was convinced that his or her own child was innocent.

The two boys, as has been described often elsewhere, sat on a specially built platform, with two social workers between them. Although in all reports they were described as being of different size and build, Jonathan slim and tall, Robert smaller and roundish, they appeared to have caught up with each other in the intervening months: they were both rather heavy and flabby—both were said to have gained weight since their arrest, Jonathan over two stone. Under close restraint, neither had had any opportunity for exercise.

But his new weight notwithstanding, Jonathan was a nice-looking boy with silky brown hair and a small childlike face: it was extremely difficult to associate that face with the acts we heard described. He behaved extraordinarily well during the long days of the sessions: except for occasionally turning around to glance at his parents, he moved little. We would hear in the course of the trial that a school psychologist had diagnosed him as hyperactive: he was certainly the stillest hyperactive child I have ever seen. A few times he, as well as Robert, played with some of the tissues their social workers held at the ready for them, creating patterns by folding them up and tearing little holes of different sizes and shapes. A couple of times I saw Jonathan open up his completed artwork and show it with a smile to the tall man beside him, who smiled back. The solid 6ft 2in man and the boy appeared close, conferred often, and the man's eyes were almost always on his charge. Repeatedly, when Jonathan seemed particularly tense, or cried, his social worker briefly held or touched him. Robert, though too heavy and his face too wide, looked nice enough the first week. But after the weekend, his already short dark hair had been almost shaved off, giving him suddenly a disturbingly neutered look—and that of a convict. I asked whether perhaps his secure unit had been beset by headlice—it seemed the only explanation for this grotesque crop. But I was told, no, he had asked for this cut.

Robert's hands were much more restless than Jonathan's. They were never still. The two boys appeared at times to compete in the Kleenex cut-outs both produced—they leaned forward repeatedly to look at each other's paper-lace and once or twice appeared to smile. They also looked at each other, quick darting looks at high points of the evidence, but, with two or three exceptions, without visible emotion.

While Jonathan's feelings about things he heard were clearly expressed in his face, Robert's was blank for most of those three weeks. His emotions were in his fingers—and in the movements of his mouth. His fingers were constantly moving, wadding-up the tissues, forming them as if with purpose into round or oblong shapes, or tearing them into bits. We were told he was in the habit of sucking his thumb and pushing his finger in his ear, but in court he did something different, stranger, with his hands, with great intensity.

Several times in almost every session, he licked the tip of each finger, then wiped them on his trousers and licked them again; then he put two or three fingers in his mouth, filling it, closed his lips around them, held them still for a moment, and then pushed the fingers to and fro or turned them around in a circle. Or yet again, he licked a finger and then drew it slowly around his mouth.

His social worker, a slim, tense-looking man, rarely looked at Robert (an interesting parallel to the reactions of policewoman Brenda M. to Mary Bell); their communication appeared limited to the five or ten times during each session when Robert, for an instant looking childlike, asked him the time. Although next to each other, there seemed always to be a small space between them which neither did anything to close. I was told the social worker was a nice man; but he didn't touch the boy, even at the very end of the trial when Robert, hearing the sentence, his usually pink face chalk-white, cried.

I had sat quite near Susan and Neil Venables throughout the trial. They were at the right, just behind and slightly underneath the platform where the boys sat. Shirl Marshall, the founder and director of Aftermath, an organization that cares for relatives of perpetrators, sat next to them. Two social workers sat directly behind them.

Neil Venables, transparently thin, his face greyish-yellow, seemed smaller than his wife; most of the time throughout the three weeks he leaned forward, his head resting almost between his knees; much of the time he cried. Susan was remarkably pretty and, I thought, remarkably composed. We knew that the couple had lived apart for years and I thought it was touching that Susan, when Neil cried, leaned forward, her dark hair brushing against his face, and whispered to console him.

Where Neil, however, looked gentle, soft and devastated, Susan seemed angry; she had what I was certain was a nervous habit—of fixing her make-up time and again. Whenever anyone spoke to them, or they got up to go outside or downstairs to see their boy, she appeared to lead; Neil followed. Oddly, for it somehow didn't fit the picture, when, as happened repeatedly every day, Jon turned around to look for or at his parents, his father often met and held his glance; his mother looked away or through him.

On the surface, the police were quite positive about the Venables, who had been very helpful to them during the incredibly difficult interrogations. But they did not feel like this at all about Anne Thompson, who had not only been absent during the first week-and-a-half of the trial but had refused to attend many of the interrogations in February.

The fact that, as the Thompson family solicitor, Dominic Lloyd, told me, she had broken down after being present at the first interrogations, did not appear to impress the otherwise immensely humane police. "Can you imagine," said Detective Sergeant Phil Roberts, one of two officers who interrogated Robert Thompson, "a mother who lets her child go through this without her?" ("I saw her collapse," Dominic Lloyd said. "He didn't.")

Until I met Shirl Marshall, Dominic Lloyd and the boys' barristers, I had only heard Anne Thompson described as a "slut", a "shrew" and a "slag". This was not the way they felt, and it was not the impression she conveyed to me when I saw her.

Forty years old last December, Anne is a big woman, dark-haired with a pale complexion: I found her unexpectedly attractive. She sat, always next to a psychiatric social worker who had been assigned to her some time before the trial and continued to work with her afterwards, two rows behind the Venables and out of reach of Robert's eyes if he had tried to look at her, which he didn't. Nor did she move, or stretch to look at him. She sat very quietly throughout the proceedings. From time to time—and there was good reason—she cried, and when she did she sat totally still, tears pouring unchecked down her cheeks. In the end she would fumble blindly for a handkerchief, wipe her face (which would emerge looking curiously young and naked), and then clench her hands and soaking handkerchief in her lap, her knuckles white with tension.

Anne Thompson had expressed a wish to meet me quite early on, even before the trial ended. She had seen my book about the Mary Bell case and told Dominic Lloyd that, with the knowledge I had gained, I could perhaps help her. She was, however, extremely upset for weeks after the trial, and it was mid-January when we finally met and spent a day together.

Sue and Neil Venables agreed to meet me shortly after that, when—just as in Newcastle 25 years ago—someone who knew them became convinced that the wrong approach to the trial needed to be publicized, and that both parents' stories were essential if this was to be understood and the boys were to be helped.

The attractive couple who came up to my room at the Adelphi in Liverpool had very little in common with the man and woman I remembered. I had of course expected them to have regained some equanimity: no one can continually manifest pain, even when they feel it. But Susan and Neil seemed almost like different people.

Sue was as attractive as I remembered her, only more rested and strangely gay. She is 37 but looked years younger. She wore tight-fitting black trousers—she is very slim—a black and gold blouse, black suede bootees, a short white belted raincoat and a Spanish hat; she would not have been out of place having tea at the Savoy.

Neil, in a dark suit, shirt and tie and beautifully polished shoes, was handsome, appeared to have filled out and grown several inches, and also looked much younger than his 41 years. Both of them readily told me about their childhoods. "I was spoilt when I was young," Neil said. "We had a very happy childhood, me and my younger sister. My father worked on the docks, nobody drank, nobody beat anybody. I did OK in school, and at 15 I left and got a job as a panel-beater for two garages."

The money hadn't been "brilliant", so his mother, who worked at Jacobs' biscuit factory, got him a job there driving a fork-lift truck. "It was an 8-to-5 job: I didn't mind it, did I?" He constantly repeated his statements in the form of questions to Sue. He laughed. "Once I was out of bed, I didn't mind, did I? But until that point, no, I wasn't that keen on it."

Neil's parents were both dead: his mother died in 1977, when she was 51, after a complicated bypass operation; his father 14 years later in 1991. He wasn't working now, he said. He'd lost his job when he was 30—in 1983—and hadn't worked since.

Was it his health that had stopped him working? I asked. Although looking infinitely better than during the trial, he is still very thin. "No," he said, "I'm perfectly healthy," and Sue laughed fondly. "Mr. Perfect," she teased him, "that's you. He wrote after 300 jobs," she added quickly. "I even tried for a £2-an-hour job sweeping streets," he said. "But then I said, no, I wouldn't get out of bed for that . . ."

"You were OK," she said. "You worked when you could, didn't you? Well . . ." she threw in, disconcertingly, "I made more money than he did," and she laughed again, a somehow unconvincing laugh.

To all appearances she was always shoring him up, but after a while I began to wonder: was she supporting him because he was weak, or was he submitting to her to allow her to appear strong?

Susan Venables was born in 1957. Her one brother is three years older. They were quite well-off, she said; her father was a building contractor and they lived "in a big house three storeys high".

Her father was also a musician: he played the guitar. "After a while he started a band and then he did building and the band."

Sue loved school, especially the last years. "Dad always worked, mum was a part-time barmaid. Dad got the band together when I was 12 or 13, and when he was off on gigs and mum was working, I'd stay with schoolfriends. I loved it. I still have some of my schoolmates now; one of them got in touch with me through the *Daily Star* when it all happened, just to say hello and that she didn't believe a word of it."

At 15, she started work at Littlewoods Pools as an inspector and copy typist and stayed there until she was 22. They had married in 1975 when Sue was 18 and Neil 22. "We had four years on our own; that's not bad," she said. In 1979 they had their first son, Paul; Jonathan came in 1982 and their daughter, Sandra, in 1983. Paul was born with a cleft lip which was operated on when he was 11 months. "He was a terribly unhappy baby and little boy till he was four or so," Sue said. "He was just so frustrated: he couldn't speak, couldn't express himself at all, though he seemed to know inside what he wanted to get across. Anyway, it was just dreadful; he never stopped crying . . . it drove me berserk."

I asked what she did about it.

"Oh, I just put him in his room and closed the door on him, left him to scream. There just wasn't anything *to* do. I was never out of hospital with him."

What had she done with baby Jon when she had to take Paul to hospital? Did she take him along?

She reacted as if she suspected a trick question: "Never," she said quickly. "I never took him along. We don't think Jon suffered from all that. He was a new-born baby.

"I just loved Jon," Sue continued. "I loved him to death. He was the best, the sweetest baby—he was great . . . pleasant, smiling of a morning, wasn't he?" Neil nodded.

"He never gave me a moment's trouble. He just sat there in his push-chair or carry-cot and smiled and gurgled. He walked at 11 months, spoke well at 15, was potty-trained at two years. He was just brilliant."

To complete the family picture then, a year later, in 1983, they had Sandra: "Now I had my daughter.

"I remember Jon at 15 months, with Sandra in her little cradle, they'd sit watching the children's programmes on the telly while I was working in the kitchen. They were like little peas in the pod: he'd always look at her, look after her, say 'Baby', and touch her and if she cried, he called me—'*Baby cry*'."

It would actually be almost two years before they realized that Sandra, too, had some problems. "We didn't suspect that at all. Contrary to Paul, she had been a happy baby—I just got to notice—probably because Jon had been so advanced—that she was lazy, though of course, she was much better than Paul . . ."

"Much better," Neil echoed. "And she talked. And she was happy—you know, she was lovely, she still is . . ."

And then she swerved back to Paul. "I tried him in an ordinary nursery when he was three, then asked for a psychologist to assess him. She did a brain scan—normal. So then she suggested special education, and after he went to Meadowbanks with the small classes, one-to-one attention, a lot of help and special tuition, and he calmed down; got much better . . . He's 15 now; gets his own bus.

"Sandra could probably have coped in ordinary school—she was assessed and went there from five to seven; but then the class went bigger and bigger; she couldn't keep up nor get the attention she needed and she was always struggling and got so upset. So we got her moved to Meadowbanks, too, and she was happy as a lark there. She's 10 now . . . reads at seven.

"I sometimes said about Paul, 'I hate him, he's overruling my life . . .' The doctor said 'That's just in your mind: you really love him . . .'

"Of course, I never stopped asking myself," Sue said, "did I do anything to harm them when I was pregnant? Well, I had been ill at the beginning of my pregnancy with Paul and was put on antibiotics; but later the doctors assured me they had been very mild."

There appears to be no clear explanation of the origin of the two children's retardation, or, if there was, the parents were not told. Susan's early handling of her screaming baby was not necessarily wrong. In principle experts have long found that it is often safer to leave crying babies who are not physically at risk, not wet, hungry or otherwise physically uncomfortable, on their own for a while in a warm and familiar place, rather than expose them to the danger of one's own frustration.

But listening to this account, it becomes obvious that Jonathan, born in 1982, must have spent his first years in an atmosphere of tremendous maternal tension.

However loved these children were—and one doesn't for a minute doubt Susan Venables's love—forcing this middle child, Jon, for a long time, perhaps unconsciously, to compensate his mother for her two problem children, put an enormous weight of responsibility on this child virtually from the time he was born.

By 1984, the pressures became too much for Susan herself. "I'd had five years of it by then. He . . ."—she nodded in Neil's silent direction, but with a smile—"he was OK: he was out working all day . . . Well," she added quickly, with one of those endearing bursts of self-correction she sometimes showed, "Not that all right then: he'd no sooner come in the door and I'd gab away about all the awful things that happened—whether it was my continued failing with Paul's potty-training and of course by then Sandra's too . . . or whether it was just . . . oh, everything . . . just the inside of the house where, 27 years old, I was all day with three kids—oh, it just went on and on and I felt completely trapped . . ." "Well," Neil said. "That's it, isn't it? I worked, and the house and the children were her job. I didn't want all that every night. I just told her to get on with it."

It was at first hard to imagine Neil taking the quiet and almost humorously firm position he depicts here, but later I would change my mind. When Sue readily admits "I nagged the moment he came in . . ." the situation must have been much more traumatic than that, above all for young Jon.

On the face of it, Susan and Neil present themselves as an exceptionally well-behaved, now well-adjusted couple; but it isn't hard to visualize the chaos of their marriage, with the three small children listening to Susan's despair and Neil's recriminations.

Did you ever hit her? I asked him. He shook his head, and Sue came in at once with another of her disarming funnies. "I'd be more likely to have hit him," she said and they looked at each other tenderly. "But I didn't, did I?" SHE ASKED HIM. "Not really?".

"No," he agreed: "Not really."

"I felt closed in," she went on, "and took it out on Neil. I'm a chatty sort of person; I need my girlfriends, an occasional game of darts, a meal out. Neil doesn't."

"I expected my wife to be at home, looking after me and the kids," Neil said again with unexpected firmness. "I said 'That's your job—like my mother's. Get on with it . . .' "

"We were very young when we married," Sue said, as if summing up. "When the kids came I felt I was a prisoner in my own house. I needed other people. We had a lot of rows through 1983. My dad had died of cancer so my mum was alone. So I decided to move to my mum's, with the kids. Neil had been made redundant. So we sold the house."

"I got myself a bedsit," Neil inserted.

"After I left I was much better," Sue said. "Neil was much better, too, we were more relaxed. Neil came up on weekends, took the children out."

"Sometimes Paul or Jon stayed overnight," Neil said. "In the morning I'd go and get the others and we'd go places together."

"I explained to the kids that we each had our place," Sue said, "that their dad loved them and would see them. Jon appeared to have no reaction—very bubbly, happy. Neil was always there. I went to see him with them. We were always friends . . . we slept together, we went on holiday together. I was at my mum's about three years. We got divorced during that time. After that I got a place of my own. But he was always my best friend."

Why did you bother to get divorced? I asked her. She giggled. "It just sort of happened. I never picked up the papers; they're still in court."

But then, perhaps you never were really divorced?

"Oh yes, we were; I got the decree nisi; the lawyer told me. I just didn't pick up the papers."

Neil grinned. "I had a good time, went to a club . . . oops, perhaps I shouldn't be telling you that."

They went on sleeping together. "We didn't the first 12 months," Sue rectifies.

"I did meet another girl," Neil said.

"But I told her there was no chance I could marry anyone else and have children with anybody else. Nobody but Susan . . ."

Sue said, "The kids were happy, we were happy . . . my mum helped me to up the Income Support—he had dole."

"I had these friends," Neil said, "older with grown-up children. They were like a mother and father to me . . ."

"But we tell each other everything," Sue said. "Always did, always will. When I was working, I rang him up every day from work."

"We were working towards a reconciliation," was what Susan Venables later told the police, social workers and the media.

I have no doubt that this is how Sue and Neil interpreted—to themselves—their ten-year make-believe separation: their marital relations stopped only briefly; they had separate flats, but shared both; the children, theoretically alternating between them, in fact wandered to and fro with them; and they all went on holidays together.

It seems at first mature and even sophisticated. But what it sounded like when Sue and Neil, who, although nice, are neither of these two things, ebulliently related their married–unmarried life to me, was two people rather desperately role-playing a kind of fantasy life. How would this curious confusion, added to his siblings' problems—his mother's principal preoccupation, to his cost—have affected Jon, especially once he started school and saw how other children lived?

"When Jon was at Broad Square Infants," she said, "he was OK. The bad things started when he was seven and went to Junior School. We had moved to a bigger house, a new area for us. Neighbours down the road who had four or five kids in the family called Paul names . . .

"Jon was very unhappy when he came home to tell me. I told him 'Words can't hurt you—ignore them.' But perhaps being in a new street and another part of the school was too much for him?"

In 1989, a social worker was introduced to the Venables family to help arrange respite fostering for nine-year-old Paul who was troubling his mother with sudden bouts of tantrums. This is a weekend away once a month in a foster-home to give the mother a rest.

As the social worker would later state to the police, this measure worked well for Paul. But he soon realized that their real problem was Jon, "along with difficult relations between all the children in the family, and other youngsters in the road where they lived . . ."

As time continued, he stated, "more and more of my attention when visiting the family was focused on [seven-year-old] Jon who was becoming an unhappy young man and as a result was creating disruption both at home and in his school. This was in spite of his mother's best efforts to read what was happening to him and try to provide some answers . . ."

"When Jon moved to the school at Walton," Neil said, "he stayed with me for three days, then Sue came to stay for the other four days." (So Jon was, in effect, living with his father.)

The Venables insist that the rumours which circulated among the media during the case, that they had these two establishments in order to double their income from the state, were wrong. "It was not for money reasons," Sue said.

"Neil had his dole . . . I had the Income Support: it didn't make any difference in money. And the proof is, when we got back together, we declared it and now we have Income Support together as a family and that's just about £5 less. So it wasn't money."

"We were lucky," Neil put in. "Sue's mother always helped—she saved some money, so we were able to have family holidays."

"We go to Butlin's," Sue said. "It's very good. They have everything for the kids . . ."

It was at the very end of our long time together, when they were already putting on their coats, that Sue suddenly said: "Of course, I've had a lot of medical troubles . . ."

What sort? I asked.

"Oh, this operation and that . . . Of course, very early on I had myself sterilized. But there were other things . . ."

Could Jon have seen her in pain? I asked.

"Yes, he could that. He did. But . . . I always talk to the kids about everything, frankly you know, so I told them that it was OK, that I'd be OK in the end; and of course Neil was always there for them."

Later, I was told by a reliable source that Sue's medical problems included two "traumatic" incidents in 1990 or 1991 which Jon would have been aware of.

Jon's problematic behaviour at school had not been so conspicuous until then, but the statements later made to the police by his teachers at Broad Square Primary indicate their increasing alarm in 1990 and 1991 at Jon's "inappropriate" and "aberrant" behaviour.

First, his form teacher:

> In September 1990 I had responsibility for the Year 4 Class. In my class at that time were a total of 24 children, one of whom was Jon Venables. I was aware that [in his previous class, in 1989] there had been behaviour problems.

And between September and Christmas of 1990, she said, Jon became a problem in her class, too.

> It was after the Christmas break in January 1991 I noticed that Jon was acting very strange. He would sit on his chair and hold his desk with his hands and rock backwards and forwards and start moaning and making strange noises. If, as happened, I moved him from the child next to him and sat him next to my desk, he would then start fiddling with things on my desk and knock them to the floor. He would also bang

his head on the furniture to a stage when it must have been hurting him. Jon was always complaining that other children were picking on him whilst he was outside of class and he would then cry. There were other incidents in respect of Jon, who would not do anything that was asked of him. He wasn't doing any work in his books and, though capable of doing more, he was what is known as a "Low Achiever".

Susan Venables would later tell me that she had never been informed of any of these problems. The form teacher continued:

Once these incidents started coming to light, I got Mrs. Venables to come into my classroom and I discussed this behaviour with her. She told me that she was having problems with Jon at home at that time. He was being abusive to her. His mother was coming into the school regularly by this time and I told her that Jon could not go on the school weekend trip. As a result of this I had a visit from a male social worker who was already working with the Venables family. [He] wanted to come on the school weekend trip, taking responsibility for Jon, but it was refused.

"All that isn't true," Sue exclaimed. "I didn't want him to go on that trip and I asked for my £8 back." Interestingly, the teacher added that Susan Venables had told her that Jon had expressed the wish to be in the same school as his siblings. This suggests the possibility that some of his earlier behaviour—for example the rocking and the banging of his head—could have been imitating Paul's tantrums before Paul was helped by being sent to a caring school and on special holidays. If it was so, this "cry for help" was not heard.

"After March 1991 things got gradually worse," the teacher continued.

One of the things Jon used to do was to go round the room, revolving along the walls pulling work and objects off the walls or displays. He would also lie down inside the group of desks, lodging himself inside so that it was difficult to get him out. I had other parents coming into class complaining, as Jon was attention-seeking all the time. On occasions Jon has cut himself purposely with the scissors; he also cut holes in his socks, stuck paper all over his face. Anything near him he would use as a weapon to throw across the room at other children. On one occasion I even got Jon and put him outside in the corridor . . . there was an incident when he hung himself upside down on the coat pegs like a bat.

"I knew nothing of any of this," Sue Venables told me when I read her these statements, "nothing about any of this behaviour. Cut himself? He never had any cuts. Hang himself up like a bat? Never. Oh, he might have rocked in his chair, his desk—we all did naughty things like that, didn't we? But 'cover his face with sticky paper'? Why would he do a silly thing like that? And 'holes in his socks'? Wouldn't I have seen them? But, most important, his teacher never mentioned any of this to me . . ."

"I did in fact keep my own log of the numerous incidents that had occurred with Jon," the form teacher noted. "But after leaving the school I destroyed this."

What had brought things to a head was when Jon apparently attacked another boy in class. Jon had taken a 12-inch ruler and held it against the boy's throat; the form teacher "and another woman who was in the class at the time" had forcibly to pull Jon away. "I took Jon immediately to the Head and to my knowledge, he was suspended. I have not seen him or any of his family since."

In the 14 years I have been teaching, I have never come across a boy like Jon . . . He caused me such anxiety . . . It was so stressful trying to contain him. So much happened whilst I was there involving Jon, I am not sure if in fact he was seen by the school psychologist, but I did complete a form for him . . .

"None of this was told to me," Sue Venables said again. "All I got was a letter from the school—the only one I ever had—saying

Jon was suspended for two days for disruptive behaviour. Anyway, after that letter I kept him out of school for ten weeks."

Did she mean to say he had no schooling then? I asked.

"I taught him myself," she said. "He was that good a reader, it wasn't hard. And the school never phoned once to ask where he was." The Deputy Head of Broad Square School also commented clearly on Jon's behaviour:

> Until September 1990 Jon's anti-social behaviour was just of an annoying nature, but not apparently serious. However, when he went into [his next] class, this pattern continued and became of much more concern from January 1991 onwards. During this time, with Jon's mother's consent, he was referred to the school's psychology service. I am aware that he was the subject of a report from them in which mention was made of his bizarre behaviour and the need to modify this in the school. This report was dated May 1991. Mention was also made of the possibility of hyperactivity. In this period from January 1991, Mrs. Venables was in school on a regular basis.

And she concludes:

> I am aware that there was an incident in the class surrounding Jon Venables which resulted in him not completing his academic year and to my recollection we were not notified as to his whereabouts. He was certainly not expelled from this school.

The Venables' social worker certainly also seemed to be under the impression that Susan was aware of Jon's difficulties:

> Susan Venables . . . was, in considerable distress over Jon. She saw him as being on the receiving end of a lot of peer-group pressure . . . I was aware of Jon's behavioural problems in school and, as a result of discussions between myself and his mother, a change of school eventually occurred in

September 1991, when he started at his present school, St. Mary's in Walton.

The social worker also added that Jon's behaviour, both at school and at home, became much more manageable then and that, believing the family to be coping, he didn't see them for more than a year until Christmas 1992.

It is difficult to reconcile Sue Venables's claim that she had never been told about any of Jon's troubles at school with the teachers' statements. She doesn't lie—I cannot say this firmly enough: she is, I think, someone who is and always was over-taxed, by life, by her own feelings, by two children born with problems.

Depression is the consequence of being unhappy with one's self; the defence against allowing it to continue and overwhelm one is to deny all that is wrong. My feeling is that Sue—who should have had help for many years—has created a falsely gay and happy exterior to hide, primarily from herself, her sadness inside. Neil, who undoubtedly loves her, has, I think, to her detriment and his diminishment, "enabled" her—assisted her—in this self-deceit.

When Jon finally manifested the trouble which had been building up in him for years, she could not face it: she denied its existence.

Jon changed schools in the autumn term of 1991. "They put Jon one class below his age because there was no room in his real class," Sue said. "He made friends with those smaller children. And then in September 1992 he started to become friends with Robert. I asked him why. He said he was sorry for him because his mum didn't care about him. To tell you the truth, sometimes when I saw Robert out in the street without a coat and all that, I felt almost like bringing him in and giving him a good hot bath, feeding him and giving him a coat. I asked Jon once, didn't Robert have a coat, and he answered 'His mum doesn't care'."

Sue said that Jon had four or five friends he was always with. "He didn't see Robert outside school. But one evening, soon after

Jon got in the church choir, he came out of choir practice and saw Robert waiting for him and ran away back into the church. After that he didn't want to go to choir practice any more because he was afraid that Robert would pick him up there. He was dead frightened of Robert."

"He has that good a singing voice," she said, "but that's all over, too, isn't it? He loves reading, our Jon, doesn't he?"

"Loves it," said Neil.

What does he read? I asked.

"Roald Dahl," she answered. "I think he read all of those."

"Since Christmas 1992," the Venables' social worker stated:

> I became gradually aware that problems regarding Jon were re-emerging. These were in the form of peer-group relations in his class and truanting. From Susan I was given the impression that another youngster by the name of Robert had a strong hold on Jon leading to his truanting. There were also signs of general disobedience both at home and at school . . .

What about Jon's truanting? I asked Sue Venables. "When Paul had trouble at school—though that was rare," she said, "they used to call me and I would go and pick him up. But nobody ever called or wrote me about Jon."

The newspapers would later report that Jon had truanted 40 times in the autumn term 1992.

"But Jon was never off 40 times truanting, so I don't know where they got that from. He had an eye operation—he was off for a few weeks with that and I sent a note." (Jon had a squint for which he had surgery, the consequences of which could have been a two- to three-week absence from school.) "I went to every open evening the school had," said Sue. "[The teacher] never told me that he had played truant . . . all we ever knew about were the four times he truanted as of January 1993; before that we never heard of anything—we never had a letter."

This appears to be quite true. In the police statement given by

Robert and Jon's class teacher, she says that while she had been aware that, prior to Robert Thompson joining her class in September 1992, there had been attendance problems with him, this was not the case for Jon Venables. During the autumn term of 1992 (3 September to 18 December), she stated, out of a total of 140 half-days, Robert missed 49 and Jon 50. But she specifically says that there were (only) five half-days when both boys were missing at the same time. As no one has claimed that Jon ever truanted without Robert, this would suggest that Mrs Venables is right, and that 35 of his absences during the autumn term are accounted for by his operation.

The class teacher went on to state that during the spring term (as of 4 January 1993 to 12 February—the day of the crime) "there were 60 half-days: Robert missed 37 of these; Jon six, for two of which I had a parent's note. The four occasions Jon truanted in January to February coincided with four of Robert's truancies." (The school's head teacher had stated that "on the first day of term, Jon's parents actually brought him back into school after picking him up in the district".)

It would thus seem that Jon truanted altogether nine times between September 1992 and February 1993—Robert 86 times.

"I would like to add," said the class teacher in her statement:

> that the day before Jon and Robert went missing on 12 February 1993, Jon behaved the worst that he had ever behaved for a whole day whilst he was in my class. He was excited and fidgety and appeared as if he couldn't contain himself. Robert was his normal self. I remember remarking to other members of staff how awful Jon had behaved that day.

"I didn't realize Jon was upset the day before it happened, like one of his teachers said afterwards," Sue said. "But on the morning of Friday he said he felt sick and didn't want to go to school. Much later he told us he felt scared of Robert but not that day.

"I said, of course you are going to school, this very minute. So then he asked whether he could bring the gerbils home from school for half-term and I said all right, and then he asked for a note for the school giving permission."

What did you do that day? I asked.

"Took care of the kids, like always," Sue answered.

When the child's body was found on the afternoon of 14 February, his torso still fully dressed but covered in blood, the lower half naked, the police had immediately suspected a sexually motivated murder and put out an alert for a known sex offender.

"But he turned out to have a firm alibi," said Superintendent Albert Kirby, who headed the investigation. He has handled, in the past, some of Liverpool's most complicated homicides, among them, in 1991, a murder investigation codenamed "Operation Clementine", which involved a satanic child-abuse cult.

Kirby is tall, slim and articulate. He detests violence in films and on television and believes firmly in a disciplined and structured family life: he and his wife Susan have a son in his third year at university. He is teetotal, a devout Christian and active in his church.

"I don't have words to describe what I felt when I saw what had been done to that baby," he said to me one night in Preston during the trial. "I think it's fair to say that few of us slept that night, or very much for weeks afterwards.

"Perhaps an adult perpetrator would have been easier . . ." he hesitated, then went on ". . . to bear." He was talking about the psychological and emotional aspect, not a moral one. He shook his head. "I just don't think that any of us will ever get over it: the violence done to the baby, the suffering of his parents and . . . well . . . the confrontations with the two boys. They were so . . ." he still sounded surprised ". . . so small; they had these young, young voices. When I looked at them the first time, I just thought 'it's impossible'. And in spite of the videos, we kept thinking, yes, perhaps hoping, that others . . . adults, had been involved."

Those security videos, taken on the afternoon of 12 February last year—on the face of it of two untroubled young boys taking a little brother for a walk—appeared on TV screens all over the world and elicited an enormous response in Liverpool. Hundreds of people phoned through to the special murder line the police had set up.

"That one doesn't half look like you," Ann Thompson had said to her ten-year-old son Robert that Saturday, pointing at the flickering image on the screen, "Were youse in the Strand yesterday?" "No," Robert had replied, staring at the television.

When Ann Thompson came to meet me 11 months later it was at the comfortable house of her young solicitor, Dominic Lloyd, and his wife, Lori. She brought three of her seven sons. Two others, Malcolm, now 16, and Brian, 15, have been in voluntary care since 1992; 18-year-old Richard works in another part of England.

Eleven-year-old Robert Thompson is, of course, now locked up in a secure unit where, his mother told me, he keeps things he likes in his room: Airfix kits, clay models he has made, and his collection of trolls. Some of them are on a table opposite his bed so he can look at them, others are "standing guard"—peeping out in a line from under the bed. Six other boys, all older than Robert, share his new home, but they don't bug him: "They've got their own troubles and the staff are very good." Robert has flashbacks about the scene at the railway and nightmares about James. "But he's said from the start, he didn't do it," Ann Thompson's voice was stubborn. "And I know what's in his heart and believe him."

(Jon Venables is in a much larger unit, with more boys, though they, too, are all older than he. Jon also has dreams, according to his mother, Susan, but they are of saving James and of the world becoming a "chocolate factory". "He has a collection of teddy bears in his room," she laughed, "he has them lined up around his bed, to keep the baddies away.")

The three boys who arrived with Ann Thompson live with her in the house on an estate in another county she was moved to after Robert's arrest. Her oldest, 20-year-old Michael, is a pale, thin, desperately diffident young man who has not yet held a job and despairs now of ever being able to go into catering, his only interest. He is manifestly in charge of the children. "He took on the father's role years ago," Ann said.

Nine-year-old Christopher, closest in age to Robert, has not been back to school all year and will hardly leave the house. He now has a tutor. An otherwise nice-looking little boy, he has gained about 35 pounds since the murder. "I can't find any trousers for him," Anne said, "so they just have to gape."

He seemed to me almost an indescribably unhappy boy, lost by events which only allow him obvious reactions: "I hate him," he says conversationally about Robbie during lunch when he shovels in prodigious amounts of carbohydrate and cholesterol. Can't you control what he eats? I asked Ann. She shrugged. "Do you want me to take that away from him, too?"

Her youngest, 18-month-old Tom, her only child born outside her marriage, is a cheerful smiling baby. In the 11 hours Ann and I spent together that day, he hardly slept but didn't cry once.

Ann Thompson, like Sue Venables, looked enormously better. Her hair freshly washed, she had lost some weight and wore well-cut fawn trousers and a loose black top.

Nothing she said or did during that long day changed the impression she had given me two months earlier in Court. There is no doubt—as she would tell me herself—that she had never been able to manage her life, or give to her children what they needed. But there is an honesty about her to which I found myself drawn. I told her right away that I first wanted to talk to her about her own childhood and her life as a girl and young woman, but for the first hour or so she kept swerving back to recent events, above all, of course, to "Bobby".

"He was difficult, you know, but he was loving," she said. "If I was watching the telly, he'd come and sit near me, and play with my ear . . . he was always putting his finger in ears, I don't know why."

I asked her if Robert had always made the odd hand movements I had noticed in Court, licking his fingers, putting his knuckles or two or three fingers into his mouth; wetting a finger and drawing it around his mouth.

No, she said, she'd never noticed it, but "he often has chapped lips".

Did he hug her, kiss her, or she him?

"No," she said. "Not big boys like that. But if I had migraine, he'd say to the others 'Shut up, mum's not well . . .' "

Without warning, she swung to the days of the trial.

"One day, downstairs, during a break, he said to me 'I

sometimes feel like crying up there.' So I said, 'Why don't you then?' and he said, 'What, cry in front of all those people? They'd think I'm a baby.'

"The newspapers wrote, he didn't seem to feel anything," she said. "But they don't know: his tension showed itself in breathing. He has asthma anyway and sometimes I could hear him wheeze from where I sat.

"Did you know?" she asked, suddenly starting to cry, "that he went to buy a rose and put it down in the grass where people had collected flowers for the baby?"

"Yes," I said, "I knew."

"Why would he do that if he didn't care?" she said.

I told her that Mary Bell, before she was arrested for the murder of two little boys in 1968, had gone to the funeral of one of them.

She looked at me for quite a while then without speaking. Finally, she said, "The day after he was arrested, I went to see him and told him that people were saying I had interfered with him."

" 'You?' he asked. 'What do they mean?' And I said, 'They think I touched your private parts.' 'You did not!' he said. He was furious," she said, sounding pleased.

She went on to ask me what I knew about child abuse. Had I talked with children who had been so abused? Had I ever met anybody who had abused a child?

It preoccupied her a great deal and she came back to it several times. Was it possible, I finally asked, when she raised the subject for the fourth time, that Robbie's father could have abused him when he was small? "No," she said. "No, he wouldn't have . . . well, except of course when he was drunk. God knows what he'd do then."

I asked whether Ann could think of anyone else who might have hurt Robert, an uncle, male friends – perhaps older boys? She shook her head. Could she think of anything else that might have happened to make him so unhappy?

She shook her head again. "Perhaps there wasn't anything," she said then, rather quietly and maturely, I thought. "Have you thought of that? Perhaps it was only because his dad left us."

Ann Thompson has always lived in Liverpool. Her parents are now 60 and 61. Her father was a lorry driver and has retired. Ann, now 40, is the middle child of three, with an older sister and a younger brother. They had lived simply when she was small. In the first house she remembered, "we had a tiny kitchen, an outside toilet, two bedrooms—one for parents, one for the two girls—a small living-room and a tiny yard." When Ann's brother was born, they moved to a three-bedroom house. Ann was frightened of her father for as long as she can remember. "There must have been a time, when I was really small, when he didn't beat me," she said, "but I can't remember it.

"I only remember the beatings, always with a belt; he'd take off his belt, you know, with a big sort of movement, and I had to stand there, waiting; it was the most frightening thing in the whole world." He only beat her, never the others. "I *was* a very defiant person, certainly, you know, when I grew . . . in my teens," she said. "But as a little girl? Well, anyway, it happened and, no, my mother didn't defend me: she was dead frightened of dad herself: he beat her, too, specially when he was drunk, which was often. I remember once, we were in bed; it was late evening and he came in drunk and started on her and she came running into our room in her nightdress screaming for help and I jumped out of bed and he lifted up the belt and said 'You make one move and you'll get it instead of her', and then he beat her as she lay across my bed. I don't think my parents knew the meaning of the word love . . ."

On the face of it, they were comparatively well-off because her father was always in work. "There was always food on the table, we had a Christmas tree . . . turkey . . . Easter eggs; you know, we had all the externals of normal life, including church every Sunday in our Sunday best."

At school "I was thick as two planks," she said. Her siblings liked school and were very bright. Her brother is now boss of a timber firm; her sister works in a factory, on the assembly line. "But only for a bit," she said quickly. (It was interesting that although she said she hadn't seen any of her family since Robert's arrest, she was careful to ensure that I understood her sister is too good for factory work.) "Just for the moment," she said again.

"They were clever about spelling—but I was always older up there," she touched her head, "than they could ever be."

She sounded relieved to go back to her childhood. She'd had friends . . . they played in the street, never in each other's houses. Much as in the majority of homes now, family life—without any meaningful verbal exchange—took place around the television screen.

"I was all the time unhappy" (the specific use of the phrase "all the time" rather than the more generalized "always" seems to emphasize the conscious continuity of her unhappiness and this is strongly borne out by her next sentence): "I was a bedwetter till 15."

Did her parents consult anyone about this?

"Oh yes, they sent me to the doctor; he sent me to the hospital, they gave me pills and all that . . . and the next time when it happened, as it always did, my dad beat me. I was so afraid of him, I only had to think of him to wet myself."

With this, the family was very prudish, she said, never saw each other undressed, any subject touching on anything to do with the body was taboo. "We didn't have a Childline," she says bitterly. "Who could we tell if we were beaten? I ran away when I was 16."

Where did she go?

She laughed, mocking herself. "Nowhere. Just over the road. And then—ha!—he had already caught me, dragged me back and beat me. I still got beaten at 17—a week before I got married.

"I talked to him three or four weeks ago," she said suddenly. "And I told my mother that he has been carrying on with another woman for 20 years and still is. I told her where she could find and ask her."

Why had she suddenly called her parents when they hadn't talked to her since Robbie's arrest, and in fact very little before that, either?

"There was a piece in the paper" (when she refers to the paper, she always means the *Liverpool Echo*) "with an interview with my father where he says that I never asked them to mind my kids." The implication was that if they had had a hand in their upbringing, this wouldn't have happened. "But it isn't even true—I did ask them, but they never would . . . the only one [of her boys] they would ever see was Malcolm, and that very rarely.

"Robert and I were married on my 18th birthday."

Yes, she said, her parents had attended the wedding. "Robert was 18, too, an apprentice electrician. He earned 15 shillings a week then. At the wedding party my dad said 'Now you're on your own. I give it 12 months.'

"Well, he was wrong there, wasn't he?" she said it with a sad kind of pride.

"We stayed married for 17 years."

Not surprisingly, she keeps coming back to her ex-husband, Robert, who walked out on her and his six children in 1988. He was a hard-working electrician and in the second half of their marriage the money was all right. "I was in love with him," Ann says. "In a way I still am. But our first nine years were difficult. We were just too young, we had little money and then—of course, now I know we had all these children too quickly. All these babies . . ." she repeated in a tone of wonder.

But why all the babies? I asked.

"I wanted a daughter," she said, dreamily.

"It's so hard to know what went wrong," she went on, searching. "I think we lived too near his parents, and then Robert's father died and left his wife with eight young children. His mother was a good woman—kind, but I never felt welcome in her house. It seemed to be because my family had more money, more possessions."

Even so, until Robert left, the various members of the families did see each other. "Afterwards, they were gone."

According to her, the last seven years of their marriage had been "all right": Robert was working and earning, and the six boys, too, were doing all right, at least, there were no complaints about them from school. They loved going camping in the summer, which the family had been enjoying for several years. Her husband drank quite a lot, it was true, she said. "But everybody in Liverpool drinks."

The women too? I asked.

"To be truthful, yes, by comparison with a lot of other places, probably quite a lot."

So would it be fair to say that even in their best years, the children would have been witness to a lot of drinking?

"I suppose so," she said. "But you know, because everybody does it, it wasn't special."

On these summer camping trips, she said, they swam and played games, people went fishing and even climbing.

However, it was evidently not these pastimes which principally occupied her husband Robert in the summer of 1988.

"We had a lot of friends on the campsite," Anne said, "among them a very nice, well-off older couple who we saw a lot of. They were grandparents in their fifties.

"But I didn't think he was seeing her separately," she said then. "For God's sake, she was 52 to Robert's 34. I had no idea there was something between him and her and when somebody suggested it—almost as a joke you know—I tried to ignore it. It was such a lovely summer. The children had such a good time and everybody was nice to everybody else.

"And then, one day, he just came with all her belongings and put them in our van and said if I said one word, just one single word, he'd take the van and go off with her. So I said nothing—he slept with her in a caravan; I slept with the kids in our eight-bed tent."

After they went back to Liverpool, they had another seven weeks together. "It was bad weeks. He never talked to me, or the kids. He went to work, then stayed out drinking, then came back just to sleep. Later I realized he had long decided to go and was only waiting to hear that she had found them a place to live."

She didn't think he saw the other woman during that time—she lived in another town. A personal ad in the *Liverpool Echo* under the title "Connection" brought things finally to a head. "It must have been a pre-arranged signal," Anne said. "He saw it, rushed out, came back at 3am, we rowed all night, and then in the morning he was gone. He left £5 on the kitchen table. That's all I ever had from him for the kids.

"I found out that they had gone to Southport and, later, that woman's desperate husband told me they had moved to Accrington, Lancs. At one point the older boys had a phone number for him and they used to ring him, but after a few months he must have moved because they couldn't get him any more. I later told the social services where he was, but they never could find him for child support, I don't know why." She snorted bitterly. "Now that the *Daily Mirror* found him, they've got him and now he has to pay. But to me, just for Christopher. I think he should be got for all those back years.

"I thought Robert loved the children," she said. "But he can't do, because he walked out and left them. They only saw him once more, when his mother, their grandmother, died three years ago. Then they saw him across her grave, but he never looked at them or said a word to them."

Some weeks after the murder, when the *Daily Mirror* had found Robert Thompson and informed him of what had happened to his ten-year-old son who bore his name, Liverpool police officers went to see him in the white-fenced cottage with ruched curtains he shares with the new Mrs Thompson. Detective Sergeant Phil Roberts described it as a *"Woman's Journal* home"—spanking clean, with pretty bits and pieces and lots of framed photographs of young couples and children—though none of them Thompson's boys.

"I asked him why he'd left his family," Phil Roberts said. "He said that in 1988 he had to make a choice: to let Ann destroy him, or to save himself. He decided to save himself. I asked him about the kids, but he had nothing to say. He obviously had no answer—who would?"

A few weeks later, Robert Thompson telephoned solicitor Dominic Lloyd asking to see him. "We met in a neutral place," Lloyd said. "I didn't get the feeling he knew exactly what he wanted, aside from feeling an obligation to get in touch. He asked about the kids, claimed Ann had made it impossible for him to see them after he left the family, and kept saying 'You know what she's like'. But he said he wanted to see Robert and also Michael.

"I went back and asked both of them. Michael really did want to see him. Robert went from hot to cold to warm, 'Yes, no, maybe'. But anyway, I never heard from his father again until after the conviction, when he again said he wanted to see the boy. I told him I'd have to make enquiries; now that he is convicted, the situation about visiting him is different. I did, but again, he hasn't called me back."

"I called him three of four weeks ago," Ann Thompson told me later. "I told him he deserted the boys; he left Robbie. I said there was no way he was going to see him now."

There certainly seemed to be a bad star over the Thompsons: a week after Robert had left them, on 16 October 1988, the family returned home after visiting their grandfather to find their house had burned down in an accidental fire. They lived for a while in a hostel before being rehoused in the Walton terrace next to the railway yard where, four years and four months later, the tragedy was to happen.

During the 18 months after Robert Thompson's departure, the family fell apart. "Everything went to pieces," Ann said. "I went on the booze, and within two weeks the kids, who had never done anything wrong before, were in dead trouble. Once it started, it didn't stop." She is amazingly honest about her own inadequacies: "I drank from morning to night, went to bed with a bottle of gin under my pillow and woke up taking a swig from it." Were there a lot of men in her life? I asked.

"Not the way you mean," she said, and smiled. "There were, but they were just . . . pals."

Drinking pals?

"Yeah." And then she added: "There was one, Roger, I had sex with," she giggled, "and now there is Bob, Tom's dad. He's OK with the other kids, too, so that's good. And—he's company. It's . . . it's very lonely where we are now. I go to car-boot sales to get stuff to make it more homey," and she showed me a photo album she had brought, with pictures of the inside of her new house, which she had obviously tried hard to make her own. "I love plants," she said. "My house was full of them, but when they moved us, they forgot them, and they take so long to grow."

Those bad 18 months had brought the "Social" in, she said. "They'd never been to us before, but after that, they were around every week, ten of them in five years.

"The first one was a doctor's daughter, very la-di-da," she said. "She'd breeze in, not a hair out of place, say 'Have you paid your bills?' and breeze out. I didn't need that, or rather, I needed something else as much and even more than money."

It is unlikely that Ann, in deep depression and drink, was clearly aware of this different need then, but she was certainly able to respond when the Liverpool Family Service Unit—a voluntary organization particularly well staffed to deal with complex family situations—sent them a young woman called Jackie.

"She was different," Ann said. "She kicked her shoes off, asked 'What's for tea?' and settled down to chat."

By this time, Richard, the second oldest boy then 13, had, very sensibly one might think, run away and gone to live with his paternal grandmother.

"Social services got in touch with me," Ann said. "And I gave my permission." Richard has, in fact, gone on to become so far the one well-organized boy in that family. He lives with the family of a "very nice girl", who, Ann said, he's in love with.

Except for the Family Service Unit and then the psychiatric social worker who supported Ann throughout the trial and now continues to help her, she is very bitter about all authorities, most of whom, she feels, have let her down.

"One day, while things were at their worst," she said, "Richard got sent home from school because he didn't have shoes. Well, it was true. He'd grown out of his and I didn't have money to buy new ones. But I wanted him back in school at once, so I went straight to the social services either for shoes or for money to buy some. The social worker said no, they couldn't help me, because I had 'dealings' with the Family Service Unit.

"Is that a way to act?" she asked me. "I mean to say, I wasn't asking for a video or a washing machine, just a pair of shoes so that the kid could go to school." The Family Service Unit then got her the shoes, she said, "without harassing me or making me feel guilty or talking down at me as if I was dirt."

There can be little doubt that the Thompson family became a considerable problem to the various services involved with them at that time; not much doubt, either, that Ann Thompson, in her anger over being deserted and her despair over how to cope, became very demanding—people do.

Social services in these economically deprived cities deal, of course, with countless similar situations and, understaffed and— more important—undertrained, frequently go wrong in their choice of priorities and assignments of individual social workers to a case. The "doctor's daughter" first sent to Ann Thompson by the Liverpool social services may have been quite as committed to her calling as the Family Service Unit's Jackie: she just didn't suit Ann Thompson—she was in the wrong slot. Mrs. Thompson was evidently both very thorny and very vulnerable—the two often go together—and, feeling bad enough about herself, reacted negatively to censure. "Three months later," she said, "one of the social workers came and said my sister-in-law had reported that I had battered my children with a stick. I made the kids strip then and there—there was not a mark on them." If the mind boggles at this thought, it is true, too, that confronted with what were doubtless outraged social workers—Malcolm had repeatedly complained about Michael beating him, and so had Brian—she didn't have many choices. "But I did have a terribly difficult time managing Brian," she said, "so I finally asked for him to be taken into care and not long afterwards Malcolm went into voluntary care—I think Brian told him about his comfortable room and all the clothes he got and attention and pocket money so he thought why not me, too. But it was all right with me; those were the two who fought most, and the places they got sent to were good.

"Don't misunderstand me," she then said. "They all loved each other, but they all paired off, age-wise."

None of this is quite as others describe it: first of all, it doesn't sound to me as if there was much, if any, love between these brothers. When I asked Ann to tell me about each of the boys, she could only say they were good kids, really, and remind me of Bobby's concern for her migraine. She couldn't really speak about them as individuals. The children doubtless mirror her emotional confusions—as children will—and are equally bereft.

Brian and Malcolm went into voluntary care, but not until 1992, much later than Ann recalls or admits. And in the children's homes, too, they remained troubled: both, Ann said, at some point took overdoses of Paracetamol. As for Robert, he was now swiftly approaching crisis point.

Teachers from the boys' school, and neighbours, all noted the amount of bullying in the family, with each pair of older boys bullying the pair next to them down the line in age. Thus Michael, 14 when his father left, lorded it over ten-year-old Malcolm and nine-year-old Brian. Malcolm and Brian in turn bullied Robbie between the age of five and seven; and Robbie, by the time he was eight and nine, bullied his little brother Christopher. There is a confusing story, which Ann denies, but others confirm, that towards the end of 1991 or the beginning of 1992, Richard, back home at that point, called the neighbours for help because Michael, then 17, had "chained him, tarred and feathered him, and hung him upside down in the back garden". It is difficult to visualize this, looking at the thin, limpid figure of 20-year-old Michael, who appears absent even when he is there. Still, whatever happened, Richard left soon afterwards. This incident is also supposed to have led to a further break between Ann and her parents, who have claimed to have felt increasingly embarrassed by the family's conspicuous conduct.

The teachers of St. Mary's Church of England Primary School in Walton, Liverpool, commented on the bullying tactics of the Thompson boys in statements to the police after the murder. "To my knowledge," said one of them:

> I first came into contact with Robert Thompson in September 1989 although I had contact with the family as far back as 1982. During this period of time it has been a continual battle to bring to the attention of the social services and other services, the problems surrounding these children in the Thompson family. I have on a number of occasions informed the social services about the bullying tactics that have applied to each of the boys in the family in relation to the direct younger brother. In respect of Robert, there have been a number of occasions when it has been reported to me that he has been bullying his younger brother, Christopher, telling him that if he didn't truant from school with him that he would break Christopher's glasses . . . Mrs. Thompson is aware that this has been going on, because a meeting took place between her, her social services worker and the Educational Welfare Officer on the 4th of February 1993.

Reading this report, which specifically says that Ann Thompson was aware of what had been going on, must make one wonder why, if the Thompson boys' bullying was known to the school for years, Robert's bad behaviour was known as of 1989, and his truanting habit specifically as of September 1992, it took until 4 February 1993 (only eight days before James Bulger's murder), to set up a meeting with the boy's mother.

As in all family tales, there is a good deal of confusion about exact dates, but it is established that when Ann Thompson became pregnant with her last baby, Tom, around November–December 1991, she stopped drinking.

"How did you manage that?" I asked her.

"Well, it wouldn't be good for a baby, would it?" she said, and added, "I wasn't an alcoholic, you know. I just drank."

Had it never occurred to her before she became pregnant that her drinking was bad for her other children?

"I know what you mean," she said slowly. "Yes, I think I knew that in my mind. But when I got pregnant, I knew it in my body, and that's different."

I think, quite aside from "wanting a daughter", it has always been Ann's body which knew that she felt well—perhaps safer—when she was pregnant; many women do. And life in the Thompson household may always have been calmer and even more orderly in those months, possibly another instinctive reason why she continually became pregnant.

By September 1991, Jon Venables had been moved to St. Mary's, and he and Robbie Thompson—both held back a year because they were academic "under-achievers"—had been put in a class where they were the oldest boys, perhaps a natural link. That first year, however, their class teacher was a man who had previously worked with maladjusted children and believed strongly in structure and discipline. Although all the teachers' statements mention Robert's tendency to lie, and Jon's "frequent . . . odd and . . . inappropriate behaviour", there is nothing in any of the statements that indicates any specific trouble that year.

> Robert is cunning, [said one of them] Jon . . . would
> never have eye contact during conversation, showed very
> little emotion and could turn on the tears as he wished . . .
> He is often involved in fights and has a very short temper.

The male class teacher found Robert "a quiet, often shy little boy making the bullets for the others to shoot . . . I knew he was from a problem family." And the boys' second class teacher, who had their care from September 1992 on, stated:

> Prior to Robert and Jon coming into my class, I was aware
> that Jon had behavioural problems and that Robert had a
> non-attendance problem. In respect of the two, I would say
> that Robert was the motivator of any minor problems or any
> truancy, and that Jon is the type of boy that would go along
> with that. [But then she contradicts herself . . .] It is Jon
> that has caused me the most trouble in the class with his
> behaviour, not generally naughty but . . . disruptive and
> awkward. Robert was fairly easy to handle.

From her dealings with both boys she could say that she never saw them involved in any violence in school and that neither boy showed any "inclination to violence or aggressive tendencies".

Their playground supervisor agreed. Robbie, she stated, was "a normal child, who never gave any trouble." But her remarks about Jon suggest that, contrary to Sue and Neil Venables's belief, the symptoms of Jon's problems had not abated after changing schools:

> When [Jon] first arrived at the school he reacted in a
> strange way [to being reprimanded] he would turn around
> and butt the wall with his head, fall onto the ground
> throwing his arms around . . . I personally think that Jon
> had a problem and shouldn't have been in the school.

(Much later, I would hear from police and lawyers that during pre-trial interrogations and meetings in the detention room below the Court during breaks, when asked difficult questions, Jon would show the same symptoms of disturbance he had manifested in both his schools: throwing himself on the floor, throwing his arms and legs about and banging his head against the wall or floor. "It was really quite alarming," said one of the lawyers.)

According to Ann Thompson—and the school reports appear to confirm this—the truanting only started in September 1992, which, according to both the school and the parents, was the time Robert and Jon had become friends.

"Robbie did truant without Venables," Ann said, "but only after Venables came to the school. He was more out of school than in. When they told me, I asked that he be sent to another school where he could be monitored. The head said 'He'd have to see a child psychiatrist for that', and I said, 'Fine, he can see one'. And then she said, 'He wouldn't pass the test to get into one of these schools', so I asked why, and she said 'Because he is a normal ten-year-old child.' I've thought and thought about that answer," Ann said, "about their indifference; about their negligence; but most of all about their obvious ignorance about children such as Robbie."

Had it not occurred to her, I asked, that she herself perhaps didn't do enough for the boys, and, as we have seen, especially for Robbie? She answered only indirectly. "When, at that school meeting I went to, nobody thought of anything to do," she said, "I thought I'd try another way: I said to Robbie, 'If you stay in school all week I'll give you a present at the end of it.' That was just that week—when it happened."

So much has been written about the people of Liverpool, the police, and of course the dreadful unhappiness of the Bulger family in those five days after 12 February last year before the boys were arrested, it is almost strange how much of a grey area it remains as far as the boys themselves are concerned.

We have all read that the two boys were found at about 7.30 pm that night by Susan Venables in the video shop where they had just earned £1 by doing an errand for the girl who looked after it. We know—and both Sue Venables and Ann Thompson have now confirmed it to me—that they were filthy, their hands and clothes "covered in mud", with large splashes of light-blue enamel paint on their jackets. "I was livid," Susan said. "It was never going to come out." But more than that. She was so furious, she said, at Jon's having again sagged off, with Robert, she screamed at Robert to get away from Jon.

Robert would run home and tell his mother that Susan had hit him, and, as proof, showed a bleeding scratch he had sustained earlier on in the railway yard. Ann, furiously, supported by a neighbour, marched him to the police station to put in a complaint of assault against Susan. The police told her there probably weren't grounds. Susan, too, had pulled Jon along the street to the police and told the constable on duty to give him a warning about sagging. "I really was beside myself," Sue said. Ironically, this meant that both boys appeared in Walton Police Station within an hour of the killing. "When I got him home," said Sue Venables, "the television was on, and they were showing that photo of missing baby James. I was hitting Jon—yes, I was—he was crying and both of us, Neil too, were yelling at him. He was on the floor and I still beat on him and I pointed at the screen and said, 'Look. Look at that. Here's that little baby missing and you, you, you are out in the street with that Robert!' I didn't know any more what I was saying, but I told him to get upstairs to bed, and he snivelled and said, 'But I haven't had my tea', and Neil said 'And you won't get any tea, either. Go to bed and think.' Well," she said, "then he cried and cried in bed, so I got sorry for him and brought him a cup of tea. Then he went to sleep."

Susan Venables told me that Jon stayed in bed late the next morning and that they had then, as always on Saturdays, driven out to see her mother for the day. "He did watch all the news about the baby," she said, "and he talked about him a lot. But otherwise, he wasn't any different from other days. He certainly didn't see that Robert. After what I done to him the night before, he wouldn't have dared."

Well, perhaps not. But Ann Thompson remembers clearly that Jon came round on his bicycle about 8.30 or 9.00 on Saturday morning, wanting to know where Robbie was and could he come in. "I told him to go away, and that his mum was apt to hit Robbie if he played with him. I shooed him out and he turned around on his bike and went. Then I told Robbie he had been."

Is it likely that these two boys didn't meet during the five days they had left? Jon would later say Robbie had told him that if anybody asked, to say Christopher had been with them all of Friday. So when he was questioned, that's what he did. Robert, however, did not mention Christopher in his interrogations. He knew quite well that that lie was pointless: Christopher had been in school and everybody knew it.

Police officers were called in from all over the Liverpool area. Detective Constable David Tanner, who had worked with Kirby on previous occasions, was one of them. He is 6ft 4in, a gentle giant, and was on the detail sent out to arrest Jon Venables that Thursday, 18 February, at 7.30 in the morning.

"When he came down those stairs in his pyjamas," Tanner said, "I thought it had to be a mistake." A few minutes later, when the officers asked to see the clothes Jon had worn the previous Friday, he threw his mustard-coloured anorak to the floor at their feet. His mother promptly reprimanded him, but this expression of childish anger didn't worry Tanner. "I'd seen worse," he said. When they got back to Lower Lane Police Station (the boys were to be held at different stations, later at different special units, and never allowed to speak to each other) and colleagues asked Tanner what he thought, he told them it couldn't be this boy.

"That morning," David Tanner said, "we went through both the Venables' flats, searching for anything relevant." (In his final words at the trial, the Judge, indicating his understanding that the two boys had watched a violent video called *Child's Play III*, which, he said, could have affected their actions, had issued what was probably the most impressive warning ever pronounced publicly in Britain against violent and suggestive videos in the home.)

Having learned of Neil Venables' addictions to videos—he was said to have rented 400 of them in the course of the past year—and knowing of the police suspicions about the motivations for Jamie's murder, I asked David Tanner whether, in their search of the Venables' homes, they had found anything indicating any kind of perversion, including pornographic films.

"Nothing," he said. "And believe me we were looking for it. But the films Neil had there were quite innocuous."

Neil Venables told me that although he had indeed seen the film the Judge's remarks had made so notorious, a neighbour had rented it, not he, and that, anyway, Jon could never have seen anything violent without his knowledge.

This, of course, is nonsense—and not only in Jon's case; it applies to most of our children. Jon told the police that he had often seen satellite films while his dad slept in the morning. I think it is very likely that Jon—and Robert—saw that particular film . . . many children I questioned later had. But when I watched it myself, I did not find it so very terrible, nor could I detect the particularly clear parallels to the crime the tabloids made a great deal of. And, oddly enough, just like the often frightening Grimm's Fairy Tales, *Child's Play III* had—though it was perhaps not very strong—a moral aspect.

But I think Mr Justice Morland had a very clear purpose when he brought up the point of violent videos in the home: he wanted to remind us that children are malleable and highly subject to influences, particularly now from films. Stable children—and adults—exposed to violent films, run the danger of becoming emotionally desensitized by a surfeit of such visual experiences, but they are unlikely to be permanently harmed by them. Unstable children, however, from chaotic backgrounds, are extremely susceptible to their mesmerizing effect. It was about this vulnerability to visual violence, I think, that the Judge was trying to issue a warning and provoke a debate.

Almost from the very beginning, after James's body had been found, Superintendent Kirby had arranged for counsellors to be available to support his team. "Don't misunderstand me," he said. "Morale, as far as determination was concerned, was very high, never higher. But at the same time, there was an enormous sense of . . . distress doesn't describe it; it was more than that: dismay."

What they felt, he and others told me, was a terrible unease, about human beings, about life, about themselves and about their own children. From the moment it began to look likely that a child or children had committed the crime, meetings had been arranged with psychologists and psychiatrists who prepared the team for what they might have to expect; how to conduct themselves with children and parents, and where to draw the line between accusation and compassion.

After the boys' arrest, agreement was obtained from their families and legal advisers to install downstream monitoring equipment to enable the interviews with the children to be listened to from outside. It was this that would enable David Tanner and Detective Sergeant Michelle Bennett, who were assigned to listen to the interviews with Jon Venables, to realize on the afternoon of the second day, 19 February, that the boy's desperate need to confess was being hampered by his mother's constant re-assurances.

Robert Thompson—his police interrogators were to call him Bobbie—and Jonathan Venables, known as Jon, had been arrested at 7.30 a.m. on Thursday, 18 February. During that afternoon and evening, and on the subsequent two days, each boy was interrogated three or four times every day, for about 40 minutes at a time. The police were extremely careful with the two children, before every interview meticulously repeating the prescribed cautions. The interviews with Jon were conducted by Detective Sergeant Mark Dale and Detective Constable George Scott, with his mother or father and solicitor Laurence Lee present.

The police officers who interviewed Robert were Detective Sergeant Phil Roberts and Detective Constable (now Sergeant) Bob Jacobs. Robbie's mother and his solicitor, Dominic Lloyd, or his assistant, Jason Lee, were always present, except when Ann Thompson felt ill, when a policewoman replaced her.

The police's preoccupation with the sexual element of the crime had manifestly not escaped Robert's attention. On the second day when Anne came to see him in the child detention cell, Robert said at once: "He [meaning a police officer] said I'm a pervert. They said I've played with his willy."

His mother had, of course, initiated such talk between them, by telling him the previous day what was being said about *her*;

even so, it seemed surprising that he should bring the subject up about himself.

There was to be an enormous difference between the two boys' approach to the interrogations. Both their voices were tiny, light, almost toddler-age. But while in Jon one heard mainly his terror, in Robert, despite the infantile sound of his voice, there was energy. "I found it . . ." tall, handsome Phil Roberts hesitated, "frightening at times," he said. "Yes, frightening."

As it started, Robert's story was not very frightening. Moreover, as far as it went (here again, an interesting parallel between Mary Bell's and Robert Thompson's response to interrogation) it was, quite carefully, almost true. "He really was very intelligent," said Phil Roberts. "Very canny."

They had sagged off from school on Jon's initiative, Robert said, gone walking along this road and that road, over a bridge, over a flyover on a backway to the Strand (Bootle Strand, the big modern shopping centre). Sometimes it took just an hour to get to the Strand, sometimes, like that day, he said, much more. Once they got there, they went to McDonald's—not to eat, just to keep warm and sit down. "We went to about five shops, the Buckingham Bingo and the library."

They had spent half an hour at the library, he said. They were allowed to read books there. He read nursery rhymes.

Jon, talking primarily to Detective Sergeant Dale, was more expansive and quite breathless in his descriptions. He'd been walking to school that Friday, he said, "and then he [Robert] came the back of me and . . . said do you want to sag off and I went 'all right' . . . " And Robert's brother, little Christopher, had been along, too, he said, until six that night.

They had played "in the subways" and in derelict factories, and in a park (he went on without pauses) and under a bridge, and on swings, and in a big block of flats where they'd gone on the lifts, and then they'd gone "robbing" in stores—Mars Bars, which he liked, and trolls which Robert collected—and then they'd gone to the Liverpool football ground and then the cemetery, "and Robert said, 'let's look at the names' and he said, 'do you want to get that flower,' and I said 'no, no, it's people's memories . . .' and then I showed Robert me nan's and grandad's [graves] and then he showed me his uncle's, his nan, his mum's uncle [gradually he gets confused] his dad's, dad's grave and his mum's, mum's grave . . . then there was a fire and then it was going darker and then we went to the video shop . . . and, I forgot: before that, we'd got the paint and he threw it over me . . . paint all over me arm and on me school pants and I said me mum's going to kill me . . ." (here he had realized that the police would have found the blue paint on his clothes which they had thrown at little James and tried, nowhere near as adroitly as Robert, to adapt his story accordingly) ". . . and Christopher was laughing and then we went back to Walton Village and . . . Christopher said it was six o'clock and he was going in now."

And then, he said, they still went on for another hour, ending up in the video shop where his mum (who was sitting there, nodding) found them. "And you [to his mother] took me to the police station and he [the duty officer there] said if you do it again, you'll go in a home. And then you took me home and then I went to bed."

This story—little bits of truth mixed with large chunks of past experience and imagination—had taken almost an hour. Its whole purpose was to keep him away from the Strand, where Robert, much more defiant, and much more sure of his ability to outwit the police, in his account admitted arriving within minutes.

The second day, 19 February, was decisive. Both children were interrogated three times: Jon from 11.06 to 11.50; 12.23 to 12.56; and 15.57 to 16.30. Robert from 11.35 to 12.28; 14.14 to 14.57; and 15.00 to 15.11.

Throughout that morning—in Robert's case also the early afternoon—both boys desperately denied anything but the most marginal contact with James. In each 300-page transcript of each boy's interrogations, their denials, almost eerily voiced virtually in the same words, stretch over 100 pages.

Robert: "I never took James on to the hill." "I never went on the hill." "I never had hold of his hand" (on four different occasions). "I never had no paint." "I never touched the baby" (again in four different interrogations). "I never killed him."

Jon cried more often. His need for his mother's approval was paramount, and it was always her he addressed whenever he mentioned the baby: "We never got a kid, Mum." "We never."

"I'm telling you, please." "I never got him." "Never a kid." "Mum, I never." "I never took him by the hand, I never even touched the baby." "I never touched a baby." "I never took the baby, Mum . . ."

That afternoon, Detective Sergeant Roberts had been asking Robert Thompson about the things they had "robbed" during their tour of the shops in the Strand that Friday, such as the tin of blue paint which Robert said Jon had "thrown in James's eye."

"Did he or you take anything else?" asked Phil Roberts.

"No."

"Did either of you take some batteries?"

"No."

". . . You went all red in the face there."

"What?"

"I noticed you went a little bit red in the face. What about these batteries?"

"I never took anything."

"When somebody gets embarrassed about something, they go red in the face. Do you understand?"

"Yeah, but I never took no batteries." (Cries wildly.)

"Well son . . ."

(Almost a screech) "I never took no batteries."

"Who took the batteries, then?"

"I don't know" (sobbing) ". . . Yeah, well Jon might have took them . . . Why do we want batteries? It wasn't me . . . He might have stuck them in his pocket . . . I never. It weren't me . . ."

And that afternoon, questioned again about the batteries, Robbie said again Jon might have taken them. "For his game gear, cos that's what he plays on most . . ."

"What are the batteries like he uses for those?"

"Pencil."

"The little thin ones, are they?"

"Not the . . . little thin ones."

"No?"

"They are about that thick" (he indicates with his hands).

"Are they the round ones—you know, are they shaped round?"

"Yeah, round."

"How would you put it—with a little . . . nut . . . at the top?"

"A lump at the top . . . And no lump in the bottom . . ."

After six more pages in the transcript, Robert, with enormous determination and skill, led the police officers away from the dreaded batteries by initiating a discussion about what one would think would be the worst thing for him to talk about—blood.

During the 33 minutes of Jon's second interrogation that day, he had become increasingly distressed, bursting into tears every few moments and beseeching his mother with that repeated "I never touched him" to believe him. And Susan Venables tried desperately to help him: "Calm down first," she said.

"No, I can't, I never touched him . . . we just went home and I . . . I left Robert on his own until he came back to Walton Village."

"Tell me the truth now, please Jon," his mother urged.

"I never killed him, Mum. Mum, we took him and we left him at the canal, that's all [he now admitted for the first time taking James] . . . I never killed him, Mum."

"I believe you," Sue assured him.

"You think I done it," he cried. "I'm telling youse . . ." He starts almost to hyperventilate. "Don't," she tries to quiet him, "we don't, Jon. Come on."

"I want to go home. I've already told youse what I know. Ooh . . . you're going to put me in jail . . . I never Mum," he wails until his "I never, I never" no longer sounds like words but one long cry.

"I know you wouldn't hurt a baby," his mother said.

"This was where we broke it off," David Tanner told me. It was early evening and we had been talking for an hour, sitting in his small office at the police station in St. Helen's. Even though it was six weeks after the end of the trial, it had been extremely difficult to get any of the police officers who had been closely involved with the boys to talk to me. Superintendent Kirby had finally persuaded a few of them to help me. "Go easy," he had warned me. "Some are still very upset."

David Tanner had been all right for that first hour while we discussed Liverpool, unemployment, violence, the decision he had made before this happened to ask to be assigned where he was now, where it was quieter, and nearer home.

He is a powerful-looking man, but quiet, with warm eyes. The moment we began to talk about those days in February a year ago, they filled with tears. He tried to joke, "Just a reflex", he said, and added that his wife would tell me there was a softy inside that big man. I didn't think so. There was a very human being inside that man.

He and Detective Sergeant Michelle Bennett had stood outside the door of the interrogation room and listened in over the downstream monitoring. Michelle Bennett, herself a mother of young children, had been assigned to look after Susan Venables. "She is very, very good," David Tanner said. "But she found it very arduous."

To comfort Susan Venables? I asked.

"No," he said, "to like her."

As they listened to the increasing tension in Jon's voice, they knew they had to do something. "By the end of that second session," Tanner said, "it was clear to us that the boy had a desperate need to confess, and the mother's reassurances were stopping him."

They had taken Susan Venables to another room and explained to her that she wasn't doing Jon any good by helping him suppress what he was trying to get out. The police by this time knew that James's blood had been found on both boys' shoes and other things. "It was particularly difficult," David said, "because we couldn't tell her about this evidence.

"We told her that what she and her husband had to do was to sit down with Jon and assure him that they loved him, and would continue to love him whatever happened. I think she trusted me," he said. "It took almost an hour, but then it dawned on her that what we were saying was right. She went to find Neil and explained it all to him and he finally agreed."

It was decided the parents would talk to Jon in the juvenile detention room where he had meanwhile been given lunch.

As they went in, Susan turned around and told Tanner that

she wanted him to come in with them. "I hadn't expected it," he said.

The experience, it was clear, had been extraordinarily upsetting. Tanner's lips kept trembling as he described it to me. "There wasn't much of anything in that room," he said. "Just a mattress on the floor and a bench at the far side of it. That's where they sat down, with Jon between them. I sat down on the mattress, at the other end. They both put their arms around him and kissed and cuddled him. It wasn't very long at all," he said, "he ended up sort of curled up on Sue's lap and he was crying and crying and they said over and over that they loved him and would always love him and then, really very quickly, he said: 'I did kill him.' It was so quick and he was crying so hard, we thought perhaps he hoped we wouldn't hear but of course I did and Michelle and Mark Dale who were standing outside the door did too and it had an enormous impact on us . . ."

The parents came out then—Michelle took Susan to freshen up while David Tanner took Neil to the interview room. "I told him that Sue had done enough for a bit and that it was time for him to take over. I said 'It's time for you to be a man'. He went back to Jon then and a little later he came out and he looked white. 'Do you know what they did?' he said, sounding stunned. 'My God, he just told me.'

"It really was all quite . . . quite terrible," Tanner said, and we both sat quietly for a while. "We really couldn't make do with Susan," he finally said. "We couldn't understand how she was . . . well . . . constantly repairing her make-up—it seemed so extraordinary." A nervous reaction? I suggested. "Well, it didn't feel like that to us."

Neil's weakness, too, he said, had made them feel uncomfortable. "But they were honest, you know, in wanting Jon to tell the truth . . ."

Jon repeated his confession into the tape shortly afterwards. That afternoon, and the next day, they tried to lead him further, but—even worse than Robert—there was one thing he simply could not get out. It took more than two hours not to say it; he told them everything in those hours: how it had been his idea in the Strand to walk towards James but ". . . Robert's to kill him," and then, bit by bit, he went over the whole walk and finally the railway yard and the bricks, and the metal bar, and the kicks, from both Robert and him, and the taking off of the trainers and socks—*he* did that—and his pants and his underpants—"*Robert* done that—and, and, and . . ."

"There was something else, wasn't there?" Mark Dale eventually interrupted him. "You left it out, haven't you, and you know it's important, don't you?" And it took another long detour, via yet more awful things he enumerated in his attempt to escape pronouncing what he just couldn't seem to bear saying.

"We found batteries there, didn't we," Mark Dale finally said. And after countless more "I never, no batteries, never batteries," and "Robert . . . not me," he almost screamed, sobbing. "They're *his* batteries . . ." and then, at last, they ended it.

In the final interview with Robert Thompson, the police expanded their questioning about the batteries into a long conversation that brought up various sexual aspects of the attack. Detective Sergeant Roberts told Robbie about some of the things Jon had said during his interviews—a tactic both police teams used to elicit more information from the boys.

"Can I just say to you what Jon has said . . ."

Robbie interrupts him: "Most probably that I've took everything off him and that I've been playing with him."

Jacobs: "How do you know that?"

Robbie: "Cos I know he's going to say that."

Roberts: "Playing with what?"

Robbie: "His privates, that's what you said before."

Roberts: "What do you mean, privates?"

Robbie: "What I say."

Roberts: "What, like his penis, that's what you're saying?"

Robbie: "Cos Jon's not going to own up, is he? It wasn't me."

Robbie was now crying. He said that they were just going to accept everything Jon was saying, and blame everything on him.

"Well," said Roberts. "You say you had hold of [James's] body. At any stage . . . any time, have you put your hand into his mouth?"

Robbie: "No."

Roberts: "Because what happened left a mark."

Robbie: "In where?"

Roberts: "Where his mouth had been pulled down."

Robbie: "On his lips?"

Roberts: "In his mouth."

Robbie: "Or his tongue?"

Roberts: "In his mouth."

Robbie: "On his lips?"

Jacobs: "*You* tell *me*."

Finally, Jacobs asks him: "Have you put your hand in his mouth at all?"

Robbie: "No."

Half an hour later, this conversation ends with a strange remark by this ten-year-old when Detective Sergeant Roberts discusses with him some "muck" he'd had on his face at the end of that day.

Roberts: "How did you get the muck on your face?"

Robbie: "I don't know, it blows all around."

Jacobs: "No it doesn't blow all around. You get . . . dust, but it doesn't make dirty marks."

Robbie: "What do you mean dirty marks?"

Jacobs: "You know what dirty marks are, don't you?"

Robbie: "Like sex marks."

Jacobs: "Like what?"

Robbie: "Sex marks. Dirty."

Until one or both of these boys one day tells his own story, we can try to fit together various pieces—the parents' stories, the teacher's descriptions, what witnesses saw—but we will never really know what went on inside those ten-year-old minds that dreadful Friday and the days which led up to it.

Superintendent Kirby, who thought of little else for almost a year, is convinced that they had long planned to murder a child that day. Two weeks before, Robert had bullied his little brother into truanting one afternoon and abandoned him crying by the Leeds–Liverpool canal which borders the Bootle Strand shopping centre. "That was the place where on 12 February they tried to make James lean over the water in order to push him in," Mr. Kirby said. "I think leaving [the young brother] there was a rehearsal."

Just before taking James, Robert and Jonathan had tried to lure away another little boy whose mother luckily found him in time.

Kirby is certain that they were determined to kill. He feels that four things support this view. First, when he considers the rehearsal for later events—Robert's abandonment of Christopher in January. (Jon was not involved in this nasty caper, and Christopher, though very distressed, sensibly enough went across the street to the Bootle shopping centre and asked a security officer to help him; he called the school and Christopher's class teacher was despatched to the centre manager's office to collect him.)

Kirby's second point is that the other boys at the school had claimed to have been invited to join Robert and Jon's "gang" of two "because we are going to kill someone". (This statement actually came from only one boy in the school and was not used by the prosecution.)

Kirby's third and fourth reasons are statements made by Jon under interrogation: Bobby, Jon said, had wanted to throw the baby into the canal but when James wouldn't "bend over the water", he had decided to "get him knocked over by a bus".

When this, too, failed—perhaps because there were too many people around on that late Friday afternoon: three witnesses would testify that they saw Robert and Jon pull James *back* from the road on three occasions—they took him down to the railway yard near Robert's home in Walton where, like many other boys, Robert was apparently in the habit of playing. His alleged "den" was unfortunately never found—or, perhaps, particularly looked for. If the children's psychology had played a stronger part in the investigation, it would have been realized that the contents of a child's den—a place where children invariably hide secrets—could have been revealing.

Although I do not see eye to eye with Mr. Kirby on premedita- tion to murder, I, too, thought that it was unlikely that the boys would have dragged the tired, often crying toddler on a more than two-mile trek, ending up in the railway yard, unless they had a purpose.

It has to be remembered that these were not stupid boys:

intelligence tests given to them before the trial by psychiatrists Dr. Susan Bailey (to Jon) and Dr. Eileen Vizard (to Robert), concluded that Jon was of average—and Robert of "Good, at least average" intelligence (a fact which was amply confirmed by his interpolations during interrogations). If one or both of these boys wanted to kill a child, there were (and I apologize for the word) easier ways to do it, not least by pushing him in front of an oncoming car.

The more complex the intention, of course, the more need there was of seclusion. (Martin Brown, the first of the Newcastle victims, it will be remembered, was killed in a derelict house; the second, Brian Howe, on an expanse of waste ground used by children as an adventure playground. In these cases, as I have pointed out, there was no frenzy: Mary Bell's pathology, deriving from her emotional abuse as a small child, was, one might almost say a "tactile" fascination with death, but—different from these two boys—not with pain.)

I suggest that if both boys', or one boy's, intention was to *kill* James, they would not have planned on the ferocious manner of his death; frenzy can occur, but it can't be planned.

What *can* be planned is a sexual attack. This, contrary to killing, requires time, isolation and, as one knows from countless testimonies of child-victims, often darkness. ("They did it all in the dark," one of the Court attendants in Preston said. "I can't get over that.")

The exact sequence of events on that dreadful night has never been discovered, or divulged, but although Jon at one point in his testimony claimed the contrary, the police believe James's clothes were removed before the killing. They undressed James and they manipulated his penis and foreskin. This much the jury was told. But because this was all they knew, and were facing the moment of having to confront the awful violence of the killing, they may well have almost disregarded what could have appeared to them as no more than a distressing interlude. The fact that it was far more than that, was suspected but not fully known. Also, however, it was not acceptable—or bearable. The police, finding the half-nude child and a number of batteries nearby, did, as we know, immediately suspect a sexual motive. James's anus and back passage were examined, the batteries were tested for body fluids, and the boys were repeatedly interrogated about the batteries, responding on each occasion with enormous distress and, of course, total denial that they had been put to any use whatsoever other than "throwing them at the baby".

The post-mortem report states specifically that "the anus showed no external injury" and that "detailed examination of the rectum . . . shows no tearing and no evidence of bruising."

It would, however, appear that in fact a tear *was* found in the child's rectum and photographed ("Yes, we have it," a police spokesman confirmed last week), but that the pathologists suggested it could have been "a result of constipation". When the forensic examination of the batteries revealed nothing, this explanation, though unsatisfactory to many of the police officers and most of the lawyers on the case, was accepted.

"The batteries had been exposed to humidity (dew and perhaps frost) for two days before James's body was found," Superintendent Kirby said. "They showed nothing. In any case," he added (Kirby himself was not at all happy to leave aside this aspect of the case), "there was no doubt they had killed the baby. There was no point in dragging the horror for the Bulgers out any further."

This was absolutely true. But there was quite a different piece of possibly related evidence which, unaccountably, was entirely ignored. Superintendent Kirby told me he had not known of its existence and, indeed, only one of the several forensic reports mentions it: "A small quantity of faecal material in the form of a stool was present under a brick on the other side of the rail adjacent to the body: blood drips were present on the outer aspect of the rail just above the faeces."

Bacterial analysis of such material, which swiftly decomposes, is difficult, but the apparent proximity of blood should have alerted the finders: although faecal material cannot be subjected to DNA testing, blood of course can. Whatever the reason, it would appear that this material was not analysed, and, particularly, not subjected to comparison with the content of the child's intestines in order to ascertain whether it was his. It could have been that little James's bowels had reacted to fear, or to the insertion of a foreign object (which the police had suspected all along); it could have come from the boys, or, of course, though less likely just in that spot, from someone else altogether. But nobody knew, and nobody tried to find out. Perhaps it was too distasteful. Anyway, in a situation where bricks played a primary part in the child's murder and where, at the conclusion of the deed, a bizarre attempt was made to hide his face with bricks, it is surprising nobody wanted to admit that the finding of this material "under a brick" next to the body was sufficiently significant to merit examination.

Late in January 1994, Superintendent Kirby told me that, as of a few days earlier, in the helpful atmosphere of the secure unit, Jon was beginning to open up. And a week later, talking to his father, Jon finally spoke about the batteries. "He said," Neil Venables told me, "that they had pushed batteries into the baby's mouth."

This voluntary disclosure of a heretofore not understood (though suspected) violent act was not only a hopeful sign for Jon, but takes us considerably further in the analysis of the actual crime. For what this admission now explained were the terrible injuries to James's mouth described in the pathologist's report but not properly understood until now. "Dissection of the face reveals evulsion of the lower lip and facial structure from the left side of the jaw over an area of three inches."

Most psychiatrists working on child sexual abuse, faced with evidence of a hard object being forcibly introduced into the mouth of a child, would consider as a first hypothesis that the perpetrator was committing an act of sexual abuse. There may be those who will feel—or even prefer to feel—that this terrible attack was not sexually motivated but part of the frenzied violence which killed James. I don't believe this is so. But I think, too, that the two sequences cannot be separated: one, I believe, arose out of and was dependent on the other.

The pattern of sexual abuse is thoroughly familiar by now to all those who work in this field. Children who abuse other children have almost invariably been abused themselves. (This will not necessarily apply to children who are present, but who do not actively participate.)

The 1957 Act of Parliament says that "Where a person kills, or is a party to the killing of another, he shall not be convicted of murder if he was suffering from such abnormality of mind (whether arising from a condition of arrested or retarded development of mind or any inherent cause, or induced by disease or injury) as substantially impaired his mental responsibility for his acts and omissions in doing or being a party to the killing."

If all the sexual components of the attack on James Bulger had been known, would the psychiatrists have been able to express a different opinion than that they had seen no "abnormality of mind" in Jon Venables and Robert Thompson?

If the defence had known all the sexual components of the attack, could they have based a plea in mitigation on diminished responsibility?

And if the prosecution had been equally informed, could they have agreed to such a plea for manslaughter instead of murder, thereby accepting that an inner disturbance which drives a ten-year-old to commit serious sexual and then frenzied physical attacks resulting in death can or must be considered "an abnormality of mind" admissible for treatment under the Mental Health Act?

I am told by eminent jurists that, under British law as it stands, the answer is no. The law relating to diminished responsibility, which alone would allow a verdict for manslaughter, does not admit that children who sexually abuse children can be suffering from an "abnormality of mind".

("I think Bobby needs help, and he's been needing it for a long time," Anne Thompson had said to me. "I asked them—give him help; they said he can't have help because he hasn't been found guilty. I said, if he isn't guilty, he should have help anyway, and if he is guilty, he needs help, now. But I might have been talking to the wall; nobody listened.")

I began this account with a plea for a change in the British legal system as regards trials of children who have committed capital crimes. I suggested that the way most Western European countries, and most North American states, handle this difficult problem is more enlightened. By having Family or Juvenile Courts deal with these cases after the social enquiry has been completed and therapeutic treatment substantially advanced, they are taking into account the changing moral climate and precepts of our society. Let me emphasize that I am not suggesting that children who kill, or for that matter deliberately hurt or harm others without causing death, do not need the strongest possible indication from society that they have done the most terrible wrong. For this purpose, and for this purpose alone, there is something to be said for maintaining a relatively formal setting; so that the seriousness of the occasion imprints itself on their minds. Paradoxically, one of the perceived dangers of the European model is that the length of time and lack of formality risks undermining that impression. The French call it banalization.

Perhaps this is a chance to create a new system combining the best elements of both. This present case, because of its extreme nature, has demonstrated most forcibly what is wrong. It is wrong to treat children as adults and to demand that they comprehend the language and thought processes of adults. It is wrong to sit children in a dock for weeks on public exhibition.

However talented police interrogators may be, it is wrong that they should question children for days on end about an act, a deed, a crime, without the training or authority for a parallel goal of understanding. It is wrong to use tricks, emotion or a parent to coerce a child, for however necessary and right it may seem in the essentials of the moment, the child will never forget.

Truth must emerge not through the pressure of, or the longing for, love, but out of an inner need. The admission of guilt, and the relief of remorse, are only given to human beings through self-knowledge. And children, just as human, only smaller, have exactly the same needs.*

* First published in the *Independent on Sunday Review* on 6 and 13 February 1994
© Newspaper Publishing plc, 1994

It is the end of July 1994 as I finish the new introduction to this book, and a new conclusion to this appendix. Eight months have gone by since the conviction of Robert Thompson and Jon Venables, both 11 years old, for the murder of two-year-old James Bulger and the sentence of detention at Her Majesty's Pleasure.

The sentencing in cases such as this is no simple matter under British law: the original recommendation is made by the trial judge and then confirmed or altered by the Lord Chief Justice. Then, however—and again Britain stands alone in the practice—the Home Secretary of the *day*, i.e. the executive branch of government, has the deciding voice.

In this instance, Mr. Justice Morland let it be known in December 1993 that he considered eight years to be the proper minimum sentence for both boys in respect "retribution and deterrence"; two days later, the Lord Chief Justice increased this to ten years. James Bulger's parents, Denise and Ralph, immediately launched a campaign, eventually supported by over 250,000 signatures, calling for the two young murderers of their child to be jailed for life. And earlier this year, the two boys' lawyers initiated an appeal to the European Court in Luxembourg, on the basis that the boys' rights are being infringed by the British legal system which allows a politician to set prison terms. The European Court has accepted the case and will presumably hear it in the course of the coming winter.

Last week, as I write this—on 22 July 1994—Mr. Michael Howard, the Home Secretary, announced that the boys are to serve a minimum of 15 years' imprisonment. He said that he had taken the judges' views into consideration but had increased the sentence because of "the special circumstances and the need to maintain confidence in the justice system". Equally, however, he said, the strength of public feeling had affected his decision.

It is, of course, impossible for anyone who murders, including Mary Bell and these boys, to "pay" in terms of years of imprisonment, for killing another human being. In that sense, eight or ten years are as irrelevant as 15—or life.

The fact remains, however, that these were damaged children and, as such, as we see with Mary Bell, can be helped to grow up into something approaching normal adults. Under the British system, the sentence imposed for deterrence and retribution is the minimum: in practice this means that they now cannot be considered for probation and release until they are 26 years old. By then they will have served their first four years in secure units, where the emphasis is on education and—if they are willing and lucky—therapy. At 15 they will presumably be moved to a secure youth facility, already essentially a prison, and at 18 to a maximum security prison. While secure units, whether they succeed or not, are theoretically treatment-oriented and certainly benign places, even the best prisons are penal institutions, largely punishment-oriented and filled with angry men or women prisoners. It requires enormous strength for a young person to withstand that anger and maintain any change and improvement he has achieved. The sentence for retribution and deterrence is, I repeat, the minimum: even at the end of it, the prisoner will only be released if he is considered safe to be returned to society.

This would have applied just as much if the judges' recommendation had been accepted. The Home Secretary's increase to 15 years, therefore, really is nothing but a political decision, a sap to the voters who consider these two 11-year-old boys to be "evil".